DATE DUE

Literal Figures

Thomas H. Luxon

Literal Figures

*Puritan Allegory and
the Reformation Crisis
in Representation*

The University of Chicago Press
Chicago & London

Thomas H. Luxon is associate professor of English at Dartmouth College.

The University of Chicago Press, Chicago 60637
The University of Chicago Press, Ltd., London
© 1995 by The University of Chicago
All rights reserved. Published 1995
Printed in the United States of America
04 03 02 01 00 99 98 97 96 95   1 2 3 4 5
ISBN: 0-226-49785-2 (cloth)

Library of Congress Cataloging-in-Publication Data

Luxon, Thomas H., 1954–
    Literal figures : Puritan allegory and the Reformation crisis in representaion / Thomas H. Luxon.
        p.   cm.
    Includes bibliographical references (p.) and index.
    1. Bunyan, John, 1628–1688—Criticism and interpretation.
2. Christian literature, English—Puritan authors—History and
criticism.   3. Christianity and literature—England—History—
17th century.   4. Puritan movements in literature.   5. Mimesis
in literature.   6. Reformation—England.   7. Allegory.
    I. Title.
PR3332.L89   1995
828'.407—dc20   94-30412
                                                              CIP

⊗ The paper used in this publication meets the minimum requirements of the
American National Standard for Information Sciences—Permanence of Paper for
Printed Library Materials, ANSI Z39.48-1984.

Most of chapter 1 reprinted with permission of Johns Hopkins University Press
from "'Not I, but Christ': Allegory and the Puritan Self," *ELH* 60 (1993): 899–
937. © 1993 by The Johns Hopkins University Press.

Chapter 5 reprinted from "'Other Mens Words' and 'New Birth': Bunyan's
Antihermeneutics of Experience," by Thomas H. Luxon, in *Texas Studies in
Literature and Language,* vol. 36, no. 3 (Fall 1994). By permission of the author
and the University of Texas Press. © 1994 by the University of Texas Press,
P.O. Box 7819, Austin, TX 78713-7819.

To Ivy . . . . in flower.

Contents

Preface

This project began, longer ago than I care to say, with what appeared to be a very simple question: if John Bunyan's work, as has been generally supposed, represents a kind of literary flowering of English Puritanism, a Puritanism theologically rooted in Calvin and Luther as anglicized and popularized by the sectarian movements of the revolutionary years, then what is he doing writing allegory? No mode of discourse is more consistently vilified by Reformation authors from Tyndale to Milton than allegory. The "single literal sense"—the "tongue sense"—of Scripture was virtually a mantra of Protestant and Puritan hermeneutics. The so-called plain style was a homiletic credo. Among the radical millenarians and chiliasts of the midcentury to whom Christopher Hill traces Bunyan's first experiences of popular religious discourse, allegory and so-called typology were despised as the rhetorical tools of a repressive church-state regime. As Luther and Tyndale accused the pope of locking up the Word with the mystifying "keys" of allegories, tropologies, and anagoges, so English Puritan sectaries accused their bishops and their king of distorting the Word for political and pecuniary ends. Literalism, even at times a kind of hyperliteralism, was the rallying cry of advanced Puritanism. Quakers, in some ways the most radical of Puritans, epitomized this broad commitment to literalism in their stubborn resistance to symbolic forms *tout court*—their promotion of silence in worship, their refusal to use traditional names for days and months, to use contracts, or to recognize symbolic forms of authority in dress and title.

So how does it happen that Bunyan, not unapologetically, writes allegory and that his allegories are so widely hailed not just as literary masterpieces, but as artifacts of English Puritan culture? Does Puritanism, beneath the surface of its literalist mantra, harbor a deeper commitment to allegory than we have hitherto supposed? This is the hypothesis *Literal Figures* pursues throughout its first three chapters. Chapter 1 uses the historical episode of William Franklin, a pseudo-Christ who rose to some prominence in 1649, heuristically to raise an array of questions about how the antiallegorical prescriptions of Protestantism gave rise to what appeared to many as monstrously radical hyperliteral enormities, especially in the matter of Puritan concepts of personal identity. It is significant, though not surprising, that William Franklin and his companion Mary Gadbury—the "Spouse of Christ"—are accused by more mainstream Puritans of suffering from "Allegorical Fancies." Chapter 2 takes issue with the widely received doctrine, both then and now, that Protestant figuralism—typology— is a distinctly nonallegorical mode of representation that somehow maintains and privileges a clear sense of what is literal and what is historical. Chapter 3 begins to plumb the depths of Puritanism's commitment to, and denial of, allegorical modes of thought by analyzing crucial passages from Luther, Calvin, Tyndale, Whitaker, and other English Reformers. Their attempts to deny or explain away the allegorical nature of Paul's "new-birth" midrash on Genesis and Hebrew history suggest that the crisis over representation endemic to Protestantism has roots in Christianity's earliest formulations. Chapter 4 refocuses attention on narratives of identity, personal and national, this time by comparing the Pauline and neo-Pauline stories of new birth to the ancient Hebrew narratives they claim as typological models. The final two chapters of *Literal Figures* reread Bunyan's autobiography, *Grace Abounding to the Chief of Sinners,* and both parts of *The Pilgrim's Progress* as texts deeply anxious about the potential of language to represent the "gospel-sense" of revelation and spiritual experience, but at the same time eager to employ the Pauline allegory of new birth to solve, or at least to allay, these anxieties. These readings also suggest how broadly dependent early modern concepts of identity are upon allegorical schemes of ontology, and how these schemes persist even in recent critical interpretations of Bunyan's work.

The simple question that initiated this project—what is a Puritan literalist like Bunyan doing writing allegory?—took shape for me only after I completed a dissertation on Bunyan at the University of Chicago. In fact, Richard Strier, one of my directors, repeatedly pressed this question on me in one way or another, but I succeeded in dodging it long enough to take my degree. Richard may not agree with the ways in which I have pursued his question, but I am now grateful to him for planting it. Sadly, my other supportive director, John Wallace, has not lived to see this project completed.

A year-long fellowship from the National Endowment for the Humanities in 1986–87 enabled the primary research upon which *Literal Figures* is grounded. Much of this research was conducted during four of the most pleasant months of my young career, spent at the Huntington Library in San Marino, California. There, Virginia Renner and the entire library staff helped to make scholarship comfortable and productive. There also, I enjoyed stimulating exchanges with Paul Stevens, Bill and Camille Slights, and Richard Helgerson. I am also indebted to librarians at the Houghton, the Folger, and the British libraries, as well as to the staffs at the Dartmouth and Haverford College libraries.

Dartmouth College has provided me with more support, both financial and intellectual, than most young scholars dare dream of. The Burke Initiation Award made travel to libraries and purchases of books and computer equipment easy. A Junior Faculty Fellowship, combined with sabbatical leave in 1992, provided me with enough time to complete the book's first draft. Since then, my colleagues in the English and Comparative Literature departments, past and present, have been energetically supportive. Many have read some or even all of the chapters and have offered valuable critiques and suggestions: Peter Saccio, Lynda Boose, Don Pease, Peter Bien, Peter Travis, David Kastan, Blanche Gelfant, Jim Heffernan, Peter Stallybrass, and Matthew Rowlinson. Jonathan Crewe deserves special mention in this regard; his uncanny ability to condense and distill the heart of the matter from the most disjointed drafts made this book possible. Summer sojourners at the School for Criticism and Theory have also played key roles in this book's development, especially Stephen Greenblatt and Daniel Boyarin. Daniel's work on Paul and midrash is acknowledged throughout the book, but I also want to thank him for saving me from more than one embarrassing error and for the sudden warmth of his support and friendship. Other friends who raised spirits as well as ideas are Marianne Hirsch, Leo Spitzer, and Larry Kritzman. My students Michele DeStefano and Jonathan Eburne were more than dedicated research assistants. Two anonymous readers for the University of Chicago Press offered cogent critiques and helpful suggestions that have made this book far better than I could have managed alone. Norma Roche edited the manuscript with a keen eye and a clear head. The infelicities, exaggerations, and errors that remain, of course, are no one's but my own. Earlier versions of chapters 1 and 5 have appeared in *ELH* and *Texas Studies in Literature and Language,* respectively; I am grateful for their permission to reuse much of that material here.

No one has contributed more to this book—materially, intellectually, and spiritually—than Ivy Schweitzer. Since I cannot even begin to describe the ways she has helped me realize this dream, a simple dedication will have to do.

One

"Not I, but Christ": The Puritan Self— Escape from Allegory?

Who, being in the form of God, thought it not robbery to be equal with God.

Philippians 2:6

If subversion is possible, it will be a subversion from within the terms of the law, through the possibilities that emerge when the law turns against itself and spawns unexpected permutations of itself.

Judith Butler[1]

If the Bible is true, then I'm Christ. But so what? You know being Christ ain't nothing. I claim my father sits on the throne. Doesn't yours? Isn't your father God?

David Koresh, Leader of the Branch Davidians, Waco, Texas, February 1993

One day in July 1649, William Franklin told Mary Gadbury that his outward body had been "destroy'd" and had been replaced with the spiritual and glorified body of Christ. He had "closed with Christ," body and soul.[2] According to her confession, recorded by a hostile but clearly fascinated witness, Gadbury found Franklin's claim difficult to credit at first. Indeed, she says that she laughed in his face. But within a short space of time, probably no more than a few days, she came to recognize in Franklin the man of her hopes and dreams, indeed, the man of all Christendom's hopes and dreams. By Christmastime, Franklin and Gadbury, now announcing herself as the "Spouse of Christ," had gathered to themselves a number of disciples, including a Hampshire minister, William Woodward, and his wife Margaret. Humphrey Ellis, a Congregational minister, was alarmed enough by the couple's success to compose a rather detailed (62-page) account of their activities and trials. By some accounts, their followers numbered in the hundreds even after they and their chief supporters had been apprehended and imprisoned (Ellis, 47).

Franklin was not the first English pseudo-Christ, but he appears to have been one of the first of a flurry of pseudo-Christs and ecstatic women prophets who commanded the anxious attention of the English public in the years immediately following the execution of Charles I.[3] For example, Thomas Tany dated his bodily conversion from November 1649, saying, "I have been emptied of temporalls, but am filled with the eternall being, . . . I am One."[4] Over the course of his seven-year career, Tany, calling himself ThoreauJohn, also claimed to be high priest of the Jews, king of England and France, and even King of the Jews.[5] In 1650 John Robins was reported to be raising the dead and announcing himself as Christ.[6] According to Lodowick Muggleton, who believed himself to be "one of the two last Prophets & Witnesses of the Spirit, being the Third & last Record from God on Earth," Robins preached "that he was that first Adam that was in that innocent State; & that his Body had been Dead this Five Thousand, Six Hundred and odd Years, & now he was risen again from the Dead; And that he was that Adam Melchisadek that met Abraham in the Way."[7] His wife Joan, like Mary Gadbury before her, believed she was about to give birth to Christ, a Christ in "substance," rather than one of "types and shadows."[8] Mrs. Richard King and Mary Adams made identical claims in 1651. Joan Garment, whose husband Joshua was a minister and disciple of John Robins, and Mary Vanlop both claimed that the man they followed was the "true god to serve" (*Grand Blasphemers*). Anna Trapnel accompanied Baptist leader Vavasour Powell to Whitehall in 1654, only to fall into a twelve-day trance, during which she uttered a series of fifth-monarchist prophecies denouncing Cromwell and the army for threatening to betray Christ's kingdom on earth.[9] In 1656, the Quaker James Nayler rode into Bristol on a donkey as women followers strewed palms in his way.[10] This list is far from complete, but the literature from which it is drawn suggests that even if the early interregnum years were not unusually blessed in the frequency of such episodes, they certainly attracted more widespread attention, both popular and official, enthusiastic and anxious, than before or after.

Most of the stories involve sexy bits. The "Abominable Practices" men and especially women were supposed to have enacted with their bodies were as much a concern and attraction as the "Horrid Blasphemies" they uttered with their mouths. The 1654 *List of Some of the Grand Blasphemers,* published by "The Committee for Religion," for example, seems especially interested in the sexual behavior of women, especially "Ranters, Quakers and Seekers."[11] Almost all of its examples betray the fear that the radically "inward" religion of Puritan "heartwork" threatened to become, at least on its radical sectarian vanguard, very much an "outward" bodily—"carnal"—experience: women claiming that the men they slept with were Christ or God, that they were literally pregnant with Christ, or that the routine practices of everyday life were as worshipful as, or more so than, organized "ordinances."

Mary Gadbury's situation epitomizes this fear. A married and deserted woman, she appears to have shared a bed for several months with William Franklin, the man (also married) she believed was Christ. However, she insisted that her relations with this Christ were not "carnal," but "spiritual"—that since Franklin's body had been replaced by the glorified spiritual body of Christ, any physical relations with such a body must, by definition, be spiritual relations. Ellis, who recorded her testimony and coerced confessions, invites his readers to scoff, along with the courtroom audience, at what he takes to be Gadbury's transparently self-serving and lust-serving confusion of the carnal and the spiritual. He recounts:

> She answered, to free her self from being accounted a harlot, . . . that he knew not such fleshly relation, that she companied not with him as a carnal, but as a spiritual man; . . . she companied not with him in an uncivil way, but as a fellow-feeler of her misery; at which last word the whole Court laughed exceedingly, some saying, *Yea, we think you companied with him as a fellow-feeler indeed.* (Ellis, 50, italics in original).

The court's laughter at what seemed to many, perhaps even to Ellis, an exceedingly pathetic account of a woman who imagined Christ as a fully present, even touchable, "fellow-feeler of her misery," both marks and masks a perennially troubling—because imperfectly suppressed—contradiction in Puritanism. This is the contradiction between Puritanism's homiletic encouragement of an "experimental" rather than merely "notional" understanding of and relationship to the Word incarnate and its commitment to a two-world dualistic ontology according to which the experience of the body in this world is, at worst, wholly to be despised, and, at best, an allegorical shell whose temporal blessings are no more than a dim figure of the eternal blessings of the world to come. John Bunyan, for instance, defined a notionist as one who knows the Scripture only "in the notion, and hast not the power of the same in [his] heart," having a head "full of the knowledge of the Scriptures," but a heart "empty of sanctifying grace."[12] Once the allegorical shell of bodily experience has been cracked by hermeneutic contemplation, it must be resolutely tossed away: "For we must hold," taught Calvin, "that our mind never rises seriously to desire and aspire after the future, until it has learned to despise the present life."[13]

With this doctrinal privileging of experience over notions, Protestant and Puritan preachers encouraged their flocks to so experience the Word in Scripture that they might say, "Jesus Christ . . . was never more real and apparent then now; here I have seen him and felt him indeed" (*GA,* par. 321). On the other hand, no version of Christianity is more committed than Calvinism to the absolute separation between this world and the next, where Christ's glorified body resides exclusively—no more miracles, no eucharistic real presence, no ecstatic raptures.[14] God is everywhere represented in his creation, especially in "man," but our ontological realm and God's remain as distinct from each other as figure and thing figured, except in the single exceptional case of Christ's sojourn on earth. Even in his Christology Calvin emphasizes the distinction between, rather than the combination of, the divine and human.[15] The divine is never human; soul is never body; this world is never changed into the next, or mingled with the next; the eternal does not participate in the temporal. The divine may manifest itself in the human, "hid under a humble clothing of flesh," but the two remain as distinct as sign and thing signified. In this world is no fulfillment, only signs and shadows.

Despite this doctrinal distinction, the expectation of fulfillment—of a new creature in a new heavenly kingdom—ran high in the late 1640s and early 1650s, and many people simply announced that the fulfillment had arrived. The king, after all, was himself a sort of pseudo-Christ, both before the dramatically public execution of his body and after. The frontispiece to Charles I's *Eikon Basilike,* in what can only be described as a Laudian fantasy of Gethsemane, depicts the king kneeling as he prepares to crown himself with a coronet of thorns. Owen Felltham's epitaph for Charles I reads: "Here Charles the First and Christ the Second lies."[16] Appended to the 15 March 1649 edition, and all subsequent editions, of *Eikon Basilike* was an epitaph by one J. H., which apostrophized the king as "thou earthly god, celestial man / . . . king and priest and prophet too."[17] Arise Evans, who in 1647 claimed he was the Lord God Almighty, also predicted the violent demise of Charles I. By 1652, he was announcing not only that Charles II would be restored to his father's throne without bloodshed within five years, but that the king would also be a new Messiah.[18]

People like Gadbury and Franklin—the "mechanick sort" for whom life was very much life in the body, and a body frequently in pain and want—however much orthodoxy may have held their desires in check, wanted a God with a body, a God they could see, touch, taste, and feel, a God who could touch and feel them. The erotic aspects of Puritan spirituality, heretofore carefully suppressed as an allegory of spiritual pleasures, erupt in the literalized body of these radical saints. Lodowick Muggleton, I suspect, articulated what many thought but were reluctant to express when he said, "No Spirit can speak at all, or hath any being without a body: And this is the very Cause that Men find so little Comfort in worshipping and believing in such a God that is a Spirit without a body."[19]

The early Reformers had removed the body of Christ from the altar and relocated it in the Scriptures, redefining Christ's true body as a discursive body—the Word. Erasmus insisted that the "writings" of the Gospels render Christ more "fully present" than "if you gazed upon him with your very eyes." Luther removed Christ from "books" and "letters" and located him in "an oral preaching, a living word, a voice which resounds throughout the earth."[20] But Christ, the Word, once removed from the corpus on the altar, could not remain a disembodied discourse. Even leaving aside for a moment people's dissatisfaction with a "God with whom they have nothing to do," the doctrine of the Incarnation, so central and so problematic for Christianity, prohibits a thoroughly disembodied Christ. Even Luther and Calvin acknowledge this in their respective eucharistic doctrines, though Calvin leans more to the disembodied (or radically other-bodied) Zwinglian Christ in his equivocal uses of such words as "substance" and "substantial."[21] Thomas Cranmer intimates the return of the Word to physical presence when he asserts that the Bible reader who most profits is not "he that is moste ready in turnyng of the boke, or in saying of it without the boke, but he that is most turned into it, that is most inspired with the holy ghost most in his harte and life, altered and transformed into that thing, which he readeth."[22]

From Luther to radical Puritanism, the body of Christ had been successively displaced from the altar bread to the Scriptures and to the oral Word. Radical millenarians and chiliasts threatened to reify Christ's body in the believer's own body at just that moment in history when Descartes was busy doubting that he had a corporeal body at all.[23] What Francis Barker calls the "Cartesian moment," the birth of the modern self as a self entirely separable from the body, had been implicit in Protestant discourse at least since Calvin. To Puritans, this incorporeal self is Christ. Thus, according to Edmund Calamy, "a Christ-seeker and a true self-seeker are terms convertible."[24] When Calamy announces that "The Soul of Man is the Man of Man," he no doubt oversimplifies Calvin, but he does not contradict him.[25] Protestantism made union with Christ chiefly an "inward" matter, apart from the body's "vileness."[26] But Christ is, after all, supposed to be God incarnate. Thus, to be truly Christ, he must have a body, either his own or the believer's. Franklin, quite understandably, lost track of the fine distinctions with which theology had circumscribed the force of the doctrine of incarnation. He came to believe what Puritanism both proclaimed and withheld.

Paul's claim, "I am crucified with Christ: nevertheless I live; yet not I, but Christ liveth in me" (Galatians 2:20), is the biblical ground for believers who claimed identity with Christ. As such, it was appropriated by any Protestant who believed in his or her (usually his) own conversion and regeneration, by the powerful and powerless, literally and figuratively, explicitly or implicitly. Yet this claim produced radically different social practices, with significantly different meanings and results, for king and "mechanick," man and woman. In the light of Paul's words, Charles I earned the status of martyr; Charles II used them to secure his throne; William Franklin languished in prison for several months and then vanished into obscurity; Mary Gadbury was committed to Bridewell, where she was whipped into confessing her-self a fraud, then recommitted to be whipped again for the offenses she had confessed (Ellis, 51–52). Being made one with Christ was not the same for everybody.

Interest in early modern religious radicals has run high in recent years, spurred largely by Christopher Hill's *The World Turned Upside Down* (1972). Unlike Norman Cohn, who, in *The Pursuit of the Millen-nium* (1957), interpreted medieval and early modern chiliastic move-ments as history's largely neglected early warnings about Nazi and communist fanaticism, Hill wants to read seventeenth-century reli-gious radicalism as a largely positive anticipation of modern popular revolutions, effectively challenging the modern state even in its rel-ative infancy.[27] My interest in people like Franklin and Gadbury is motivated by a desire to account for John Bunyan's nervous and con-tradictory relation to allegory, a mode of thought and expression about which Protestant Reformers issued frequent and strident warn-ings. If, as Hill has argued, Bunyan is best understood as a belated ver-sion of the millenarian radical who learned his religion from the notoriously chiliastic army preachers but lived to see the disappoint-ment of millenarian expectations, we need to know what part allegori-cal thought played in these radicals' religious and political discourses, as well as in those of their hearers and followers.

Franklin and Gadbury are good examples of millenarian expecta-tions carried to a logical and very personal extreme. Though they are often dismissed as crazies and even frauds of the popular religious left, it is my working assumption that they and people like them offer us a valuable glimpse of how the most troublesome religious and political issues of the period took shape and motivated action among the "me-chanick sort," the undereducated working and often vagrant class with which Bunyan explicitly identified himself.[28] Did they share the resistance to allegory so prominent in Reformation and Puritan dis-courses? How did they interpret Scripture? How did they understand and act upon Calvin's re-allegorized relation between God and the self, between this world and the promised "world which is to come"? What role, if any, does allegory play in refiguring the human body, male and female, in its relation to God and to God-incarnate? Explor-ing these questions will shed new light on the role allegory plays in

Bunyan's strident rejection of the most radical modes of Puritan thought and practice.

For the rest of this chapter, then, I will use the episode of Franklin and Gadbury, as it is recorded by the more orthodox Puritan Humphrey Ellis, as a kind of heuristic paradigm of the Reformation, and especially the English Puritan, crisis in the theory and practice of representation. Protestantism repeatedly promised to liberate or cleanse the Christian faith from the riddling allegories and equivocating tropes of "Papist" scholastic theology and hermeneutics. Franklin and Gadbury, perhaps, took this promise too literally, but that, surprisingly enough, is not the charge leveled against them by Ellis. His charges and their responses foreground on a popular level the problems and contradictions that had been brewing in Reformation thought at least since Luther. In the chapters that follow, I will undertake readings of Luther, Calvin, Tyndale, William Whitaker, and John Bunyan that probe some of the more learned, and so more subtly masked, manifestations of the Reformation's anxiety over allegory, symbolism, and typology.

Allegorical Fancies

HUMPHREY ELLIS, THE WINCHESTER PARSON who wrote up the only detailed account of Franklin and Gadbury, levels four startlingly contradictory charges against the pseudo-Christ and his followers. He lumps them together with a whole host of "abusers of the Scriptures" who flourished in England in the late 1640s and early 1650s: Anabaptists, Seekers, separatists, chiliasts, even "Jews and Papists."[29] The specific abuses of the Scriptures he charges against Gadbury and Franklin are: (1) they perversely interpret Scripture according to "Allegorical fancies," (2) they apply specific portions of Scripture too directly to themselves, (3) they reject and condemn the Scriptures altogether even as they use "seeming Scripture-Gospel expressions" (Ellis, 7), and (4) they exhibit a deceitful theatricality in their use and abuse of Scripture and Scripture language calculated to lend to their actions and speeches the authority of the very Scripture they abuse and reject. Finally, Ellis accounts for his special interest in Gadbury and Franklin by identifying them as particularly striking examples of the Scriptures' fulfillment:

What our blessed Saviour hath foretold to his Disciples, should come to pass in the latter Times, and to be a great and manifest sign of his Coming, and of the end of the World, (*viz.*) That men shall say, *Lo here is Christ, and lo there: that false Christs, and false Prophets shall arise; Mat. 24:23, 24;* the same may be seen truly verified in these times of ours; and the fulfilling thereof, even in the literal sence of it, will be discovered in this following *Relation.* (Ellis, 5)

Are the implicit contradictions in Ellis's charges truly contradictory or only apparently so? Is allegorical interpretation of the Scriptures also a sort of rejection of the Scriptures? In what sense is the long-standing Protestant tradition of taking Scripture promises personally not only a perversion of the Scriptures, but an implicit rejection of them? How can Scripture be interpreted to authorize its own rejection? Most puzzling is how Franklin and Gadbury's allegedly "Allegorical" perversions of the Scriptures result in a literal performance, "even in the literal sence of it," that is, a fulfillment of the Scripture's own prophecies.

A closer look at Ellis's charges and at Franklin and Gadbury's countercharges demonstrates that alleged crazies and frauds did not threaten orthodoxy from outside the Puritan tradition, but very much from within it. In Franklin and Gadbury, Puritanism spawned strange and "unexpected permutations of itself," scripting, in Judith Butler's provocative words, parodies or pastiches of Puritan orthodoxy out of that orthodoxy's own suppressed contradictions.[30]

Ellis complains that Franklin "would oftentimes alledg Scripture in his discourse, and speak much in the language of it, but very strangely abusing, perverting, wresting it from the true sence thereof by his Allegorical fancies" (Ellis, 48). The charge of hermeneutically perverting the "true sence" of Scripture had long been a mainstay of Protestant attacks against the Roman Church and sectaries alike. It is also, as we shall see, the implicit charge that Christianity more generally levels against the Jew. "The Holy Spirit," claimed Martin Luther, "is the very simplest writer and speaker there is in heaven and earth; therefore His words, too, cannot have more than one most simple sense, which we call the Scriptural or literal or tongue-sense."[31] William Tyndale also insisted that "the Scripture hath but one sense, which is the literal sense."[32] English Reformers from William Whitaker (d. 1595) to John Weemse (d. 1636) all felt obliged to announce that the Scriptures were perspicuously and singularly literal and to denounce the alleged duplicities and equivocations of medieval exegetical practice, now associated with "Papists" and "Jesuites": "There is but one literal sense and meaning of every Scripture: So should men have but one sense and meaning in their minds, and not a double meaning, as the equivocating Jesuites have."[33] Calvin dubbed scholastic medieval exegesis, the *quadriga* or fourfold method of scriptural interpretation, a "licentious system" contrived by Satan "to undermine the authority of Scripture, and to take away from the reading of it the true advantage." "For many centuries no man was considered to be ingenious, who had not the skill and daring necessary for changing into a variety of curious shapes the sacred word of God. . . . God visited this profanation by a just judgment, when he suffered the pure meaning of the Scripture to be buried under false interpretations."[34]

This charge of allegorizing the Scriptures appears with some frequency alongside the more familiar charges against sectaries of condemning the Scriptures outright as a "dead-letter," or interpreting them according to a "Lesbian rule" or idiosyncratic fantasies.[35] Bishop Samuel Parker of Oxford was still repeating the same charge in 1670: "And herein lies the most material difference between the sober Christians of the Church of England, and our modern sectaries, that we express the Precepts and Duties of the Gospel in plain and intelligent terms, whilst they trifle them away by childish Metaphors and Allegories, and will not talk of Religion but in barbarous and uncouth similitudes."[36]

According to Ellis, Franklin's chief "allegorical" fancy was his claim to have a new body, to be literally born again. Gadbury testified that Franklin had said,

> the body and nature of Franklin, born at Overton, conceived in sin, and brought forth in iniquity, the Lord had destroyed, though the destruction thereof were not, as of the body, layd in dust, visible to the creature, to be seen by it. (Ellis, 11)

As Gadbury reports his claim, Franklin equivocates a bit about the materiality of his body's destruction and replacement. The Lord had apparently destroyed the "body and nature" he was conceived and born into, but this destroyed body, of course, could not be produced;

there was no *corpus delecti* "lay'd in the dust." Nevertheless, Franklin's followers had a very literal understanding of his bodily transformation. Margaret Woodward, a Hampshire clergyman's spouse, testified

> that the man examined before us, whom we called *Franklin,* is *her Lord, and her King, and that she is saved by his Death and Passion. . . . That . . . his flesh was clean scrap't away, and his skin and bone hanged together: and his skin likewise very suddenly fell off from him, and that he had nothing left but the hair of his head, and of that one hair was not diminished; and afterwards new flesh came again as a young childe.* (Ellis, 39)[37]

Ellis transcribes a number of the judicial examinations of Franklin's disciples. They routinely identify the "one which some men call *Franklin*" as "the Son of God, the Christ crucified for our sins, now come down from Heaven" (Ellis, 39).

When haled before the justices, Franklin and his followers refused at first to give their "Names, Conditions, Callings, Habitations: they would . . . answer, they had no name, no habitation, according to the flesh" (Ellis, 40). At first skeptical of Franklin's claims, Gadbury says she asked him about his wife and children, to which Franklin answered:

> And as for the woman his wife, he owned her so to be his wife, while he carryed about that body, in which he was so joyned to her, and he then also owned his children to be the children of that body, but now they were no more to him then any other woman and children, and that he had a Command from God to separate from her. (Ellis, 11)

Franklin and his followers implicitly claim that the state and its ideological apparatuses (marriage, family, law, vocation, even religion) can no longer hale him, for he is a new creature inside and out, having been "crucified at Jerusalem" (Ellis, 41). Thus he can say as Paul said, "I am crucified with Christ: nevertheless I live; yet not I, but Christ liveth in me; and the life which I now live in the flesh I live by the faith of the Son of God, who loved me and gave himself for me" (Galatians 2:20).[38]

In what sense is Franklin's claim to be the glorified body of Christ an "Allegorical" fancy, as Ellis charges? Ellis does not elaborate much on the hermeneutic theory underlying this charge, but it is safe to assume that he sees Franklin as having confused the metaphors Paul employs to describe conversion with the literal sense intended by such metaphors. The normative literal sense of any Scripture passage, according to exegetical tradition, is the sense gathered from the explication of metaphorical expressions, not the literal sense of the metaphorical figures themselves.[39] What Franklin and his disciples have apparently done is to take the metaphorical expressions themselves in a literal sense, abjuring even the most automatic exegetical gestures of reading demanded by obviously figurative expressions. By insisting on taking Paul's metaphor of the new creature hyperliterally, Franklin has taken Puritanism's antiallegorical and antifigural emphasis to an extreme. The result of this hyperliteralism, for Ellis, is "Allegorical fancies."

We must also ask, then, how obviously metaphorical are Paul's descriptions of conversion? Paul frequently describes the Christian convert as ontologically split between two states of being. Conversion, the experience of one's true being, forces one to abjure the experience of being "in the flesh [*sarx*]":

> For we know that if our earthly house of this tabernacle were dissolved, we have a building of God, an house not made with hands, eternal in the heavens. For in this we groan, earnestly desiring to be clothed upon with our house which is from heaven, if so be that, being clothed, we shall not be found naked. For we that are in this tabernacle do groan, being burdened; not that we would be unclothed, but clothed upon, that mortality might be swallowed up of life. Now he that hath wrought us for the selfsame thing is God, who also hath given unto us the earnest of the Spirit. Therefore, we are always confident, knowing that, while we are at home in the body, we are absent from the Lord (For we walk by faith, not by sight); We are confident, I say, and willing rather to be absent from the body, and to be present with the Lord. (2 Corinthians 5:1–8)

In this passage, the convert's two ontological states are kept fairly distinct: one is now, the other is then. One's true being, both originarily and teleologically, is a condition of "being absent from the body [*sōmatos*], and . . . present with the Lord." In other places, Paul appears to announce that a convert is already present with, indeed, virtually one with, Christ as a "new creature":

Henceforth know we no man after the flesh; yea, though we have known Christ after the flesh, yet now henceforth know we him no more. Therefore, if any man be in Christ, he is a new creature; old things are passed away; behold all things are become new. (2 Corinthians 5:16–17)

Ye have put off the old man with his deeds, And have put on the new man, that is renewed in knowledge after the image of him that created him; Where there is neither Greek nor Jew, circumcision nor uncircumcision, barbarian, Scythian, bond nor free, but Christ is all, and in all. (Colossians 3:9–11)

Paul even identifies these two ontological states not simply as an "inward" versus an "outward" being, or simply an ontology of the spirit in opposition to an ontology of the body (only *sarx,* not *sōma,* is absolutely opposed to *pneuma*), but as two ontologically distinct bodies— on the one hand, the "body of the flesh [*sōmatos tēs sarkos*]" (Colossians 2:11) or the "physical body [*sōma physikon*]," and on the other a "spiritual body [*sōma pneumatikon*]" (1 Corinthians 15:44) newly fashioned by conversion.[40] The new creature produced by conversion, the experience Paul describes as being "crucified with Christ" (dying to the *sarx*) and being reborn as a spiritual body, is not merely a metaphor in Pauline discourse. From a converted perspective, understanding according to the spirit, the spiritual body is more literally a real body than the now-destroyed "body of the flesh." To read Paul's "new creature" as a mere figure of speech, signifying a personality change or a new social or ideological identification (although it signifies those, too) is to ignore the orthodox tenet of bodily resurrection built upon Paul's discourse of the new creature.

Franklin may indeed have taken Pauline expressions over-literally on occasion, but in this crucial case, which so disturbed Ellis, Franklin's hyperliteralism is quite central to Christian doctrine. Franklin's misreading of Paul—if it is a misreading—produces his conviction that his fleshly body has already been stripped away and replaced with Christ's spiritual body. His error, then, is not that of taking a figurative expression literally, but of announcing the end of that dispensation under which such a dualistic ontology was required. From Franklin's perspective, orthodoxy's dualistic insistence that Christ's kingdom is both "now and not yet," that the convert is redeemed and justified, but not yet glorified, is no longer necessary.[41]

Many people in 1649 had been encouraged from the pulpit and Parliament to see Charles I's defeat and execution as an apocalyptic event that would usher in the physical reign of Christ on earth.[42] It should not surprise us, then, if some also expected an end to the heaven/earth dualistic ontology that was supposed to characterize the premillennial life of God's "true Israel." A spiritual body, Christ's body, had been quite literally promised, and Franklin was not alone in claiming a literal experience of that promise's fulfillment.

Paul himself often sounds just such an apocalyptic note, or, at least as in the following claim, he appears to invite apocalyptic readings: those "baptized into Christ have put on Christ" (Galatians 3:27). Calvin himself did not read this as a metaphorical expression: "So he testifies to the Galatians, that all who have been baptized into Christ, have put on Christ. . . . Thus indeed must we speak, as long as the institution of the Lord and the faith of the godly unite together; for we never have naked and empty symbols [baptism], except when our ingratitude and wickedness hinder the working of divine beneficence."[43] Even modern Protestant commentators insist on the literalism of Paul's teaching about the glorified body of the convert, though they are always careful to note that "the completion of this transformation must wait upon the day of the *Parousia*": "The resurrection of the body starts at baptism, when a Christian becomes 'one Spirit' (i.e., one spiritual body) with the Lord (I Cor. 6:17), and 'puts on (the body of) Christ' (Gal. 3:27), 'the new man,' which 'hath been created' (Eph. 4:24) and 'is being renewed . . . after the image of him that created him' (Col. 3:10). Baptism begins the substitution of the solidarity of one body by that of another."[44] When Franklin understood Paul's teaching about the new creature literally, his hermeneutics was not unorthodox, though his sense of timing may have been.

In Protestant and Puritan orthodoxy, this same apocalyptic literalism is tempered by an equivocation: Christ's kingdom and the glorified body it promises are both literally "now" and literally "not yet." Andrew Lincoln, though our contemporary, puts the orthodox Puritan position of Ellis's day quite aptly when he says, "There can be no attempts to find any short cuts to glory, for although believers already belong to the heavenly commonwealth they cannot yet claim all their rights as citizens" (Lincoln, 194). It is not hard to imagine that five months after Charles I's execution, Franklin, among others, was no longer content to be a citizen without a citizen's rights, that he felt the much-heralded establishment of a heavenly commonwealth entitled him to claim those rights. For him, these included the right to the spiritual body Christ promised, a body and a life that truly matters to God because it is the body of his only begotten Son, no longer the old body and life of the flesh that was everything God was not.

Ellis also charges Franklin, Gadbury, and their followers with abusing Scripture by personalizing it and applying it "wholly to themselves" (Ellis, 15). Ellis is particularly upset by Gadbury's implicit identification of herself with the Zion of Isaiah's prophecy (Isaiah 66:7–9), a prophecy understood by Ellis as messianic. While staying at the Reverend Woodward's parsonage, Gadbury says, she was "taken as a woman in travail" with pains similar to labor pains, but "more painful." Ellis sardonically comments that she could well tell the difference, having experienced both. In the midst of her pain, she heard a voice saying, "Shall I bring to the birth, and not give strength to bring forth?" (Ellis, 20; Isaiah 66:9). Ellis explains that Gadbury understood these pains to presage "some spirituall, and not any naturall birth," and that she interpreted them as a physical sign, supported by the voice, that someone was about to be converted to belief in Franklin/Christ, the man-child promised by Isaiah's prophecy (Ellis, 21). But Ellis dismisses both the pains and the voice as theatrical pretense designed to seduce "any one like to be wrought upon," and he is especially distressed that Gadbury would have the blasphemous audacity to claim, even in a "spirituall" sense, to be travailing in the birth of new converts, as Paul imaginatively represents himself doing in Galatians 4:19.[45] In applying Paul's metaphor to herself, Gadbury has hyperliteralized it insofar as she claims to have felt physical pains and to have heard a voice, but she apparently understood both pains and voice as "of God" and "spirituall," presaging not a physical birth, but the imminent spiritual rebirth of one of Franklin's auditors (Ellis, 22).

Nevertheless, Ellis is scandalized. Phyllis Mack astutely observes that the role of the ecstatic prophet had long been described as feminized in the Christian, and especially sectarian Puritan, tradition. Women, long despised as the "lowly" and the "last," considered overemotional and thus overreceptive to supernatural influences, both good and evil, were all too likely to serve as vessels for divine revelation as well as infernal possession (Mack, 23). Paul figures himself as the Galatian converts' birth-mother and as wet nurse to the Thessalonians (1 Thessalonians 2:7). For a woman to apply the same metaphors to herself, however, automatically threatens to re-literalize, and so re-gender, the very thing such metaphors sought to neutralize—the power and significance of material, particularly *mater*-ial, generation. Paul's argument in Galatians is precisely that fleshly birth counts for nothing in determining membership in God's true Israel; the true sons of Abraham are the sons of God by virtue of having been born "of the spirit," not of the flesh. By figuring his evangelistic and apostolic role as birth-mother, Paul insists that he is more truly a mother than any carnal mother, giving birth to God's true Israel as opposed to a "carnal" Israel. For Paul, the figural mother—himself in this case—is the literal or truly real mother, the mother capable of bearing true sons to God. For a woman to make the same claim threatens the crucial distinction between the spiritually true mother and the carnal shadow of a spiritual mother. Mack's comments on this are particularly relevant to my point: "To a sympathetic observer—and there were many—these women visionaries must have appeared almost as living allegories, concrete manifestations of cosmic Womanhood [the birthing-nursing Christ/Paul]. To a hostile observer, they might just as easily have been perceived as agents of the devil" (Mack, 30).

"Living allegories" is an apt euphemism for the way Protestant typology, as Barbara Lewalski describes it, encouraged believers to regard themselves.[46] "For like as it behoved the thing too bee substauncially fulfilled in Christ, which was begun in David," wrote Calvin, "so must it of necessitie come to passe in every of his members."[47] From Gadbury's perspective of an already arrived millennium, her experience with Franklin was nothing less than the substance shadowed forth by the lives of Paul, David, Israel, and the early church. A "living allegory," to a millenarian like Gadbury, is precisely not an allegory.

Ellis thought, however, that a mother, a carnal bearer of children, cannot speak this way without threatening to dissolve the ontological distinction between this world of fleshly bodies and the next of spiritual bodies. Carnal mothers are literally the metaphor, the fleshly figures, for truly spiritual mothers like Paul. Here Ellis, not Gadbury, wanted desperately to preserve the allegory, the distinction between figure and thing figured. He took Gadbury to be acting, playing a role without announcing it as such. Or, he hoped that Gadbury was only acting. Even worse, perhaps she was possessed by a devil, and actually gave birth to a dragon or a serpent. If Gadbury really experienced a fusing of flesh and spirit, Ellis reasoned, the spirit must have been not God, but a demon:

> But one thing I may not omit here fit to be inserted, evidenced by a Constable, when the businesse concerning the pretended travails of this woman and her spirituall birth was examined and heard before the Judge of Assize, *viz.* that he heard from *Edward Spradbury* that this woman had been in travail, and was delivered; and asking of what she had been delivered, it was answered, of a Dragon, and what she was delivered of, her Lord and Christ had slain it on the bed:—Hence I suppose it was, that so strong a report was sometime raised and carried about the Countrey, as if this woman had been in some reall travail, and had been indeed delivered of a Serpent, or some such monstrous birth. (Ellis, 22)

A woman's "experimental" union with Christ's glorified body was either a theatrical fraud or literally the work of the Devil. So, apparently, thought the Justices who suspected that Gadbury "was delivered of a childe, and had destroyed it" (Ellis, 39). Margaret Woodward's testimony fed the judges' suspicions: she said she had "received what the Queen [Gadbury] was delivered of; and said, it was of that man which she called *Franklin,* but in a spiritual manner, perswading them that *Franklin* was transfigured, and had no substance left him" (Ellis, 40). The equivocation built into the word *substance* in so much Puritan discourse is put under a great deal of strain here: what is a substantial birth? Is it a birth after the flesh or according to the spirit? For Gadbury and Franklin, *substantial* is a synonym for *spiritual,* since they both reject the dualistic ontology of the premillennial past. The substance that Franklin and Gadbury, and many others, had been repeatedly encouraged from the pulpit to trust in was what Paul called "the substance of things hoped for, the evidence of things not seen" (Hebrews 11:1). Only such substance was truly real; everything else was merely types and shadows of it. Franklin and Gadbury acted on the desire to have done with this distinction, to count here and now as truly real, substantial beings.

They came by this desire honestly. As I mentioned earlier, English Protestants as early as Thomas Cranmer had encouraged pious readers to find themselves in the Scriptures, to be transformed by an experimental, rather than a merely notional, understanding of the Word. Cranmer, we recall, asserted that the Bible reader who most profits is "he that is most turned into it, that is most . . . altered and transformed into that thing, which he readeth." Did Gadbury take such encouragement too far, performing, as it were, a parody of Puritan experimentalism? Or was such encouragement never intended for the likes of Gadbury, the uneducated, poor, and even illiterate?[48] Or, more subversively, were the poor and illiterate peculiarly well positioned to experience being "turned into" the book? Were they the despised outsiders peculiarly singled out by the Gospels and by Paul for such an experience of new being?

What Scripture Gadbury knew, she learned from preachers like William Sedgwick, who claimed that Christ appeared to him in his study in 1647 and told him "that the world will be at an end within fourteen days."[49] Sedgwick preached that London was the "new Jerusalem," that the Levelers were an incarnation of "Divine Charity that lifts not up it self, but is lifted up; and being lifted up, drawes all after it."[50] In a fast-day sermon to Parliament in 1643, Sedgwick told the members that they were literally living on the verge of the physical reign of the glorified Christ on earth:

> Thou shalt be called Hephzipah, and thy Land Beulah, for the Lord delighteth in thee, and thy Land shall be marryed. Which is not meant onely of a mysticall and spirituall union of the Church to Christ, but of a visible, outward, and manifest declaration of this marriage: Christ will take his Church by the hand, and publickely owne his people. She shall be a Crowne of Glory in the hand of the Lord, and a Royall Diadem in the hand of thy God, ver. 3. Christ and his Church will stand openly hand in hand: there shall be a publicke solemnization of the marriage of the Lambe, Revel. 19:7. When the Church shall say, Loe this is our God, we have waited for him, and he will save us. As his people shall see it, so the world shall acknowledge it, and say, Thy maker is thy Husband. Men see it darkely now, and hate them; but they shall see it clearly, and honour them.[51]

Just what is this "it" to which Sedgwick so insistently refers? Gadbury eventually took it to be her life with William Franklin, her not "onely . . . mysticall and spirituall union" with Christ, but something also "visible, outward, and manifest."

In the heady millenarian atmosphere of the summer following the king's execution, people like Gadbury expected that Christ would come any day now, in the flesh, and draw all unto him. If types and shadows like the king were finally being replaced, many thought it stood to reason that their own shadowy existence would also shortly be replaced by true being and the only true self, Christ—glory in the here and now, rather than the hereafter. For a poor woman, abandoned by her husband, left with a child, reduced to selling "small Wares, as Laces, Pins, Bandstrings, and other trifles for Gentlewomen" (Ellis, 8), this was indeed a gospel worthy of faith, for it spoke directly to her and, more importantly, of her. It spoke of her as she knew—or wanted to know—herself, without the metaphysical dualisms of "inward" and "outward," spiritual and physical. She was literally the "Spouse of Christ," a physical manifestation of Christianity's favorite allegory of the Church as wife, which Sedgwick evokes in the passage quoted above. By literalizing the figure of Church as spouse, Gadbury threatens orthodoxy's allegorical ontology by which this world is merely a shadow of the next. The Church as spouse had always been figured as Christ's other, but conversion promised to make the saint one with Christ. The marriage figure covers the contradiction by replacing the promise of union with the figure of juridical or sexual union, an equivocal union that preserves the otherness of the saint in the most explicit way possible—by gendering the saint as feminine, as the Man-God's other.[52]

Being Christ's bride, a feminized position, figures the saint's preglorified condition, the condition of being as yet on earth, expectantly awaiting union with the God-Man. Once Jordan is crossed, however, there is only the risen Christ, and he is most certainly not feminine. Bride, wife, and spouse, then, are Christianity's figurations for deferred selfhood, the as yet unfulfilled self of life in the body, in this world, still yearning for the next. Gadbury's personal literalization of these figures implicitly ignores the distinction between this world and the next. For her, being the Spouse of Christ is already no longer a metaphor. This is profoundly disturbing to the orthodox Ellis for at least two reasons. First, it exposes orthodox Puritan discourse of the self as more deeply committed to an allegorical understanding of reality than it wishes to admit. Ellis, no less than Sedgwick, believes that all people shall "see it," that the union of Christ and his church is more than a mystical promise, but this "it" that everyone shall literally see must remain absolutely beyond the horizon of this world. Anything this side of the next world can only be a dim and inadequate shadow of the real thing. Otherwise, there is no use for religion at all. Second, what Ellis understands as Gadbury's blasphemous impersonation of the "Spouse of Christ" threatens to expose orthodox Christianity's implicit commitment to understanding real being as exclusively masculine. The Church is Christ's spouse or bride only by virtue of the fact that it is not yet fully one with Christ. When the promised union is achieved, there will no longer be any need for the category of the feminine. Women, it seems, are not really real; they are only one of this world's allegories of true being. Other such allegories of true being, as we shall discover in later chapters, are "the Jew," the "Papist," the misbeliever, and the "false professor."

Unless allegory meant something very different for Ellis than it did for Franklin and Gadbury, Ellis's oft-repeated charge against the couple of abusing and "sleighting" the Scriptures by "Allegorical fancies" seems exactly wrong. Or, it serves to mask Ellis's and orthodoxy's own deep commitment to a dualistic allegorical ontology. Franklin and his followers frequently responded to charges of abusing the Scriptures by explicitly rejecting Scripture itself as allegorical "types and shadows" that have been superseded by the "Substance" of their own spiritual and physical experience. Margaret Woodward, says Ellis, "told the Justices, that what was in the Scripture, of either Old or New Testament, was but Types and Shadows, which she did not now regard, having the Substance" (Ellis, 40). When the Justices at Winchester told Franklin that "he could not be the Christ, Christ being in Heaven at the right hand of the Father, as the Scripture testifieth, . . . he answered, *Those things of the Scripture were gone, and were nothing to him but types and shadows*" (Ellis, 41). Ellis reports that Gadbury had much the same attitude toward the Scriptures: "the Scripture, when in any conference alledged to her, was generally slighted by her, the greatest Authorities she alledged was her owne visions and revelations, many of which were yet in Scripture-expressions delivered by her that she might deceive the better by them" (Ellis, 19–20).

In effect, the two parties, Ellis and the Justices explicitly and Franklin and Gadbury implicitly, charge each other with having an insubstantial—that is to say, an allegorical—faith. According to Franklin's party, Ellis and the Justices still cling to the "types and shadows" of the Bible, resting their faith upon tropologies, analogies, and allegories, receiving God's promises by way of hermeneutics rather than directly from the Spirit now speaking and acting in Franklin's glorified flesh. According to Ellis and the Justices, Franklin and Gadbury have deluded themselves and their followers into believing that the promises of Scripture have been spoken directly to them and of them; they have, in effect, allegorized themselves into biblical characters—Christ, the Spouse of Christ, the mother of Christ (Ellis, 50), "the Kings daughter, all glorious within" (Ellis, 40), John the Baptist, and "one of the destroying Angells mentioned in the *Revelation*" (Ellis, 31). Franklin and his followers lodge much the same charge against their persecutors that the Reformers lodged against the "Papists" and "Schoolmen"—that of having an insubstantial, over-mediated, faith. Ellis counters by charging Franklin and Gadbury with being, or pretending to be, virtually living allegories; that is, either they are impersonating biblical characters, or they are sufficiently self-deluded to believe that they actually personify biblical characters and live "gospel" lives.

Thus, on both sides, the charge of believing allegories is somewhat like the more modern charge of suffering from false consciousness, or being ideologically deluded. It is a euphemism for misrecognizing reality. Nonconformist and orthodox alike regularly accused each other of suffering from and perpetuating "Allegorical fancies" in place of the truth, as if the single most telling sign of apostasy were the habit of twisting God's utterly plain truth allegorically. Puritans of nearly every stripe proclaimed a holy war on equivocation in matters of doctrine, worship, and faith, and allegory was taken to be equivocation par excellence. For the orthodox Ellis, true reality is always other and absent, located in that "world which is to come." Franklin and Gadbury want their heaven here and now or not at all.

In an important sense, Ellis's charge of misinterpretation misses the point: Franklin and Gadbury's faith rejects interpretation and mediation altogether, claiming that God's Word, whether in voice, vision, preaching, or Scripture, has spoken directly to them and of them without the equivocal mediations of interpretation, application, tropologies, or allegories. Theirs is a faith based on hearing a promise unmediated by hermeneutics, grounded in their own experience of the Spirit in the flesh. As radically perverse as their faith seemed to the likes of Ellis and the Justices, it is, in fact, just such a faith as Reformation teaching from Luther to Richard Sibbes had encouraged, but from which it also carefully and strategically retreated.

This equivocating encouragement and strategic retreat is, I will argue in the following two chapters, the primary ideological work of what Barbara Lewalski has called the "Protestant Symbolic Mode," or typology. Typology, I will argue there, is allegory that denies it is allegory. The same symbolic mode of thought is credited with rehabilitating the historicity, the actuality, of the "Old Testament" Israelites even as it preserves them as Christianity's constitutive other—the Jew who is but an allegory of the Christian. This argument, partly because it is so controversial and partly because it is so complex, is difficult to summarize, but for present purposes, I simply want to suggest that Ellis, when he accuses Franklin and Gadbury of suffering from "Allegorical fancies," performs a damning gesture very familiar in Christian discourse. He accuses Franklin and Gadbury of imposture in much the same way Christianity had long accused "the Jews" of being, quite literally, impostors—that is, not God's true Israel, as they supposed they were. And when Franklin and Gadbury literalize the discourse of Puritan experimentalism, they do little more than take that discourse to its logical extreme: "For me to live is Christ." Making this claim good and explaining why this conflict takes the shape of mutual accusations of "Allegorical fancies" is the task I take up in the following chapters.

Here it is necessary to point out how Puritan soteriology equivocates between announcing a new self fully identified with Christ and a new self that remains a mere worldly figure of Christ. Richard Sibbes, an unexceptionably orthodox Puritan, offers us a taste of this equivocation:

> So then a true believer, when he is made one with Christ, he reasons thus, My corruption of nature, this pride of heart that naturally I have,

this enmity of goodness, this is crucified; for I am one with Christ. When he died, I and my head did die, and this pride and covetousness and worldliness, this base and filthy carnal disposition, was crucified, and I in my head am now risen and sit in heaven. Therefore now I am in some sort glorious.[53]

Sibbes boldly announces that the new self is Christ—"for I am one with Christ"—but this new self is also spoken of as the object of Christ's redemptive agency. It is both Christ and other than Christ, other enough to be the object of Christ's adequation of it. In his formulation of the experience of union with Christ, Sibbes employs a string of equivocations calculated to avoid making a claim as boldly transgressive as William Franklin's, or even Paul's. The crucial equivocation of Sibbes's claim concerns the status of the word *I*, the location of the subjectivity implicit in such a claim. The Pauline claim is more explicit about the objective status of the self and its body—"not I but Christ in me," and "for me to live is Christ." The *I* of Sibbes's claim is never negated. It is not transformed into a "me," the fully abject object of Christ's agency. Things the *I* once possessed—"corruption of nature . . . pride of heart . . . this base and carnal filthy disposition"— are erased or "crucified," and the subjectivity revealed or liberated by this erasure of carnality, the place from which the self now speaks, is absolutely identified with Christ—"for I am one with Christ." Thus, Sibbes comes asymptotically close to Franklin's claim.

What keeps Sibbes's claim from becoming transgressively radical, like those of Franklin and Gadbury, is that he makes it indirectly. It is pronounced as the reasoning of a "he," presumably another person, a "true believer." No doubt Sibbes would class himself as a true believer, but by couching his claim *ex propria persona* and by hedging it with a suggestion of temporal deferment—"When he is made one with Christ"—Sibbes avoids the transgression of a William Franklin or a James Nayler. In the final sentence, the nearly transgressive "Now I am . . . glorious" is held in check by the interpolation of "in some sort." Sibbes's *I* oscillates between the deferred subjectivity to be realized only in the "world to come" and the very present subjectivity of a fully regenerated self. Sibbes's "true believer" announces that he has been crucified with Christ, but only "in my head," and though he claims to be risen and "glorified," this is also "in my head." This equivocation keeps *I* distinct from Christ even in the act of announcing the erasure of that distinction.

The result is that Sibbes effectively preserves a dualistic, allegorical ontology even as he announces the unmediated literalism toward which Puritan soteriology gestures.[54] He allegorizes his own authorial voice as that of a "true believer." What once defined the self—"corruption of nature . . . pride of heart . . . this base and carnal filthy disposition"—is allegorized into things the self possesses.[55] The temporal condition—"when"—that governs the entire reported speech of the allegorized self keeps the chiliastic "now" of the last two sentences in allegorical check. And, as if all this were not enough, in the last sentence, Sibbes covers his chiliastic copulative, "I am," with the re-allegorizing "in some sort," signaling Puritan allegory's crucial equivocation as it both encourages and disallows the claim of identity with God.

Why, then, we might ask, does Ellis accuse Franklin and Gadbury of suffering from "Allegorical fancies?" Why doesn't he accuse them instead of being over-literal? Again, a full answer to these questions requires a detailed analysis of Protestantism's anxiety over symbolic modes of thought, an analysis undertaken in the chapters that follow. Here it is sufficient to recall that "Papists" were routinely accused of perverting the faith by allegorizing Scripture, and Jews were accused of literally being allegories of God's providential design without knowing it. Virtually all forms of misbelief and apostasy were understood as being produced by an inadequate understanding of the one true literal sense of God's revelation in Scripture. Protestantism, especially Puritanism, championed literalism. To accuse Franklin and Gadbury of being too literal, then, might amount to a self-accusation.

We can get a sense, however, of Ellis's dilemma, the dilemma of a Protestantism that insists on literalism and personal experimentalism even as it remains committed to an allegorical understanding of reality—this world and the more real of the next—if we consider Protestantism's radically ambivalent relation to the Jew. As we shall see in more detail in my analyses of Protestant typology, Protestants, and especially Puritans, oscillate between identifying themselves with the ancient Israelite of the "Old Testament" and regarding "the Jew" as the quintessential misbeliever, Christianity's perennial constitutive other.

Medieval Christianity, according to J. S. Preus, characterized the Israelites of the Hebrew scriptures as a people "unaware that their whole history was an allegory."[56] Augustine had compared the Jew to "a blind man with a lantern who shows the way to others but doesn't see it himself."[57] In this model, the ancient Israelites, their scripture, religion, history, indeed their very being, is taken to be an allegory, a shadowy figure (*umbra*) of Christian reality.[58] The Jew, then, is Christianity's old man, bound by blindness to a "carnal" existence which he does not realize is no more than an allegorical drama of true spiritual being. Preus also argues convincingly that Luther, and the reformers who followed him, attempted to de-allegorize both the ancient Israelite and the Hebrew scriptures. Luther and Calvin attempt to rehabilitate the ancient Hebrew covenant as a real covenant, real promises made to real people.[59] For Luther, the Christian is no longer the thing signified by the ancient Israelite. "The Old Testament led him to see that he was still 'as if' (*ac si*) an Old Testament man, insofar as he had not yet attained, and God had not yet given, that which had been promised. Indeed, it was the Old Testament that unveiled the real situation of the Christian church as like the situation of the 'faithful synagogue'; even the Church was not yet the 'reale quid Israel' but a *testimonium* and promise of the eschatological Israel" (Preus, 269).

I will argue, however, that this rehabilitation of ancient Israel and its history is finally and crucially incomplete. It must remain so if Christianity is to survive. Rather than effecting a de-allegorization of the Jew, Protestantism can just as easily be seen as producing a re-allegorization of the wayfaring Christian pilgrim, who possesses a self that is never, in this world, a true self, and who regards his or her own life in this world as an extended figuration of true life in the next. "If we were well read in the story of our own lives, we might have a divinity of our own, drawn out of the observation of God's particular dealing with us," wrote Richard Sibbes.[60] Indeed, it is precisely the act of interpretation that renders the old self old and initiates the new self's being. The old self becomes an allegory out of which the new self, let us call it the hermeneutic self, "reads" divinity, just as medieval hermeneutics read out of the Hebrew scriptures a divinity its Israelite characters could never see. The hermeneutic self must now regard the old self just as medieval hermeneutics regarded the ancient Israelites. The old self is made equivalent to the "Old Testament" and the Jew. The Reformation Christian, like the medieval allegorist's Jew, must now be seen, not as fulfillment, but as figure of the fulfillment promised—and so deferred—in the world to come. The Christian must "read" his experience in this world as an allegory of his being in the next; he or she must oscillate between the roles of allegorical figure and exegete of that allegorical figure. The Christian in this world is like a personification of the glorified Christian (Christ) of the next. When allegorical personifications or figures interpret their surroundings, their own actions, and their positions in the world, they do so as characters in a play or a fiction might do, characters for whom the horizon of the fictional world in which they are staged remains finally opaque, a veil hardly even perceived as a veil, let alone seen through. Their being, actions, and even their interpretations of being and actions are never more than figurations whose proper exegesis can only be the work of another.[61]

My point is that reformed Christianity, for all of its insistence on literalism, remains profoundly committed to an allegorical ontology. It is incessantly about the business of othering. It others the self and the world into God's allegory of himself and his kingdom; it others the past as an allegory of the present and the present as an allegory of the future. And Christianity's names for the other, whether it be the old self, the other of the past, or the other of the present (as viewed from eternity), are the Jew, the Synagogue, the "carnal" Jerusalem, the whore, the flesh, and the world. In short, Reformation thought allegorizes the Christian much as medieval theology allegorized ancient Israel.

When Sibbes tries to describe the ontological states of both Christ and the Christian, he virtually repeats Augustine's characterization of the Jew. Augustine wrote: "The Jew carries a book, from which a Christian may believe. Our librarians is what they have become, just as it is customary for servants to carry books behind their masters, so that those who carry faint and those who read profit."[62] Sibbes writes:

> Who keeps Christ alive in the world, but a company of Christians that *carry* his resemblance? . . . He lives in them, and Christ is alive no other-

wise in the world then in the hearts of gracious Christians, that *carry* the picture and resemblance of Christ in them. (*Complete Works*, 4, 264, italics added)

So far as the eternally divine Christ, the other-than-human being, is in the world at all, he appears not on the altar of transubstantiation, not in a text, nor in mere words, but in mortal Christians who "carry" his resemblance in their hearts, in their inmost being. Sibbes equivocates between resemblance and being.[63] The Christ within is at once the redeemed new self and the hollow space left by the death of the old self. He is at once present ("alive no otherwise") and represented ("picture and resemblance"), that is, absent. Sibbes's key equivocation between being and representation is the phrase "in the world," an equivocation that maintains the allegorical status of the Christian's experience. The Christian, like the "Old Testament" Jew, still dwells in the shadows of unfulfilled promise. Reformation thought, I will argue, presses the boundaries of Christianity's perennially contradictory distinctions and threatens to blow it apart at its imperfectly sutured seams.

Pseudo-Christs like Franklin tried to break this endless chain of othering and equivocation by de-allegorizing their experience of conversion, announcing their experience as fulfillment in spirit and in flesh, and discarding the Scriptures as fully superseded types and shadows of that experience. Ellis, on the other hand, sees this de-allegorization of conversion as a disingenuous performance, a kind of stage-play. His challenge to Franklin takes the predictable form of Christianity's indictment of the Jew, the paradigmatic misbeliever. He accuses Franklin and Gadbury of being characters in a drama, of being allegories without knowing it.

Ellis brings his "Relation" of this "tragical story" to a conclusion by "presenting to my Reader a brief Synopsis of it, in the names of the Actors in it, with the parts acted by them therein" (Ellis, 53). Such theatrical terms appear earlier in his account (Ellis, 13, 24), but at the close Ellis makes his charge more explicit. By presenting Franklin and Gadbury's activities as a scripted drama, complete with "Synopsis," a list of *dramatis personae,* and with Hampshire as "the stage," Ellis attempts to re-allegorize the experience Franklin and Gadbury tried to de-allegorize. Franklin and his followers insisted that they were not representing Christ, the Spouse of Christ, John the Baptist, and "The King's Daughter all glorious within," but that Scripture had represented them. Now that Scripture's representations had been fulfilled in them, now that the substance had appeared in the flesh, such imperfect scriptural representations were superfluous, even misleading. Ellis's "Relation" tries desperately to return Franklin and Gadbury to the status of representations, to re-allegorize them into characters in a drama or in the "tragical story" of his "Relation." In so doing, Ellis returns them to the status assigned to the "Old Testament Jews" in medieval hermeneutics—that of characters in a drama whose message is intended for others. They are parts of a drama that they, as characters in it, mistake for reality. Like Augustine's Israelites, "they were unaware that their whole history was an allegory."

The drama of Franklin and Gadbury, however, is an odd sort of stage-play. In his "Post-script" to his introduction, "To the Reader," Ellis takes great pains to vouch for the historicity of his "Relation":

> What is here discovered in the ensuing Relation, I was for a great part an eye and ear Witness thereof; other things I had from their Confessions in their Examinations before the Justices, and from the Testimonies of divers persons of known honesty and integrity, whose Testimonies, subscribed with the hands of those from whom I received them, I have reserved by me. (Ellis, 4)

His "Relation" is not, says Ellis, "like the stories of some travellers, . . . nor done long ago, as things forgotten, . . . but things done among our selves, and that very lately, that they are fresh in the memories of most persons hereabout" and so cannot be easily gainsaid, or charged with being fictional. "Thousands in these parts can witness these things for the generallity and substance of them to be true, . . . how strange soever they might otherwise seem." The play is not a play, but part of the figural drama of history itself. Franklin and Gadbury are not so much actors, but characters in the drama of 1649–50. Insofar as they are sincere, then, Ellis implies that they are more figural than real. They don't realize that they are acting a part. Ellis himself alternates between positions inside and outside this play: inside as he visits the characters in prison (Ellis, 47) and tries to reason with them; outside as he is part of the audience this drama is intended to warn and edify. Ellis, then, occupies the multiple positions of character, audience, and hermeneut which we shall see structure the life of Protestantism's way-faring pilgrim. Ellis betrays what I will later argue is a central feature of Protestant typology: even as it tries to privilege the literal and the historical over allegories and fictions, this very effort tends to empty such distinctions of their crucial differences.

For Ellis, then, life in this world is allegory. Some characters in this allegory, like the Hampshire Christ and his Spouse, are doomed to be no more than characters. Mistaking their experience for reality, they doom themselves, like Augustine's Jews, to a perpetual lack of being, ever to appear as characters in a play whose real message speaks neither of them or to them. Others, like Ellis and his intended audience, oscillate among the positions of scripted representations of God's grand allegory, readers of that allegory, and, in the next world, union with the true meaning of that allegory. In other words, the damned live an allegory under the delusion of self-sameness, and the redeemed live a life of represented being, a life of deferred being, whose originary being is always both another's and elsewhere.

The drama of life in this world teaches us, says Ellis, what is always already and only true: "the Truth of Christ, and of his Word, the Scriptures." With allegorical precision, text and reality exchange and re-exchange positions as the "literal sence" of the Scripture's truth is verified by its allegorical representation in the drama of our experience. The text of Franklin and Gadbury's experience, and of Ellis's "True Relation" and exposition of it as a drama "thus eminently fulfilling the *Scripture,* notwithstanding their impugning of it, give us ground thereby to be setled in our faith concerning the divine Authority of it" (Ellis, 54). That is, Franklin and Gadbury's rejection of Scripture must be interpreted as a performative fulfilling of Scripture. Their claim to be the substantial fulfillment of the Bible's shadowy types is an already pre-scripted performance of a scene from providential history —God's allegorical drama of his own reality. Insofar as they are themselves characters in the text or drama of this world's experience that is correctly interpreted by Ellis, they fulfill and verify Scripture, "even in the literal sence of it," for the Scriptures promised there would be false Christs and prophets in the last days.

There is, Ellis implies, no real escape from allegory, except, perhaps, to die. In this world one is either a representation of the next world's eternal self (Christ) or a representation of one's own lack of a next-world identity, a perpetual allegory of one's own lack of being, a kind of "Jew" whose only function is to performatively represent in one's self-deluded conviction of fulfillment the fulfilling of Scripture's promise of fulfilled selfhood to another.

The re-allegorization of radical sectarianism that Ellis attempts anticipates Bunyan's later literary attempt to do the same for his account of "the Way / and Race of Saints." Bunyan describes the composition of his first explicitly allegorical work as almost a kind of automatic writing that proceeded of itself, even against his will. *The Pilgrim's Progress,* as he introduces it, is literally "another" book from the one he intended to write:

> When at the first I took my pen in hand,
> Thus for to write; I did not understand
> That I at all should make a little Book
> In such a mode; Nay, I had undertook
> To make another, which when almost done,
> Before I was aware, I this begun.

This other book, however, displaces the intended book, rendering the intended book "another." Bunyan says he "Fell suddenly into an Allegory," in which mode the "things" began "to multiply . . . so fast" that they threatened to "eat out / The Book that I already am about."[64]

In the final two chapters of this book, we shall see that Bunyan, like Franklin and virtually all Puritans, understood his conversion as being made literally one with Christ; unlike Franklin and Gadbury, however, Bunyan falls back into the allegory Protestantism requires. Franklin and Gadbury had to be threatened and even beaten back into their own flesh and into acknowledgment of the names, callings, and habitations that went with it. Ellis tries to re-allegorize Franklin and Gadbury as allegorical characters in a kind of scriptural drama because he desperately needs to mask the frightening specter raised by people like them—the specter of a world in which the Christian religion is no longer necessary, since men (but not yet women) are already gods incarnate. Franklin went to prison, but Gadbury was committed to Bridewell, where she was repeatedly whipped, and then to the common gaol (Ellis, 44–45). Gadbury never committed the grand blasphemy of claiming to be Christ, yet her punishment was far more violent and severe than Franklin's. Franklin, after all, had merely taken

Puritan piety to a parodic, though not illogical, extreme. The truly redeemed self is, after all, supposed to be Christ. Gadbury, however, had claimed to be the Spouse of Christ in the flesh. She had literalized in her body Christianity's favorite metaphor for the Church. In so doing, she risked exposing what many women of the day were beginning to suspect: that orthodoxy really had no space for a female Christian. Even her most literalized experience of Christ is not union or identity, but always as Christ's vessel, spouse, or mouthpiece. Christ's voice can speak through her catatonic body, but that body always marks her as Christ's significant—allegorical—other. The glorified Church must pass from spousehood to identity, reclaiming the true self of Christ, the Man/God. But femaleness has no telos in a glorified body; it is always but an allegory of true being. Like the damned—the world, the flesh, and the devil—the female as female cannot be Christ. Bunyan's Christiana, we shall see, experiences much the same exclusion as Mary Gadbury.

Bunyan's return to, his "fall" into, allegory transforms a radical religion and practice into mere dissent and nonconformity. Even in its dissent it affirms the two-world ontology that renders this world's experience literally unreal. Its nonconformity restores the distinction between inward and outward so that the essential conformities of physical behavior—a despising of this world and the fleshly self that lives in it—are also tacitly restored. Nonconformity and its later versions of fundamentalism become complicit with the very structures of power they once threatened to expose and overturn.[65] Millenarian literalism and the religion of glorified bodies had thrust orthodoxy's suppressed contradictions into bold relief.[66] They had threatened to overturn or render meaningless that endless string of allegorical binaries—soul/body, spirit/flesh, literal/figurative, this world/the next, God/Man—that define the Christian as a citizen not yet allowed to claim a citizen's rights, guaranteeing that the significance of life and action (even words and speech, as we shall see in chapter 5) in this world is precisely its insignificance, as the husk, once cracked open, is dispensable.

The two chapters that follow trace out in much more detail Protestantism's inevitably abortive attempt to transform Christianity's allegorical metaphysics into something more historical and literal. First, I argue that recent critics' uncritical acceptance of the Reformers' own attempts to distinguish typology as absolutely as possible from allegory have tended to obscure deeply contradictory aspects of that attempt, and finally to obscure the fact of its failure. Chapter 3 probes these contradictions as they appear in a remarkable series of commentaries, from Luther to the English Puritans, upon that most troubling bit of Pauline exegesis—his allegoresis of Abraham's two wives and sons in Galatians 4.

Because so much of the Puritan discourse of the self is enabled by the claim that Christians are God's true Israel, chapter 4 presents a detailed comparison of the Pauline discourse of the spirit-born self as Christ and the ancient Hebrew discourses of self and God out of which and against which he forges it. Both Pauline and Calvinist versions of the self, I argue, are the effective result of forcing the discourses of endless metonymic displacement characteristic of the Genesis narratives—especially the stories of Joseph and Tamar—into a two-world allegorical ontology. Metonymic displacements shift to metaphoric replacements as Paul redefines this world's birth and life as but an inadequate figure for the truly real birth and life of the Spirit.

Chapters 5 and 6 read Bunyan's most celebrated works, *Grace Abounding* and *The Pilgrim's Progress,* as culminating moments in the Reformation crisis in representation. Bunyan's extreme anxiety about equivocation in words and deeds leads him down a path toward utter skepticism, even atheism, from which he is rescued by his "fall" into allegory, a fall already evident in his autobiography. Life in "this world" is unavoidably reinstated as an allegory of true life, so Bunyan's much-celebrated "realism" literally *is* allegory. Thus, the only escape from this "carnal," and therefore utterly allegorical, existence is to be newly born into that other world, the one that is never quite present, always yet to come. Paradoxically, however, Bunyan tries to abandon hermeneutics altogether, and urges his readers to abandon it as well, for hermeneutics is that mode of understanding practiced only by those poor damned souls whose life and being is but an allegory. At once practicing and denying allegory, Bunyan preaches an anti-hermeneutics of "experience" available only to those who have been spiritually parted from this world and reborn into the next. My reading of Bunyan challenges Stanley Fish's claim that *The Pilgrim's Progress* is "the ultimate self-consuming artifact," not by denying that claim, but by demonstrating that Fish's claim, as well as the theory of experiential hermeneutics upon which it rests, is a thinly secularized version of Bunyan's own anti-hermeneutics of experience.[67] Thus, Fish's theory of "literature in the reader" is virtually a latter-day perpetuation of Puritan allegory, a symbolic practice that is not finally interested in interpretation at all, but in the evangelical project of "transforming minds" by a kind of new-birth experience.[68]

Throughout the book I pay constant attention to the ways Puritan allegory genders both the self and its constitutive others, especially in the discourse of new birth as it appears in Paul, the Reformers, and in Bunyan. If "carnal" birth is but a this-worldly figure for real birth, then woman, like the Jew and this world, is thoroughly displaced. There is no place, then, for women, as women, in "the world which is to come." Woman, as we shall see, is figured as the place of displacement.

Two

Allegory versus Typology:
The Figural View of History

And they are weaker in that they wish to seem learned, not in the knowledge of things, by which we are truly instructed, but in the knowledge of signs, in which it is very difficult not to be proud.

Augustine[1]

In the case of Franklin and Gadbury, we found the orthodox Ellis and the pseudo-Christ Franklin locked in a battle of mutual accusation. Each accuses the other of misunderstanding God's revelation by taking it allegorically rather than literally. One believer's literalism is the other's allegory. Our working assumption in chapter 1, then, was that Christianity's two-world ontology requires an allegorical discourse, and that the banner of literalism, or the "one true sense of Scripture," under which the Reformers marched had the effect, not of dispensing with allegorical modes of thought, but of installing a denial of Christianity's allegorical structures, a denial that prompted a crisis in Reformation theories of representation more generally. This chapter now turns to a more detailed investigation of that crisis.

In a brief analysis of the iconoclastic passages of Milton's "Nativity Ode," Christopher Kendrick appeals to the following axiom: "in so far as religion is dominant, it works in terms of a confluence of messages; it is by definition an overcoded, or *allegorical,* medium."[2] Thus, argues Kendrick, Milton's "Puritan call to arms" against the idolatry of the Laudian church is grounded in an allegorical reading of the Gospels. Christ's nativity, according to Milton, inaugurated a campaign of "Herculean anti-idolatry," an iconoclastic cleansing of the Augean stables of all those mediating, but hopelessly distorting, representations of God of which "the Jews" were allegedly so fond. Milton's poem, however, reads the first-century nativity of Jesus as an allegory for the latter-day rebirth of Christ in the hearts of all those truly re-formed. This new-born body of Christ must now attack the idolatry that is so widespread a feature of the Church of England under Charles I. The new "Jews" are the "Papists" and the Anglican bishops whom Milton thought little better than "Papists" in their persistent devotion to ritual and the "outward forms" of religion.[3] The new "Christ" is what Kendrick calls "the Christian reliving Christ's birth and infancy in the present" (45). In this way, the Gospels are read as an allegory of the present (in this case, 1629–30).

Of course, English reformers of the day would shrink from calling this allegorical interpretation, for that would imply that Christ's advent was little more than a prophetic fiction, "shadowing forth," but not actually effecting, the true cleansing of the temple. The favored term for this sort of symbolic application of biblical history to contemporary events was typology. Typologically speaking, Christ's nativity is a historical event in its own right, and it also prefigures the advent of the Christ "within" the hearts of the elect. Both of these, in turn, pre-figure the second advent of Christ, an event Milton and many other radical sectarians believed was imminent. This second advent would put an end not only to the idolatrous rituals of the Laudian church, but to history itself. The end of history would mean the end of prefig-urative events; the single event all previous historical events had fore-shadowed would finally "come to pass," and this event would prefigure nothing—it would just be. This event would combine being and meaning in a manner never known before, for it would literally signify nothing; rather, it would be the "thing" signified by everything that ever was.

Such a combination of being and meaning in an event or a "thing" that "is not used to signify something else," that is to say, a thing that is the end of an otherwise endless chain of recursive signification, is the stuff of Augustine's fantasy of "things which make us blessed" in Book One of *On Christian Doctrine*.[4] There Augustine elaborates a Chris-tian semiotics, dividing the world into "things" and the "signs" by which "things" are learned. "Strictly speaking," says Augustine, a "thing" would be "that which is not used to signify something else." Strict thingness, then, would be marked by a thing's utter lack of sig-nificance. It would mean nothing, but would simply be. Augustine attempts to list some mundane examples of such things, "like wood, stone, cattle, and so on." Immediately, he finds he must qualify these examples:

> but not that wood concerning which we read that Moses cast it into bitter waters that their bitterness might be dispelled, nor that stone which Jacob placed at his head, nor that beast which Abraham sacrificed in place of his son. For these are things in such a way that they are also signs of other things. (*CD*, 1.2, 8)

One wonders what things there might be that are not "things in such a way that they are also signs of other things." If the apparently mundane list of "wood, stone, cattle, and so on" requires such immediate qualification, what sort of list could we make?

Perhaps it would be a list of things that must be imagined as never used to signify something else, especially those not so used by any biblical characters. Augustine pursues this possibility when he maps onto his thing/sign binary another, analogous binary:

> Some things are to be enjoyed, others to be used . . . . Those things which are to be enjoyed makes us blessed. Those things which are to be used help and, as it were, sustain us as we move toward blessedness in order that we may gain and cling to those things which make us blessed. (*CD*, 1.3, 9)

Things that "are to be enjoyed," and so "make us blessed," are thus those things that are things "strictly speaking," and not also "used to signify something else." Signs, acknowledges Augustine, are also things ("for that which is not a thing is nothing at all"), but they are things in a different way, in that they also signify something else. Words are such things, "for no one uses words except for the purpose of signifying something." Indeed, words, though Augustine must allow that they are things, cannot ever qualify as things "strictly speaking," for words' "whole use is in signifying." Thus the only words that could meet Augustine's definition of things "strictly speaking" would be words that signify nothing, or nonsense words.

The difference between things "strictly speaking" and things equivocally speaking is gradually revealed to be the difference between all the things of this world, including words, and the "invisible things" of the next world, "our native country where we can be blessed" (*CD*,

1.4, 10). Only "eternal and spiritual" things, that is, "the Father, the Son, and the Holy Spirit, a single Trinity, a certain supreme thing common to all who enjoy it" qualify, "strictly speaking," as things— things to be enjoyed rather than used, and which signify nothing else. "Corporal and temporal things," by contrast, are things by whose use, signifying and otherwise, we come to "comprehend the eternal and spiritual." These may be thought of as things only in an equivocal sense, and though they appear to fall into a mixed class of "others which are to be enjoyed and used" (*CD*, 1.3, 9), Augustine explicitly warns that the enjoyment of such things always betrays a categorical mistake:

> Suppose we were wanderers who could not live in blessedness except at home, miserable in our wandering and desiring to end it and to return to our native country. We would need vehicles for land and sea which could be used to help us to reach our homeland, which is to be enjoyed. But if the amenities of the journey and the motion of the vehicles itself delighted us, and we were led to enjoy those things which we should use, we should not wish to end our journey quickly, and, entangled in a perverse sweetness, we should be alienated from our country, whose sweetness would make us blessed. (*CD*, 1.4, 9–10)

"Strictly speaking," then, all the things this side of one's return to "our native country," things "made" by God to signify himself, are not really things at all; they are no better than words "whose whole use is in signifying." Like words, we must allow them the equivocal status of things only to avoid concluding that they are "nothing at all," which is, "strictly speaking," precisely what they are.

Another way of putting this would be to say that the things of "this world" are only things allegorically speaking. Allegory installs precisely the equivocation needed to keep things from evaporating into "nothing at all" and words from hardening into the thingness of nonsense. Something like this Augustinian semiotics must underlie Kendrick's claim that religion, insofar as it is dominant, "is by definition an overcoded, or *allegorical,* medium."

By calling this allegorical overcoding typology instead of allegory, Reformers simply bring a certain sort of denial to bear on the equivocations that are constitutive of Christianity's allegorical metaphysics. Milton's own call for a campaign against the idolatry of the established church has the disturbing effect of rendering the gospel accounts of Christ's nativity a "shadowy type," a prophetic prefiguration of a reality that has not yet arrived, a reality always about to arrive. If the substance of the gospel's figure still lies just over the horizon of fulfillment, what is the gospel itself but an idol whose day is past, about to be replaced by the substance of experience? In Augustine's terms, the historical Nativity is a thing only in an equivocal sense, as indeed anything that is merely historical—this-worldly—must be. It is very possible to read in Milton a version of William Franklin.

Even though reformers from Luther to Milton abominated allegory and allegorical interpretations of God's Word, and even though they announced allegiance to a literalist hermeneutics in opposition to the idols forged by medieval Catholic hermeneutics, these attitudes proved impossible, in practice, to square with the insistently allegorical metaphysics of Christianity.

But what does it mean to call Christianity (not to mention religion in general) allegorical "by definition"? This might simply mean that Christianity deploys its various discursive and ritual practices quite consciously as coded versions of something else, where something else—provisionally coded as God, Yahweh, Christ, or "the world which is to come"—is taken to remain essentially beyond the horizon of any mortal's capacity to comprehend or represent it. This would be to say no more than that Christianity is a mystery religion with a strong tendency to appeal, when push comes to shove, to some version or another of what we call negative theology. If this were all that is meant by calling Christianity allegorical, then I suppose most (if not all) religions must fall into this category. But Christianity has never been content with being a mystery religion, nor has it ever allowed itself to rest for long in a negative theology.

In fact, one could argue that Christianity has from its beginnings exhibited a disturbing tendency to try to dispense altogether with codes and coded versions of the something else, and announce the immediate advent of that something else that renders codes and codedness, and the negative theology they require, no longer necessary. The Christian Gospels repeatedly strive to announce the fulfillment of Hebrew prophecy in the event of Christ's conception, birth, life, death, and resurrection: "Now all this was done, that it might be fulfilled which was spoken by the Lord through the prophet" (Matthew 1:22).[5] The desired effect is to render the spokenness of Hebrew prophecy as no more than an initiating part of God's complete performance. The Gospels strain to announce the completion of that performance, to announce that all that was said has now been done, and that therefore saying, with all the inadequacies attendant upon it, is no longer necessary. The codes (the law of ritual practices and prophecies) may pass away, now that what they only inadequately represented has arrived.

That this rhetoric of fulfillment is so often repeated in the Gospels—indeed, that there is more than one gospel that repeats this rhetoric—is testimony enough to its failure to announce the completion of God's performance. Pauline Christianity, as we have seen, tries yet again to announce such completion as it replaces the advent of Jesus with the advent of the risen Christ reborn as the Christian self. Jesus' disciples, especially Peter, James, and John, claims Paul, cling like "Jews" to the fleshly idol of a this-worldly Jesus and so miss the completing experience of the risen Christ born again as "I." The Reformers of the sixteenth century lodge much the same charge against Roman Catholics, as do the English reformers of the seventeenth century against the insufficiently reformed English church.

Kendrick links the terms "overcoded" and "allegorical" in such a way as to suggest that what is allegorical about religion is not always, not even usually, something conscious. To refer to religion as "the dominant ideology, or master-code" of seventeenth-century English society is to speak of it as a totalizing system that drives both thought and practice before it; whatever consciousness it produces must be assumed to be false consciousness. Thus Christianity's repeated attack on codedness must be seen as itself overcoded; its incessant attempts to announce the end of history, the arrival of "the fullness of time," and thus the absolute supercession of all codes and systems of representation must be regarded as an endless playing out of the central ideologeme of anti-idolatry.[6]

Puritanism is obsessed with idolatry. It is an iconoclastic campaign against virtually every conceivable form of idol that insinuates itself into faith: in ritual, the surplice and the Mass; in hermeneutics, allegorical exegesis; in architecture, statues and rood-lofts; in church government, bishops, priests, or hierophants of any description; in private meditation; and in the "carnal" imagination itself, which clings perversely to those images of God forged by what Calvin called "a perpetual forge of idols"—"the human mind" (*Institutes,* 1.11.8). If Christianity is indeed an overcoded and allegorical medium, Protestantism must finally fail in its campaign against idolatry, or it must succeed in destroying Christianity itself. Arguably, Protestantism has so far succeeded in doing both, to some degree. That Protestant Christianity survives in a form still recognizable by specific ritual practices and discourses is proof enough of its failure utterly to cleanse the temple; that Christianity is no longer the dominant ideology testifies to its qualified success in severely disabling, if not destroying, its own capacity to serve as a master-code. It has (almost) accomplished this by doggedly pursuing the task of disqualifying codedness itself wherever it could recognize it. Protestant Christianity's absolute success will be achieved only when that "perpetual forge of idols" known as "the human mind" is finally destroyed or exposed as the nothing all idols must always have been. This, of course, has not yet come to pass.

Typology versus Allegory: The Protestant Dodge

THE PRINCIPAL DODGE THAT ALLOWED Protestantism to attack allegorical interpretation as a "licentious system" devised by Satan and the equivocating "Papists" while simultaneously preserving the absolute otherness of God and "the world which is to come" is called typology. I call it a dodge because it is largely a euphemism for allegory designed to mask Protestantism's continued commitment to allegorical structures of thought and representations of reality or truth even as it constituted itself under the antiallegorical banner of the one true literal sense of God's Word.

One of the larger obstructions to understanding the Reformation crisis in the theory and practice of representation is the still widely credited distinction between allegory and typology. Barbara Lewalski, for example, bases her entire discussion of Protestantism's "Biblical Symbolic Mode" upon precisely this distinction. Reformation resistance to allegory is not, according to this distinction, a resistance to all representational modes, only to allegory as it is distinguished from typology:

Allegory was understood to involve the invention of fictions, or the contrivance of other systems of symbols, to represent underlying spiritual truth or reality. Typology by contrast was recognized as a mode of signification in which both type and antitype are historically real entities with independent meaning and validity, forming patterns of prefiguration, recapitulation, and fulfillment by reason of God's providential control of history. (Lewalski, 111)

The crucial term in this distinction is "historically real." In allegory, neither the sign nor the thing signified is taken to be historically real. An allegorical sign is a fictional figure, having no "independent meaning and validity" apart from what it signifies, or is taken to signify. Accordingly, the Song of Solomon was taken to be allegorical, a fictional representation of Christ's relation to his church. The literal sense of the fiction, what Augustine defined as the things signified by the words, is a relatively dispensable placeholder, mediating quite temporarily between the fictional figure (what the words literally say) and the "underlying spiritual truth or reality" (what the figures mean). Solomon's poetry should not be taken to represent his own historical romantic experiences. Whether or not he ever had such experiences is, according to this model, entirely irrelevant, and any discussion of such a possibility is thus considered a sign of an interpreter's vulgarity, or a hopelessly "carnal" mind.[7] The sign is fictional, not historical; therefore this is allegory, not typology.

A number of corollary distinctions are implicitly advanced in this attempt to separate allegory from typology as a distinctly "Protestant" and "Biblical" symbolic mode. The something else signified in allegory, in order for it to qualify as allegory, must be every bit as historically unreal as the fictional sign. Besides having the effect of disqualifying most straightforwardly political allegory (like, for example, Dryden's *Absalom and Achitophel*), this distinction also re-enforces on the level of axiom the two-realities metaphysics that makes Christianity itself so insistently allegorical. "Historically real entities with independent meaning and validity" are here distinguished from "spiritual truth or reality." The quasi-scientific force of the term "entities" cannot hide—more likely it calls attention to—the fact that whatever is "historically real" has been disqualified from being really (one force of the term "spiritual") real or really true. The appeal to the historical reality of typology's figures and meanings ultimately falls short of its ostensible purpose—cleansing typology of the taint of allegory—but it succeeds admirably in hollowing out the categories of the historical and the real. The overwhelming allegorical force of "God's providential control of history" has the effect of co-opting the attempt at distinguishing typology and allegory along the poles of history and fiction because the appeal to God's eternal perspective must always render such a polarity a distinction without a difference.[8]

My claim is not that Lewalski misrepresents the Protestant distinction between allegory and typology. She does not. I wish only to show that she takes it, quite on its own terms, to have been successful at preserving the historicity of figures and things figured when in fact it was not. True, reformers strongly denounced any hermeneutic practice that tended to treat the "historically real entities" of the Hebrew scriptures as allegorical fictions. I have already called attention to Luther's and Calvin's campaign to re-historicize the characters and events recorded in the Hebrew scriptures, to rescue "God's Israel" (as opposed to "the Jews") from the realm of fictional *umbrae* and return it to historical reality. By claiming, for example, that David and Israel are types of Christ and his church, rather than allegories, reformers sought to preserve a sense of their independent historicity. They are not fictional characters, but real historical characters, and though they prefigure Christ and his church, they are also real people with (so it was alleged) a historical relation to Christ and his church. Joseph, Moses, and David, therefore, all represent Christ as figures, and are simultaneously real people in covenant with Christ. In allegorical terms, they are simultaneously inside and outside of the representational structure—inside as figures, and outside as interpreters of, or as the intended audience for, the figuration. They are both readers and the thing read, characters in and audience for God's providential drama of history, that is to say, God's allegory of himself. But an important effect of these contradictory projects—preserving the historicity of God's providentially deployed figures and insisting that such figures mean or "point to" something "more real"—is that terms like history and historicity undergo a radical shift in significance.

Lewalski notes that this "new Protestant emphasis" on the historicity of God's allegory "makes for a different sense of the Bible as a unified poetic text, and for a much closer fusion of sign and thing signified, type and antitype" (Lewalski, 117). She might also have said that it makes for a much closer fusion of fiction and history, for it is hard not to recognize that one effect of what the Reformers call typology is not simply a re-historicizing of the ancient Hebrews and of their experience, but also a re-fictionalizing of history more generally. No longer is Christ's nativity, or the rites of the church, or even a believer's experience simply the reality figured by the allegorical "Jews" of "the Old Testament"; these things must now also be understood as figures of yet another, truer, reality to come. Neither Jesus, nor the church, nor Christians are final fulfillments any longer. Reality has been pushed beyond a new telic horizon. Protestant Christians may assert the historicity of the ancient Hebrews and even figure their own experiences of God increasingly on Hebraic models, but they do so at a cost. The cost is that of identifying one's self and one's own experience as figural, rather than fully real. By reducing the dispensational divide between "Old Testament" times and Jesus' advent, the Reformers effectively reduced the divide that once distinguished between God's figural self-revelation (to "the Jews") and his actual self-revelation (to Christians), with the result that what was once taken to be actual must now be understood as figural. Under the totalizing force of Christianity's allegory, the Reformers' redefinition of the historically real as figures could only have the effective result of radically emptying out the category of the historically real.

Lewalski's reading of Protestant typology depends directly and explicitly upon Erich Auerbach's formulation of the "figural view of reality" in his landmark article, "Figura."[9] There, Auerbach invokes the historicity of figural (his preferred word for typological) interpretation as the feature that distinguishes it from, and qualifies it as superior to, allegorical modes:

> Since in figural interpretation one thing stands for another, since one thing represents and signifies the other, figural interpretation is "allegorical" in the widest sense. But it differs from most of the allegorical forms known to us by the historicity both of the sign and what it signifies. Most of the allegories we find in literature or art represent a virtue (e.g., wisdom) or a passion (jealousy), an institution (justice), or at most a very general synthesis of historical phenomena (peace, the fatherland)—never a definite event in its full historicity. (Auerbach, 54)

What distinguishes typology from allegory, then, is not that it is a different mode of representation, but rather a perceived difference in the ontological status of the figures and the things figured. Typology replaces allegory's figural fictions with historical figures (the pun is instructive) and its abstract things figured with "definite event[s] in [their] full historicity." This is precisely the distinction Lewalski describes, but with an important difference: Auerbach allows that "in the widest sense," typology is indeed allegory. It is this "widest sense" of allegory that accounts for the progressive narrowing, and near evaporation, of the category of the historically real under the pressure of typology's claim to be something completely different.

The rest of this chapter will trace in more detail the process whereby this effort to locate typology's difference from allegory in the historicity of its figures and things figured de-historicizes history. Auerbach's account of "the figural view of reality" will be especially useful in this task, but I will also argue that Auerbach largely reproduces in summary fashion the theory of typology variously worked out by Luther, William Tyndale, William Whitaker, and other Protestant reformers, thus tracing the theory from the early Reformers up to English Puritans. This will leave us in an especially good position to consider the significance of Bunyan's "fall" into allegory.

Calvin's "Human Mind": "A Perpetual Forge of Idols"

CALVIN, AS FAR AS I CAN TELL, IS NOT SPECIFICALLY INTERESTED in distinguishing typology from allegory and so does not appear in the list above, even though he, like the others, worried his way quite nervously through the problem of what Paul meant in Galatians 4:21–31 by designating Abraham's complicated family history—two sons, one born of Hagar and one of Sarah—an allegory (*allegoroumena,* Galatians 4:24). Calvin's famous strictures concerning images and idolatry in *Institutes* 1.11, however, betray rather clearly some of the problems of Protestant theories of history and representation that may be taken to underlie, or produce the need for, such a privileging distinction of typology from allegory. Before considering further how the distinction stumbles, then, I shall turn briefly to Calvin's remarks on representation.

"The human mind," asserts Calvin, "is a perpetual forge of idols," so thoroughly depraved that it will not allow any representation of things divine, or even of things invisible, to remain merely representational. "The human mind, stuffed as it is with presumptuous rashness" suffers from an "infatuated proneness" to mistake any physical attestation of God's existence or presence (a miracle, for example) for the deity itself (*Institutes* 1.11.8). This is tantamount to saying that the human mind, once presented with an image of something divine or invisible (i.e., something spiritually real or true), is simply incapable of maintaining the distinction between the figure and the thing it figures. It is the unnatural state of human nature to accommodate the otherness of the divine to the sameness of fleshly perception. Indeed, "daily experience shows, that the flesh is always restless until it has obtained some figment like itself, with which it may vainly solace itself as a representation of God." "Nothing," says Calvin, is "more incongruous than to reduce the immense and incomprehensible Deity to the stature of a few feet. And yet experience shows that this monstrous proceeding, though palpably repugnant to the order of nature, is natural to man" (1.11.4).

In this context, at least, Calvin uses the term "the flesh" as a euphemism for human nature, a cluster of attributes that, however "repugnant to the order of nature," are taken to be "natural to man." This "flesh" is understood as "always restless," that is to say, it is in a chronic state of desire for "a figment like itself," and once it gets hold of such a "figment," as it always does, "adoration forthwith ensues; for when once men imagined that they beheld God in images, they also worshipped him as being there" (1.11.9). By the phrase "a figment like itself," Calvin probably means no more than an entity that, like "the flesh," is a visible, corporeal, created thing, as opposed to anything divine, which is defined as invisible, incorporeal, and, in the case(s) of God and his Son (begotten, not created) at least, uncreated. Thus the human mind is marked as fleshly because of its infatuated addiction to the sensual as its ground of reality. Human beings all have, as a matter of "natural instinct," if by no other means, some "sense" that there is a deity (1.3.1), and this instinct somehow initiates a desire to experience God sensually. This being by definition impossible, human nature follows its (un)natural proclivity to mistake "figments like itself" for God.

What Calvin has succeeded in describing here, as if it were a kind of exquisite hell, is what he takes to be the constitutive double bind of unnatural human nature. Simply by virtue of being human, one's desire for God is already sensualized (it originates, after all, as an instinctual sense) to such a degree that we always mistake any "corporeal symbol of his presence" (1.11.8) for God himself. These corporeal symbols are, like ourselves, mere "figments" or "empty phantoms," since corporeal reality is, by definition, not really real. Human beings, after all, are made "in the image of God," and so are, like the rest of visible creation, figments, at best, of God's glory. A pseudo-Christ like William Franklin, then, illustrates the epitome of this double bind when he mistakes himself for God. What else can he do?[10] It is the depraved nature of human beings always to conjure presence into the index of the absent, and then to mistake that index for the presence of the absent one.

This depraved nature, insists Calvin, is not to be confused with stupidity or a failure of intellect. "The Jews" were "not so utterly thoughtless as not to remember that there was a God whose hand led them out of Egypt before they made the calf." They simply wanted to visualize God "going before them in the calf." "Nor are the heathen to be deemed to have been so stupid as not to understand that God was something else than wood and stone" (1.11.9). Even the heathen Gentiles understood representation and could distinguish between figure and thing figured, sign and thing signified, but they, like all human beings, could not manage to stay clear on the ontological distinction between things equivocally speaking and things "strictly speaking." Calvin argues that the human imagination is so constituted that it always loses track of the distinction between things and "things," the real of this world and the really real of the next, and so inevitably takes the former for the latter.

> Read the excuses which Augustine tells us were employed by the idolaters of his time (*August. in Ps.* cxiii). The vulgar, when accused, replied that they did not worship the visible object, but the Deity which dwelt in it invisibly. Those again, who had what he calls a more refined religion, said, that they neither worshipped the image, nor any inhabiting Deity, but by means of the corporeal image beheld a symbol of that which it was their duty to worship. What then? All idolaters, whether Jewish or Gentile, were actuated in the very way which has been de-

scribed. Not contented with spiritual understanding, they thought that images would give them a surer and nearer impression. When once this preposterous representation of God was adopted, there was no limit until, deluded every now and then by new impostures, they came to think that God exerted his power in images. (*Institutes,* 1.11.9)

Representation, says Calvin, always slides into the very monism that Yahwism was invented to avoid. However firmly one tries to believe in a God whose substance is absolutely discontinuous with what it created, representations of that God will always have the ultimate effect of compromising that belief. As soon as God is defined as absolutely other, the inevitable quest for experience of that God is sure to take adulterous byways—"whoring after false gods" is, after all, perfectly human. God's display of his power and majesty in created things is always already transformed by the idol-forging factory of human imagination into God's exercise of power and majesty in created things. Thus human imagination makes God's power dependent upon what he has made; such a God is nothing without bodies to exercise power upon. God's power and majesty thus become misconstrued as consubstantial with the visible creation.

For this reason Calvin proscribed all representation except of "those things which can be presented to the eye":

> The only things, therefore, which ought to be painted or sculptured, are things which can be presented to the eye; the majesty of God, which is far beyond the reach of any eye, must not be dishonored by unbecoming representations. (1.11.12).

This is virtually a proscription against what Lewalski and Auerbach both defined as allegorical representations—"systems of symbols" specifically contrived "to represent underlying spiritual truth or reality" (Lewalski, 111). Such representations are "unlawful," says Calvin, because they invite the human mind to engage in the inevitable process of idol forging, mistaking the figure for the thing figured. This is far less likely to happen, reasons Calvin, if the things figured in paintings and sculptures are "things which can be presented to the eye" without representation or besides representation. If one can turn one's attention quite readily from the figure to the thing figured and back again, there is less danger of human imagination stepping in and forging idols. Representations, in these cases, will not generally be mistaken for the things they represent, for reality. Such a proscription seeks to limit representation (both its figures and the things they figure) to just one world of the two-world cosmic order. Representation is legitimate and allowed only when the thing represented shares the same ontological space with its representation. The represented thing, in all its thingness, must be as available to perception as its representation in order to avoid the danger of representation sliding into representation. As we shall soon see, this is analogous to the prevailing Reformation strictures on allegorical interpretations of the Scriptures. A preacher may have recourse to allegorical interpretation, but not to prove any point of doctrine. The allegory may illustrate a point of doctrine stated literally elsewhere in the Scriptures, but no doctrine that is not literally articulated elsewhere may be gathered from allegorical interpretation. Thus, a representation, to be legitimate, must share the same ontological space with the thing it represents; otherwise "idolatry has as it were raised its banner" (1.11.13).

Calvin's limitations on the uses of representation, however, almost immediately run into a problem of which Calvin himself seems to remain unaware.

> Visible representations are of two classes—viz. historical, which give a representation of events, and pictorial, which merely exhibit shapes and figures. The former are of some use for instruction and admonition. The latter, so far as I can see, are fitted only for amusement. (1.11.12)

Calvin expresses here a preference for "historical" representations, presumably pictures and sculptures representing historical events, because they are of some instructional use. Simple pictures of otherwise visible things are at best harmlessly amusing. Since Calvin includes both "historical" and "pictorial" representations under the rubric of "visible representations," that is, representations of things "which can be presented to the eye" in all their unrepresented reality, we are prompted to ask a question Calvin simply overlooks: in what sense are historical events capable of being "presented to the eye" apart from representations? From what vantage can one look back and forth from representation to historical event and by doing so avoid engaging the idol-forging propensity of human imagination? How do representations of history manage to avoid Calvin's clear proscription against representing invisible things?

Calvin seems not to notice this difficulty. Perhaps this is because his chief concern is to secure as firmly as possible the distinction between this world and the next, and historical events—however relatively absent—are not absolutely absent in any sense that interests him. History remains for him in the realm of the flesh, the carnal, the created. Like nature itself, history is just another of God's displays of his power and majesty, and as a display, Calvin appears to treat it synchronically. As elsewhere in the *Institutes*, Calvin assumes the ahistorical apocalyptic perspective promised to the pious elect, and from this perspective history is really little different from a painting. What's more, Calvin's stated preference for "historical" over "pictorial" representations complicates the problem further. Presumably, historical representations are of some use for instruction and admonition precisely because they, unlike mere pictures of things, have something important to teach us about the only thing worth knowing—God and his majesty. Elsewhere, Calvin's euphemism for history is God's "continual government of the world,"[11] and as such it is included in his vision of the "works of God" "delineated as in a picture":

> It must be acknowledged, therefore, that in each of the works of God, and more especially in the whole of them taken together, the divine perfections are delineated as in a picture, and the whole human race thereby invited and allured to acquire the knowledge of God, and, in consequence of this knowledge, true and complete felicity. (1.5.10)

As a kind of "picture" of the "works of God," history offers "knowledge of God" and the "felicity" that, according to Augustine, can be had only in the enjoyment of a "thing, strictly speaking," i.e., a thing not of this world. It appears that Calvin prefers "historical" representations for the very features that ought, by his own rules, to disallow them—they pretend to represent God's majesty. Even worse, they represent God's past representations of himself.

If we follow Calvin's logic, however, and take historical events as things that can indeed be presented to the eye, that is to say, things that are not Augustine's "things, strictly speaking," things that exist only on the hither side of true reality, then Calvin's preference for historical representations makes a kind of sense. History, like everything else on this side of the next (or other) world, is already at best a figure (at worst "a figment") of something else, something more real. So, in a strange inversion of Plato's alleged objections to representation, Calvin allows it can be useful to construct representations of history. After all, who would mistake historical events for true reality, any more than one might mistake a statue or a painting of the emperor for the emperor himself?

Typology, because it is allegedly a symbolic mode that limits its attention to historical figures that claim to represent nothing more than other equally historical things, appears to avoid nicely Calvin's dire warnings against idolatry. It invents no fictional figures, and it avoids mistaking the figures God has scattered everywhere throughout creation and history for God "himself." Both its figures and the things they represent are, in Auerbach's (slightly amended) words, "definite event[s] in [their] full historicity." If this account of typology were true, Protestantism would have succeeded in limiting representational thought quite strictly to the this-worldly side of its two-world cosmos. This would mean that the agentive role of human imagination in representation would be severely limited in an effort to avoid the nasty results of its idol-forging propensity. According to this way of thinking, all figures are ready-made, or found, figures, and the things they may be taken to represent are equally ready-made. And the relation between figure and thing figured is one forged by God, not by human imagination. If fiction plays any role at all, it is always only God's fiction (*fictus*, making), not human making. Sidney's famous "maker" is thus outlawed as worse than a "sawcie comparison," and interpretation is reduced to mere reading, or even less than reading.[12]

But, of course, typology in Protestant practice never submitted to such limitations, except insofar as it resulted in a thoroughly secular worldview and relinquished the Christian two-world model altogether. Atheism was one of the great unforeseen products of the Protestant campaign against idolatry.[13] Insofar as Protestantism avoided atheism, it exercised its allegorical imagination under the euphemism of typology, with disastrous consequences for its favorite shibboleths, history and historicity.

History Emptied Out

IT SHOULD ALREADY BE APPARENT that the terms *history* and *historicity* are subjected to a great deal of unacknowledged pressure in both Lewalski's and Auerbach's (not yet to mention the Reformers') articulation of typology as the only legitimate, because divinely authored and divinely interpreted, symbolic mode. The very feature invoked to distinguish typology from allegory—the historicity of its signs and things signified—is in serious danger of evaporating before our eyes. That Auerbach is dimly aware of this danger is evident in the way his use of the word *history* is so frequently hedged about with qualifications. When insisting on the historicity of typological figures and things figured, he usually talks of "concrete history," or "a definite event in its full historicity," as if qualifiers like *concrete, definite,* and *full* are needed to keep a concept already under threat of being emptied out from blowing away in the rhetorical wind.[14] In fact, once he has appealed to history and historicity in defining typology, Auerbach finally does allow the concept of history he has appealed to so insistently to be virtually emptied out:

> Figural prophecy implies the interpretation of one worldly event through another; the first signifies the second; the second fulfills the first. Both remain historical events; yet both, looked at in this way, have something provisional and incomplete about them; they point to one another and both point to something in the future, something still to come, which will be the actual, real, and definitive event. (Auerbach, 58)

"Actual, real, and definitive" now appear as qualifiers deployed in opposition to "historical" inasmuch as the "something still to come," the "something other that is promised and not yet present," holds hostage the actuality, the reality, and the definitiveness of any (now merely) historical event. Historical events "have something provisional and incomplete about them," not just as figures (a figure without a corresponding thing figured is, after all, not incomplete or provisional, but nonexistent), but as events. History qua history is, in this sense, not really real:

> Thus history, with all its concrete force, remains forever a figure, cloaked and needful of interpretation. In this light the history of no ep-

och ever has the practical self-sufficiency which, from the standpoint
both of primitive man and of modern science, resides in the accomplished fact. (Auerbach, 58)

Even history's much-vaunted concreteness, its definitiveness and alleged fullness, the very qualities that enabled it to serve as typology's
distinguishing feature, do not save it from being rendered by the "figural view of reality" as actually inactual, really unreal, and definitively
indefinite—fully unfulfilled and unfulfilling signs that, unless
grounded in a radically other reality, a reality one is both forbidden
and obliged to conceptualize, mean and are nothing at all.

　　In fact, Auerbach goes on to describe typological signs as figures
not only of "something other that is promised and not yet present,"
but simultaneously figures of "something that has always been":

> Thus the figures [concrete historical events] are not only tentative; they
> are also the tentative form of something eternal and timeless; they point
> not only to the concrete future, but also to something that always has
> been and always will be; they point to something which is in need of
> interpretation, which will indeed be fulfilled in the concrete future, but
> which is at all times present, fulfilled in God's providence, which knows
> no difference of time. (Auerbach, 59)

Historical events, as Auerbach's figural view understands them, are the
"tentative form" or shadowy intimation of "something eternal and
timeless," something that is always both "not yet present," but "promised" and, mystically enough, "at all times present." It goes without
saying that this "something eternal and timeless" is radically unhistorical; it is valuable as "ultimate truth" and "the real reality" in
large part because it exists outside or beyond history. It will, insists
Auerbach, have a fulfillment in "the concrete future," but this moment
of concrete futurity is implicitly an apocalyptic moment, the moment
that registers the end of all moments, the end of "concrete" history.
Once "concrete" history is over, "the authentic, future, ultimate,
truth" will reveal itself in the timeless eternal something that has always lurked somewhere behind, beyond, or mystically within the *figura* of events in history. In a curiously inverted image of the agency
behind this apocalyptic moment, Auerbach personifies the "ultimate

truth" of "real reality" as unveiling and preserving the *figura* of historical events:

> earthly life is thoroughly real, but . . . with all its reality it is only *umbra*
> and *figura* of the authentic, future, ultimate truth, the real reality that
> will unveil and preserve the *figura*. In this way the individual earthly
> event is not regarded as a definitive self-sufficient reality, nor as a link in
> a chain of development in which single events or combinations of
> events perpetually give rise to new events, but viewed primarily in im-
> mediate vertical connection with a divine order which encompasses it,
> which on some future day will itself be concrete reality; so that the
> earthly event is a prophecy or *figura* of a part of a wholly divine reality
> that will be enacted in the future. (Auerbach, 72)[15]

Understanding the figural view of reality as something significantly
different from the "spiritualist and Neoplatonic tendencies" of the European Middle Ages—that is, understanding how typology differs
from allegory—requires that we forge firm distinctions between the
"thoroughly real" and the "really real," between "concrete reality" and
"the real reality," between "earthy life" and "definitive self-sufficient
reality." Such an understanding insists that "reality" can serve as a figure for a "real reality" that "will be enacted in the future," but really
exists outside history and time altogether. Something "always present" is also always something to come. When Auerbach asks us to
imagine a personified "real reality" at some asymptotically future moment unveiling and preserving the *figura* of earthly history, he appears
to forget the degree to which his figural view of reality has defined
historical events *as* the veils that must be removed and discarded in
order that "real reality" may appear. I think Auerbach is anxiously, but
dimly, aware that the figural view of reality he describes threatens to
relegate historical events to a kind of pseudoreality of "tentative
forms," and this image is a rather desperate but unsuccessful attempt
to preserve some sense of historical events as reality.

The real reality signified in typology turns out to be every bit as
ahistorical, spiritual, eternal, timeless, ever present (and so, historically speaking, ever absent) as God and his majesty, the very things
typology was first defined as prohibited from figuring. In short, typology is the term used (by Auerbach, Lewalski, and indeed by the Re-

formers themselves, as we shall see) to denote an allegorical mode that effectively treats history as God's fictional representation of the something else that lies outside history.

Indeed, typology, to use Auerbach's word, "preserves" historical events as *figura* even as it evaporates them as history. It has often been observed that the medieval fourfold method of allegorizing the "Old Testament" had the effect of rendering Israelite history not only meaningless and useless as history, but of encouraging the exclusion of the Hebrew scriptures from the sacred canon.[16] Typology bypasses this threat by preserving history itself as God's writing, God's allegory. As such, Israelite history is still every bit as much a disposable allegorical husk as it threatened to become in the fourfold allegorical mode, but as God's allegory, and as a fiction that includes us rather than means us, only God, not human beings, can throw it away and "enjoy" the kernel.[17] The event promised by historical *figurae* is, in one important sense, precisely the throwing away of history as real reality's finally unnecessary representational husk. The end of time is, after all, the evaporation (perhaps by vaporizing) of what we have gotten used to calling "concrete" history. This is the "end of history" Puritan (and now fundamentalist) Christianity longs for. This is what Bunyan would have called the "Gospel-sense" of history.

The End of History and the New-Born Self

IF PURITAN CHRISTIANITY LONGS for the evaporation of history and the end of its constitutive element, time, its devotees also have another longing—to be saved from that evaporation. To live this world's history is to live in the "City of Destruction" and not know it; it is to be doomed forever to the status of an allegorical figure with no "independent meaning and validity," no real being. Put another way, typology redefined the "carnal" self, the self that lives in history's "City of Destruction," as "the Jew." Clearly, then, Puritan Christianity requires a new self, a self reborn outside of history, or more precisely, a self that is born by virtue of being parted from history, conceived and carried in the "fleshly" womb of history's nonbeing, and, following the "travail" (also "travell" or pilgrimage) of worldly gestation, new-born into ahistorical reality. This rebirth is, of course, also known as death, but the fantasy is that what dies is what might be called the "Jew-self," left behind in the historical "City of Destruction," still clothed with the "Raggs" of its own "righteousness" (*PP*, 8) What lives on is the new-self, born of the shedding of the "Jew-self." As we have already seen, this new-self is the most problematic idol of all, the self taken to be Christ.

Lewalski's account of Protestant typology is designed to ground her reading of seventeenth-century English meditational poetry. Thus it confines itself to largely personal or private versions of typology, what might be called a typology of the self. Auerbach's account shows much broader strokes, portraying a typology of peoples, ages, and even races. The constitutive otherness of "the Jew" is central to both.

Seventeenth-century Protestants, says Lewalski, entertained two versions of the represented self: "Two formulas were available for relating the contemporary Christian to the biblical type." On the medieval Augustinian model, we recall, the Israelite of the Hebrew scriptures was no more than an allegorical fiction representing Christian fulfillment. The Israelite, like "the Jew" (and like all the false pilgrim characters in Bunyan's *Pilgrim's Progress*) was an allegorical figure without knowing it. With the advent of fulfillment, such types and shadows could be (must be) left to disintegrate in the dustheap of "old-covenant" history, a history that was not really real. The Protestant was not nearly so secure about his or her reality, hence the proverbial anxiety over salvation and eternal security so endemic to Puritan meditation, especially notable in Bunyan's *Grace Abounding*. Thus the Protestant Christian, says Lewalski, "sees himself" in two constantly alternating versions of the "Old Testament" mirror. Typological meditation on the "Old Testament" yields two versions of the self: self as antitype and self as type; the result is a self understood as alternating between being a figure and being the thing figured by the figure with which it alternates.

> When the emphasis is on the great benefits and advantages the Christian enjoys in his religious life, the ease and comfort of the Gospel in comparison to the Law, the Christian may see himself (through Christ) as an antitype of the Israelite of old. But when on the other hand he concentrates upon his essential spiritual life and situation, his dependence upon faith and his imperfect spiritual vision in this life, he is more likely to view himself as a correlative type with the Old Testament Isra-

elites, located on the same spiritual plane and waiting like them for the fulfillment of all the signs in Christ at the end of time. The two approaches were not incompatible, and both contributed importantly to the power, profundity, and psychological complexity with which the great seventeenth-century religious lyric poets probed the personal spiritual life.[18]

"The two approaches were not incompatible." If compatibility here is measured by the frequency with which both versions of the self—type and antitype—appear side by side in Protestant literature, then we can have no quarrel with Lewalski's account. But surely there is some incompatibility between seeing one's self as both a type and its antitype, a figure and the thing figured by that figure—an incompatibility that may be smoothed over by alternating between one version and the other, never invoking both simultaneously (except as mystically paradoxical), but an incompatibility that is never fully erased. Perhaps it is precisely this felt incompatibility between understanding one's self as a figure awaiting fulfillment and as the fulfillment "(through Christ)" of all figures that constituted the effects of "power, profundity, and psychological complexity" Lewalski detects in seventeenth-century religious lyrics and in religious discourses and practices more generally.

This felt incompatibility emerges even more clearly when we consider that these two formulas of self-representation are two modes by which the Christian is invited to "view himself" in relation to one of the Christian's crucially constitutive others—"the Jew."[19] The Christian, especially the Protestant Christian,[20] is always oscillating between two ontological accounts of him- or herself. In one account, the Christian is the fulfillment of "the Jew" as type. This account sees the Israelite depicted in the Hebrew scriptures as a kind of allegory of Christ and Christians. Promises made to the Israelites—nationhood, numbers, land, "temporal blessings"—are regarded as allegories of the spiritual blessings—salvation, righteousness, eternal life—promised to the Christian. Unless converted to Christ, "the Jew" has no claim on either promise, the temporal or the spiritual, since the first was not properly a promise at all but merely an allegory of a promise, and the second—the proper promise implicit in the allegory—was made to and can only be claimed by one who has correctly interpreted—seen through—the allegory; that is, a Christian. This, in vulgar brevity, is the medieval Catholic account of the Christian's relation to "the Jew."[21] Christian and Israelite (as "the Jew") inhabit two distinct ontological realms: the latter is a figure in an allegory of promise, an allegory already conveniently textualized and made available as the Book, and the former is the thing figured by the allegorical stand-in.

In the other, more typically Protestant, ontological account, the Christian believer shares—almost—the typical status of the Israelite of the Hebrew scriptures, "*as if he* [the Christian] *were in the synagogue.* For as long as we do not receive the promises, we have not entered Jerusalem, but we stand and await our entrance."[22] I insert "almost" here, because although in this account the ancient Israelite is no longer presumed to be unaware of the spiritual meaning of the promises couched in temporal figures, still, as Lewalski points out, the first account is always available to the Protestant Christian.[23] This means that it is always possible to return the newly de-allegorized Israelite to the status of "the Jew," for as Calvin notes, the "Old Testament" covenant exhibited "only the image of truth, while the reality was absent, the shadow instead of the substance," but the "New" exhibits "both the full truth and the entire body" (*Institutes* 2.11.4). The ancient Israelite may well have grasped the spiritual substance figured by "the image of truth," but he or she had to do so hermeneutically, by way of shadowy figures.

The Israelite's faith, however much Luther and Calvin redefined it as faith in the truly spiritual object dimly figured by promises of "temporal blessings," remains, according to the Reformers, a faith in something perceived through figures, never directly. The Christian, however, can always point to the incarnate, crucified, and resurrected Christ, says Calvin, as "the full truth and the entire body" revealed without mediating tropes: "Where Christ can be pointed to with the finger, there the kingdom of God is manifested."[24] Even in the midst of contemplating him- or herself as "located on the same spiritual plane," in the same ontological realm, as the ancient Israelite, the Christian can supposedly do what the ancient Israelite never could— point to Christ with the finger—and so the ancient Israelite slips immediately back into the relative obscurity of figures, types, and shadows. In relation to the Christian, the ancient Israelite always must finally remain "the Jew," or the childish or merely potential Christian.[25] When the Reformation gestures toward de-allegorizing the ancient Israelite are carried to their logical extremes—as some antinomians and millenarians did—the need to be a Christian evaporates. Typology is precisely this arrested gesture of de-allegorization—arrested, that is, by those who wanted or needed to preserve Christianity from the full effects of their own campaign against idolatry; they initiated the gesture but retreated from its full effect.

Thus, when Protestants meditate on the self as flesh (or as not yet fully Christ), they identify with "the Jew"; and when they meditate on the self as fully replaced, reborn as Christ, "the Jew" defines precisely what they are not.[26] "The Jew," then, is nothing but the self that is hopelessly mired in history, the shadowy type or sign that must be stripped away and destroyed as the self is reborn as eternally Christ. Once this is accomplished, Christians live in a new (non)history and in a new (non)world order, which turns out to be the real reality that history and the world only dimly prefigured. This is the (non)world which is (never quite) to come, but by believing in it and affirming it, damnation of allegorical figures like "the Jews" and Bunyan's "false-professors" is justified.

Auerbach's description of typology, though he never identifies it as peculiarly Protestant, betrays much the same effect, but on a more public, even cosmic, scale. Unlike Lewalski or the Reformers upon which she bases her account, Auerbach acknowledges, if only for a moment, the deeply ahistorical, even antihistorical, force of typology —the "figural view" of history. This brief moment of acknowledgment occurs—this should surprise no one—as Auerbach explains the "origins" of figural interpretation in Pauline theology and hermeneutics (Auerbach, 49). According to Auerbach, the early Christians (Judaeo-Christians, as he calls them) quite naturally looked to the Hebrew scriptures for historical and prophetic prefigurations of Jesus as messiah, though messiah was at first understood as a second Isaiah, a second Moses, or a second David, not a replacement and annulment of such worthies. But Paul's "pronounced" hostility to the Judaeo-Christians (what Pauline scholars refer to as "the Judaisers") lends his figural interpretations (1 Corinthians 10:6, 11; Galatians 4:21–31; Colossians 2:16f; Romans 5:12ff; 1 Corinthians 15:21; and 2 Corinthians 3:14) a distinctly antihistorical spin. The historicity of the Israelites, and therefore the historical character of their scriptures, is denied, rendering the "Jews" *typoi hēmōn* ("figures of ourselves") and their very experiences as mere figures of a later, Christian, reality: *tauta de typikōs synebainen ekeinois* ("these things befell them as figures") (Auerbach, 49, quoting 1 Corinthians 10:6 and 11). Auerbach explains that Paul's figural approach to the "Old Testament" effectively erases from it any sense of "Jewish History and national character":

> . . . in its Jewish and Judaistic legal sense the Old Testament is the letter that kills, while the new Christians are servants of the new covenant, of the spirit that gives life. . . . As a whole it ceased for him [Paul] to be a book of the law and history of Israel and became from beginning to end a promise and prefiguration of Christ, in which there is no definitive, but only a prophetic meaning which has now been fulfilled, in which everything is written "for our sakes" (I Cor. 9:10, cf. Rom. 15:4) and in which precisely the most important and sacred events, . . . are provisional forms and figurations of Christ and the Gospel. . . .
>
> In this way his thinking, which eminently combined practical politics with creative poetic faith, transformed the Jewish conception of Moses risen again in the Messiah into a system of figural prophecy, in which the risen one both *fulfills and annuls* the work of his precursor. What the Old Testament thereby lost as a book of national history, it gained in *concrete dramatic actuality*. (Auerbach, 51, italics added)

What only a few pages later will be called the "concrete" or "full" historicity of figural events is here in danger of being transformed into drama—"concrete dramatic actuality"—where the terms *dramatic* and *actual* cannot help but call each other into question. Drama is perhaps a peculiarly felicitous term here, for few modes of representation play so equivocally on what it means to be real, always calling attention to the slipperiness of the distinctions between figures and things figured, representations and realities, performativity and being. It was not for nothing that the Puritan campaign against idols was often so virulently directed against drama, for the drama too persistently foregrounded the slipperiness of distinctions Puritans so desperately wanted to make firm and absolute. The "practical politics" that motivated Paul's redefinition of Israelite history as allegorical drama and the Torah as an allegory of spiritual rebirth may prove to be remarkably similar to the "practical politics" of the Puritan Reformation.

In the "figural view of reality" introduced by Paul, Israelite law and history are annulled, replaced by Christians and the life of the spirit. Seen in this way, the book is no longer a historical record of events that "will someday, in all human probability, happen again in the same or similar way" (Thucydides).[27] Just as the law of the "Old Testament" is no longer to be considered law, so the events it recounts are no longer to be considered historical. If they happened at all, the events "befell them as figures," and were written "for our sakes." With respect to the Hebrew past, Paul is both antinomian and antihistoricist. The old things and events have passed away, that is to say, they have become no longer historical, but dramatic—what might be called the Jew-drama recorded in Hebrew scripture is God's allegory of Christian actuality. Hence what Auerbach calls the de-historicized Scripture's "concrete dramatic actuality."[28]

"It was not until very late," Auerbach continues, "probably not until after the Reformation, that Europeans began to regard the Old Testament as Jewish history and Jewish law; it first came to the newly converted peoples as *figura rerum* or phenomenal prophecy, as a prefiguration of Christ, so giving them a basic conception of history, . . . which for almost a thousand years remained the only accepted view of history" (Auerbach, 53). Auerbach would have us believe that throughout late antiquity and the Middle Ages Europeans understood historical events ahistorically, not as events, but as *figura rerum,* figures of things. This would be as hard to prove as it is to believe. It is easier to believe that *figura rerum* was much more specifically the dominant European conception of Hebrew history. Auerbach omits the word *Jewish,* but it is impossible not to hear it implied. The "Europeans" he is talking about, after all, are "the Celtic and Germanic peoples" who could never, he says, have accepted the "Old Testament" as law or history: "In its original form, as a law book and history of so foreign and remote a nation, it would have been beyond their reach" (Auerbach, 52). It is not, therefore, all history that is utterly de-historicized by Pauline figural interpretation; it is specifically Jewish history. Paul, his Gentile congregations, and the newly converted Celtic and Germanic peoples of the European past remain real enough; their historicity is not challenged or emptied out. Indeed, they come to be who and what they are precisely as a result (*O felix culpa!*) of the de-historicization of Jewish history and the de-actualization of "the Jew." After the Reformation, of course, the Hebrew scriptures may once again be granted the dubious status of history because, as we have already seen, the Reformation achieves the emptying out of the category "history" as the spiritually unreal. Once history has been relegated to the status of allegory, it is safe to grant "the Jew" a history.

Immediately following his account of Paul's de-historicizing of the Jews and their history, Auerbach enters into his crucial distinction between typology and allegory, that is, "the historicity both of the sign and what it signifies." He does this apparently oblivious to the equivocal sense that he has allowed to accrue to his own use of the words *historical, historicity,* and *history.* The distinction between Jewish history and real history never explicitly emerges, but it remains just below the surface, finessing—and, for some readers, masking—the equivocation implicit in Auerbach's sense of the historical. For example, what makes typological or figural interpretation "completely different" from symbolism, says Auerbach,

> is that figural prophecy relates to an interpretation of history—indeed it is by nature a textual interpretation—while the symbol is a direct interpretation of life and originally no doubt for the most part, of nature. Thus figural interpretation is a product of late cultures, far more indirect, complex, and charged with history than the symbol or myth. Indeed, seen from this point of view, it has something vastly old about it: a great culture had to reach its culmination and indeed to show signs of old age, before an interpretive tradition could produce something on the order of figural prophecy. (Auerbach, 57)

Here, Auerbach explicitly identifies history as something "textual"; this is the sense of history that Fineman calls the generic narrativizing context, stripped of its contingency, its just-happenedness (Fineman, 53, 57). Symbols directly interpret "life" and "nature"; figural prophecy does not. Figural interpretation, it would seem, is concerned with history as text rather than as events per se. Auerbach explicitly distinguishes between "history" on the one hand and "life" and "nature" on the other: symbols make signifiers out of life and nature, but figural interpretation considers only what is text or may be thought of as textual. History, in this sense, is a "text" cut loose from the contingency, the just-happenedness, of events. What signifies is the event as "text" rather than the event as "happening." Such a sense of history as essentially textual must indeed be a feature of a belated culture, a culture whose history has passed out of touch with life and become exclusively textual, a culture that shows "signs of old age" only because what used to be the signs of its own past are now taken to be signs of a "youthful and newborn" age. In short, the belated culture of "the Jews," having reached its culmination and begun to decline into "old age," is transformed into a mere textual sign, an allegory, of the newly real "youthful peoples of the West and North" (Auerbach, 58).

This is the cultural, and deeply Eurocentric, version of the personal and private new birth Lewalski describes; it is a kind of soteriology of history itself. Christian culture is the "youthful and newborn" "peoples of the West and North" who have successfully been parted from a people whose culture has died of "old age" and is now revealed as never having been anything more than a kind of dramatic allegory of "universal history"—that is, the events of the newborn Christian people, still full of their actuality and historicity. Protestantism repeats this fantasy of the death and textualization of history when "Papists" come to occupy the place of "the Jew," and English Puritans repeat it once again, casting all misbelievers and "false-professors" along with the old "carnal self" as "the Jew." In the endlessly recursive versions of this, the place of "the Jew" is the place of displacement, occupied by whatever must be thought of as truly unreal and thus (paradoxically) deserving of the iconoclast's violence.

As with "Historical," So with "Literal"

I HAVE ARGUED THAT the Reformers' renewed emphasis on Christianity's bipolar ontology—locating the real ever more absolutely outside of time and space, as a something else very much elsewhere—had the effect of denying the historical any claim to reality. Something very similar happens to the term *literal*. My task now is to explain some of what underlies critics' frequent observations that Bunyan's allegory often seems strangely literal or literalistic, and conversely, that his autobiography often seems oddly allegorical.[29] Just as Auerbach felt compelled to hedge the term *historical* about with qualifiers like *full, concrete, independent,* so discussions of Reformation hermeneutics often speak of the "full literal" or "normative literal" senses of Scripture.[30] This is because, like the bipolar historical/fictional, literal/figurative also undergoes a kind of degeneration, not to say deconstruction, under the pressure of the Reformation's insistence on the "one, true, literal sense" of Scripture.

Typology and typological interpretation were not invented by Protestants. Lewalski is certainly correct to see typology as a mode peculiarly favored by reformed exegetes, but this favor has the effect of pressuring the typology inherited from medieval scholasticism into something rather different. Reformers wanted desperately to distinguish typological interpretation of the Scriptures from the "arbitrary allegorizing" of "idle and unlearned Monks and the Schooledoctors."[31] Luther's intense dislike of allegory and allegorizers did not stop him from admiring allegorical interpretations and even using them himself. Perhaps this is because the scholastic exegetical categories Luther inherited were grounded in a different bipolar division— that between the "literal sense" and the "typical sense."

Under the general rubric of the scholastics' "literal sense," allegory played a role, along with all the other rhetorical figures, in the production of literal meaning. Here the literal sense is understood as "the truth really, actually, and immediately intended by its author," where "author" is taken to be a text's human writer, as opposed to "the Holy Spirit."[32] This "literal sense," then, "must not be construed in such a way as to exclude figurative language from its range." Metaphor, synecdoche, even irony and allegory were generally considered fairly transparent literary devices by which writers conveyed the "literal sense" they intended. In Matthew 5:13, for example, Jesus expresses himself figuratively by calling the Apostles "the salt of the earth." To understand such a sentence in its "nonfigurative sense" would be absurd. The sentence does not "first class the Apostles among the mineral kingdom, and then among the social and religious reformers of the world, but the literal meaning of the passage coincides with the truth conveyed in the allegory" (Maas, 693). Such devices were considered part of the "immediately intended" literal sense. "The fable, the parable, and the example" may appear to offer two senses—a literal and a figurative—literarily speaking, but theologically speaking, the "literal sense comprises both the proper and the figurative."

This may appear obtuse to a linguist or to a literary critic whose chief concern (traditionally speaking) has to do with only one author and so one set of intentions, however complex and problematic critical access to these might be. But scholastic theologians used the literal/typical bipolarity to distinguish between the meanings intended by biblical authors and those intended by "the Holy Spirit." The "typical sense" was defined as "the Scriptural truth which the Holy Ghost intends to convey really, actually, but not immediately" (Maas, 695). It is easy to see that this bipolarity identifies two sets of real, actual intentions—the writer's and God's. The writer's intentions are taken to be "unmediated," thus treating language, and even rhetorical (literary) devices, as virtually transparent. The Holy Spirit's intentions are admitted to be—defined as—mediated, and here the medium is identified specifically as what we normally refer to as reality itself, not language or, more broadly, human representations of reality. The Holy Spirit produces meaning from the literal sense in three modes—allegorically (truths to be believed), anagogically (boons to be hoped for), and tropologically (virtues to be practiced). "Typical sense" allegories, unlike "literal sense" allegories, are "not to be sought in the literary expression, but in the persons or things expressed" (Maas, 695).

This formulation of two sorts of allegories, one grounded in a writer's intention and the other in God's intention, will be recognized by most as identical to Dante's two types of allegories—the allegory of the poets and the allegory of the theologians.[33] Thomas Aquinas insisted that the second is more properly termed God's allegory, since God alone has the power "to signify His meaning, not by words only (as man also can do), but also by things themselves."[34] In other words, what distinguishes God's mode of speaking or writing from human modes is that it is always mediated, the mediatory problematics of human language being largely ignored here. Further, insofar as it is a distinctly divine mode, its meanings are mediated by things, persons, and events, not by words. God may stoop, from time to time, to human forms of communication (words), but his distinctively divine mode is metalinguistic, using the things signified by words as if they were words. This, we are told, humans cannot do.

The scholastics' "typical sense" is what Reformers preferred to call the spiritual sense. The spiritual sense, then, is much like the metalanguage Roland Barthes calls myth, a language that takes first-order language's things signified and deploys them as signifiers in a second-order language, or metalanguage. Augustine and Aquinas differ from

Barthes by insisting that only God can speak this metalanguage, only God can signify in myth, and further, by insisting that what God does so signify is actual, that is, truly true and really real, as opposed to merely historically or linguistically so.[35] The truly real things signified by God's own special language, then, are of an ontological order beyond the horizon of human power to signify; they are objects, not of human perception, but of human faith, hope, and desire—that is to say, they are constituted as deferred, and so perpetually absent from human experience and from the power of humans to represent them. In short, God does not speak literally in Scripture or anywhere. The Holy Spirit's meaning is, by definition, mediated and not literal, but "typical."

For a whole host of reasons, religious, political, and economic, reformers were impatient with the notion of a God who never speaks literally. Charting these reasons is beyond the scope of this present study. For present purposes, it is enough to recall how insistently they raised the banner of "the one literal sense and meaning" of Scripture.[36] Samuel Preus's detailed account of how Luther gradually developed and refined the concept of *promissio* is particularly relevant to this discussion, for it traces Luther's pursuit of a way to understand Scripture words as God's Word of promise directed immediately toward human beings, promising them "the goods" of salvation and eternal life. This concept raises the ancient Israelite "out of the theological and historical limbo of 'umbra' to which the people of Israel had been consigned in most medieval exegesis" to the status of one who, like the *post-adventum* Christian, hears God's words of promise and by believing them, takes them literally (Preus, 268). Likewise, the Christian, who under the medieval hermeneutic model was obliged to understand God's promises as made directly to Christ and only tropologically applicable to believers in their *conformitas Christi,* found him- or herself in a state of being "'as if' (*ac si*) an Old Testament man, insofar as he had not yet attained, and God had not yet given, that which had been promised" (Preus, 269). Luther's concept of the Scriptures as a record of God's unmediated promises threatened to undo the medieval letter/spirit, literal/typical bipolarities whereby God was forever banned from speaking, and humans banned from hearing, directly literal promises of salvation and eternal life.

The "sola fide" and "solo verbo" hallmarks of Reformation theology thus threatened the entire theological and ecclesiastical structure of Christianity. Hermeneuts and hierophants could no longer hold God's Word and grace hostage to their intellectual or theological credentials. "Faith now depends not on some interpreter's gnosis about signification but on Christ's person and word" (Preus, 250). If one can but read or be read to, one can hear God's Word, and hear it sacramentally: "The Holy Spirit is the very simplest writer and speaker there is in heaven and earth; therefore His words, too, cannot have more than one most simple sense, which we call the Scriptural or literal or tongue-sense."[37] Luther and the reformers who followed him desperately wanted a Holy Spirit who spoke not "typically," but literally.

To the degree that Protestants realized this desire for a God who speaks literal promises directly to human ears and hearts, they also succeeded in emptying the term *literal* of any meaning, much as the term *historical* was emptied out. For what are the things God literally promises? Things invisible, incomprehensible, radically absent from this world, located more securely than ever beyond the horizons of human understanding. Moreover, these are now the only things worthy to be called real. The real, the true, and the literal have all been evacuated from this world and projected into the next, with the result that the Protestant Christian's grasp on reality is by way of faith (*sola fides*) and word (*solo verbo*) alone.

> All our goods are only in words and promises. For heavenly things cannot be shown as present; they can only be proclaimed by the word. Therefore, he [the Psalmist] does not say, "I see, therefore I show it as a work," but, "I believe, and therefore I speak." But those who boast of their own goods, and glory in something present—they do not have faith of those things, but sight. But we believe, and thus cannot show it by a work. That is why we only speak and bear witness. For faith is the reason why we cannot do other than to show our goods by the word, since faith rests in what does not appear, and such things cannot be taught, shown and pointed to—except by the word.[38]

The literal and the real are literally gone from this world, except insofar as they are spoken of and witnessed to by those who admit they cannot see them, show them, or point to them. This desperate desire for a God who speaks literally has paradoxically, but inevitably, resulted in the allegorization of everything this side of eternity. As Preus observes, "This lends new weight to the notion that Christ pre-eminently and ultimately 'is,' while we and all else 'signify'" (Preus, 195).[39] Is it any wonder that radical sectarians like Thomas Tany and William Franklin understood being itself to be conditional upon being Christ? Protestantism, radically understood, condemns its faithful to a perpetual struggle to be made real, which is identical to the struggle to be made Christ.[40] Justification and new birth is now the process by which one becomes truly real. Nothing else really is.

Once we imagine a God who speaks literally to human beings, promising them real things, indeed, promising to make them real if they only believe these promises of things that they cannot see, know, be taught, point to, or comprehend, then we no longer have any need for hermeneutics at all; this for either—or paradoxically both—of two reasons: (1) God's literal promises are absolutely clear and so require no interpretation, simply belief, or (2) they require only belief and not interpretation precisely because the things they promise cannot ever be literally understood, comprehended—in a word, known. By erasing the difference between the "mystical" or "typical" sense and the literal sense, the Reformers foregrounded the mediating, and therefore equivocal, qualities of language largely ignored in scholastic typology. If God's Word speaks literally of "things invisible," then he can never expect a "fit audience" among mortal beings. Human language, like Calvin's "human mind," becomes the key obstacle to God's effective revelation. No doubt this realization is what powered the seventeenth-century search for an ur-language, or the original pre-Babel language of creation.[41]

Precisely this impasse is wonderfully illustrated in Luther's exegesis of Psalm 2:7. This is one of the few Scripture passages that occasioned endless medieval scholastic debate about whether Scripture can ever be understood as having more than one literal sense.[42] The stakes in this scholastic debate seemed already to be fairly high; for Luther and Protestantism, the stakes approached an asymptotic limit. Aristotle, after all, had pronounced, "not to have one meaning is to have no meaning."[43] If the Holy Spirit speaks its "typical sense" by deploying the literal sense as its sign or lexeme, then identifying more than one literal sense runs the risk of doubling the Spirit's intended meanings for any given passage of Scripture. Since the Holy Spirit already intends a triple "typical sense" of any given literal sense (allegorical, anagogical, and tropological), this would mean that any passage with a multiple literal sense must now yield at least six "typical" senses, possibly more. This potentially endless multiplication of the senses of Scripture—the book that tells believers what must be believed, done, and hoped for—is precisely the sort of bogey Luther set out to destroy in his campaign for the "one true literal sense" of God's Word. It is much the same bogey that threatens Bunyan more than a century and a half later when "similitudes" began to "multiply," to "breed so fast" that they threatened to prove "*ad infinitum,* and eat out / The Book that I already am about."[44]

Psalm 2 has traditionally been classified by Hebrew scholars as a "royal psalm," probably composed for a coronation.[45] In verse 7, the persona, the voice of the new king, announces Yahweh's "decree:" that the king is "this day" (presumably the coronation day) made "my Son": "I will declare the decree: The Lord hath said unto me, Thou art my Son; this day I have begotten thee." Modern Hebrew scholars perceive a tension in this announcement between the respective forces of the words "decree" and "begotten." Yahwism defined Israel's kings as sons of God by adoption ("decree"), rather than by generation ("begotten") as was the common belief among the monistic Canaanites, in direct opposition to whose beliefs Yahwism defined itself. In this passage the persona, apparently the new king, anxious to assert his *bona fides,* finesses the crucial distinction between a king who is a son of God by decree and a king who is son of God more literally (and Canaanitishly) by divine generation. "In Canaanite culture," writes one modern commentator, "the king was believed to be an offspring of the gods and to have been suckled at divine breasts" (Dahood, 11–12). Hence it is possible here to see the king as appealing simultaneously to the strict Yahwists and to the more heathen-inclined in his potential power base by quoting as a "decree" the Lord God's affirmation of his begetting. The generally accepted interpretation of this verse understands the king as reporting the Lord God's metaphorical use of the word "begotten" to imply his adoption as a son of God, and thus as the legitimate King of Israel.[46] Like any religion claiming a corner on "universal truth," Yahwism was often obliged to co-opt by metaphorization many of the most persistently appealing features of the pagan religions that served as its constitutive others. Hence the survival in this coronation formula of the Canaanitish term "begotten" as a figurative expression for the Yahwist concept of adoption.

From the first century of the Common Era right down to and including Luther, Christian exegetes never understood the term "begotten" in Psalm 2:7 as anything but literal. Psalm 2 was always identified as a "Messianic Psalm," and as such was always taken to refer, quite literally and directly, to Christ.[47] The early church described by Luke in the Acts of the Apostles understood this psalm as God speaking quite literally, however ventriloquistically, "by the mouth of thy servant David" (Acts 4:25) about Christ. For these earliest Christian exegetes, this was not a matter of typological interpretation, but simply the literal sense of the Hebrew passage. David's words could not possibly have referred to himself as son of God, they reasoned, since David died and "saw corruption" (Acts 13:33–37), and in another psalm of David, we have been assured that God "will not suffer thine Holy One to see corruption." Thus Psalm 2 is not about David, not even as the literal base of an allegorical or typological sense. David's words (or the Lord's words in David's mouth), Christian exegetes agreed, were simply talking literally and prophetically about Christ.

The scholastic argument, then, is not about typology or allegory, but quite simply over what one should understand as the literal sense of "begotten." When God announces that he has "begotten" his son "this day," are we to understand simply that on a certain day (presumably the day upon which God ventriloquized this announcement through David) God reproduced himself by whatever divine means, that Christ was literally begotten by the Father? This seems to be the interpretation suggested by Hebrews 1:5. But there might be equally literal senses intended by the rhetorical figures whereby Christ's resurrection is understood as a kind of divine begetting (Acts 13:33). The verse could also refer to Christ's "eternal priesthood" (Hebrews 5:5), taking "begotten" as a rhetorical figure for his ordination. Others alleged that it must also be understood as referring to Jesus' nativity, in which case "this day" refers, quite specifically, to the day upon which Mary became impregnated by the Holy Spirit. All of these are advanced as candidates for the literal sense of "begotten" in Psalm 2:7 (Maas, 694). Not even Luther, whom Preus credits with lifting the ancient Israelites out of a "theological umbra," entertained the possibility that the Hebrew word for "begotten" here might be a metaphorical co-optation of heathen religious beliefs about the divine nature of kings.

Strangely enough, the literal sense of Psalm 2:7 favored by scholastic and reformed exegetes alike is that it announces, quite literally and directly, the "divine generation of the Son." It is hard to imagine a more mystical or spiritual concept, one more difficult to comprehend literally, than that of Christ's divine generation. How does one think historically or literally about God begetting his son? Upon whom or what is the son begotten? Thinking literally about such a matter would appear to invite precisely the kind of "carnal" imaginations about God and his activities Calvin so abominated. At cruxes like this, the distinctions between the literal and historical sense, on the one hand, and the mystical and spiritual senses, on the other, slide into meaninglessness.

Luther, who was fond of asserting that "the Holy Spirit is the very simplest writer and speaker there is in heaven and earth," slices the Gordian knot of scholastic argument over the literal sense of Psalm 2:7 by asserting that the "one most simple sense" of the passage is that it refers to "the eternal generation" of the son and as such, the sentence "cannot be understood or comprehended by human reason."

> The professors have disputed in various ways about the phrase: "Today I have begotten You." For some expound it as concerning the nativity of Christ, others concerning the resurrection, and the time of the New Testament. But we should keep it as it is, ῥητόν, or literally. For the Hebrew word means expressly "to beget." In this passage it cannot be understood with regard to the natural or temporal nativity (for it speaks not about men but about God), and consequently it signifies the eternal and invisible nativity. As a result it is the kind of word which cannot be understood or comprehended by human reason. The Son makes it known to us, but unless we believe it, we shall never understand it. It is truly a word brought to us from that "unapproachable light in which God dwells" (1 Tim. 6:16). When it is spoken among men about men, it is understood. But here, when the eternal Father, who is a Spirit, speaks this word about His own Son, it cannot be understood.[48]

Luther's appeal to the Greek, *rhēton,* to keep the "express" meaning of the Hebrew word "as it is, ῥητόν, or literally," is rooted firmly in the

New Learning, the recovery of ancient languages. Luther imagines himself as rescuing the grammatical-literal sense of the Scriptures, God's promises, from the darkness of medieval linguistic ignorance and allegorical accretions. The crucial things to be believed, *quid credas,* must all be literally and simply expressed in the Word, not deduced from allegorical exegesis.[49] The humanist's recovery of the ancient biblical languages, Hebrew and Greek, held out the promise of recovering the experience of God's promises to Israel and to the Apostles in all their immediate literalness and historicity. Hence Luther's appeal to "keep it as it is, ῥητόν," meaning exactly to the letter, the exact literal content of some piece of speech or writing without interpretation. God literally begets his son today.

But to "keep it as it is," is precisely to render it incomprehensible, thus straining the sense of *literal* past the breaking point. To understand "begotten" literally in this context, says Luther, is to take it as "the kind of word which cannot be understood or comprehended by human reason. . . . it cannot be understood." The literal sense here is mystical.

Liddell and Scott's *Greek-English Lexicon* tells us that *rhēton* means not only the quality of being stated "expressly," "distinctly," articulated without ambiguity, but also describes something "that may be spoken or told" or "that can be enunciated," not just in the sense of "communicable in words," but also in the sense of permitted to be said and heard, as opposed to things *arhēton,* which are unfit to be pronounced or heard, as well as "inexpressible."[50] Luther acknowledges, however, that when we understand "begotten" as such an utterance, it is not only incomprehensible, but unhearable "as it is":

> Moreover, you see in this very passage a two-fold address. The first is internal, when the Lord speaks with the Son. We neither hear nor understand it, but it is understood only by Him who speaks it and Him to whom it is spoken. The second is external, when the Son speaks with us: "The Lord said to me, 'You are My Son.'" We hear this, indeed, but we do not understand it either; for it wishes to be and can be understood by faith alone. I, therefore, take this passage as a reference to the eternal generation. (*Luther's Works,* 12:52)

The passage represents a speech event whose content is literally unhearable except by the divine addressee and his Father. The reader or hearer of Scripture can only hear this as reported speech, in quotation marks. Without quotation marks, it is simply inaudible, even unspeakable. Even with quotation marks, heard as reported speech, the content of this speech "cannot be understood." Thus, Luther tells us that the speech of God cannot be heard, let alone understood "as it is," but only as it is reported, represented, by the Son. And even as it is reported (as opposed to "as it is"), it is a pronunciation of something literally unpronounceable, unsayable, incapable of clear articulation. Paradoxically, to take the passage literally (*rhēton*), then, is to hear what is *arhēton,* to hear without understanding, without "ears to hear."

It is significant that the word *beget* should be the occasion of so much strain on Luther's use of the word *literal.* When this word "is spoken among men about men," says Luther, "it is understood." We know what it means for a man to beget a son. A man begets a son when, through coitus with a woman, he impregnates her with his seed. To understand this of God, however, is truly unthinkable. What woman? What seed? How? To understand this passage and this word literally of the "eternal generation of the Son" as opposed to the historical nativity of Jesus, then, is to risk unseemly, even heretical, notions of God. God the Father is a Spirit. We may not think of him otherwise even though we must. By insisting on the single literal sense of this passage, Luther manages to produce what can only be called a non-exegesis. The literal sense spoken in this verse, taken "as it is," cannot be understood, cannot even be heard without distortion, "for it wishes to be and can be understood by faith alone." This is a (non)hermeneutics of piety; one must simply believe that the unhearable and unsayable is both spoken and heard quite literally. Hermeneutics is traded in for a sacramental—and therefore mystical—experience of the Word.

There is in Luther's (non)exegesis of Psalm 2:7 a deep irony. Yahwism set its spiritual and radically non-human God over and against the monistic (and sexually active) pagan gods and goddesses whose fertility gave birth to (as opposed to created) the world.[51] Israel's King is a son of God by adoption, not generation. The psalmist-king speaks the word "begotten" in an attempt to render heathen monism unreal, a metaphor, a figure of speech. The "reality" is that God adopts his king-sons. The heathen idea of divine kings, suggests the psalmist, is attractive (and in this case politically useful), but only when understood metaphorically. Luther's literalism undoes the metaphor in the name of a religion that, not unlike paganism, wants a king who is divine, a literal Son of God. We may recall Lodowick Muggleton's observation that people never give up the desire for a God with a body: "No Spirit can speak at all, or hath any being without a body: And this is the very Cause that Men find so little Comfort in worshipping and believing in such a God that is a Spirit without a body."[52] Christianity's God *begets* a Son even before he *creates* anything. Indeed, he is eternally (perpetually?) begetting his Son. But this, says Luther, is precisely what is unknowable, unhearable, unspeakable, for reformed Christianity is more committed than ever to the Yahwistic principle that God is absolutely and radically other than his creation. Apparently, Christianity both wants and doesn't want to know it wants a sexually active God, a God with a body, a historical body in time and space.[53]

The literal sense, said Aquinas and the scholastics, is also the historical sense of Scripture's words, the immediate sense for which they were spoken or written at a particular time or place. According to Luther's reading of this passage, what is literally signified—the eternal generation of the Son—is absolutely ahistorical. To think historically about the Son's eternal begetting is to imagine not only a sexually active God, but one perpetually so:

> if we wish to speak *as it is,* the Son of God will be born and has been born today, daily, and always. For eternity has neither past nor future. In this way the expression "today" must be understood as time *as it is* to God, not to us. For God is *not speaking with us* but with Him who is outside time in the presence of God. (*Luther's Works,* 12:52, italics added)

Literally, "today" must be understood as meaning "today, daily, and always," for God's literal sense of time "as it is" is that it isn't. The literal sense of "today" as it is spoken by God to the Son is no sense, for "today" as "something different from yesterday and tomorrow" is a difference "unknown in eternity." Where there is no difference, there is no meaning. The literal sense of "today," then, is a null set. When we hear the word in our historical literal sense, we are hearing something other than what God meant or the Son understood:

We recite these words like parrots without understanding. For we are
temporal, or more exactly, a small piece of time. For what we were has
departed, and what will be, we are still lacking. So we possess nothing
of time except something momentary, what is present. (*Luther's Works,*
12:52–53)

What is "momentary" is precisely what, in God's literal sense,
does not exist. From God's perspective, time is nothing. From God's
perspective, where everything is seen "as it is," we possess "nothing of
time" (which is really nothing) "except something momentary" (and
as such, is also nothing). "What we were has departed, and what will
be we are still lacking," and what we are at this moment is a "small
piece" of nothing, infinite lack. So "we recite these words like parrots"; the words as we speak them and hear them are pure signifiers
without things signified, a *lexis* without signification much like Aristotle's notion of *phōnē asēmos* or the sounds made by brutes.[54] Luther
invites us at this point to think of human language as utterly brutelike
compared with God's, so that the humanist's perennial distinction between humans and beasts becomes precisely the same as the distinction between God and humans. Thus the category of the human is
here threatened with as complete an evaporation as anything Foucault
or Derrida has suggested. Luther invites us to imagine that the words,
spoken originally by God to his divine Son, and now recited by us as
we read the Scriptures, are only truly meaningful to God and his divine Son. We are like parrots, to whom the words signify nothing. Performing the words may express a desire for bits of birdseed or signs of
approval from the one who trained us to mimic these sounds, but the
words as words are, to us, mere nonsense.

Pressing his case for literalism all the way to its limit, Luther
stumbles onto Christian metaphysics' self-projected and self-constituting
horizon—the boundary that installs difference between sense and
sensible, sense and non-sense. And, like Calvin after him, Luther
quickly retreats from this discovery, desperately trying to leave the
boundary uncrossed, to cover his own transgressive tracks. Having
stated unequivocally that Psalms 2:7 is "a reference to the eternal generation," and that it "cannot be understood with regard to the natural
or temporal nativity," Luther senses that if this is so, the passage refers
to nothing that any human could count as a thing signified. So he pro-

ceeds to supply for the passage exactly the other literal sense he earlier ruled out:

> His nativity is a twofold one, outside time and within time . . . this Person born of the Virgin Mary is at the same time true man and true God. Beware of debating more subtly how this was done or could have been done. With simple faith follow the Word, which so teaches us about these things; and avoid arguments. (*Luther's Works*, 12: 53)

Luther had a very specific reason for his earlier rejection of "the natural or temporal nativity" as the literal sense of "begotten": "for it speaks not about men but about God." By definition, both Yahwistic and Christian, God is not natural, nor are his activities temporal, and he certainly doesn't beget anything in the sense the word bears when uttered by or "about men." But Luther seems to realize, without explicit acknowledgment, that Christianity requires a "two-fold sense" if its discourse is not to slide off into utter nonsense, nothing more than a parrot's interminably asemous phonemes. Since he has already declared himself against the "two-fold" senses of allegory and the scholastic distinction between "literal" and "typical" senses, his only recourse is to admit two literal senses—God's literal sense and human literal sense. Luther could save the appearances here by an appeal to allegory, claiming that human language is an allegory of God's language, but such an allegory could only be decipherable by God and his Son, leaving no room for Luther's central doctrine of the promise. A promise that cannot be comprehended by the promisee is worse than no promise; it is a cruel and cynical taunt, like speaking ironically to a toddler about his or her keenest desire, secure in the knowledge that you will be misunderstood. Luther quite rightly despises such a God. But his solution, to call two separate (infinitely separate) senses a single "two-fold sense," exposes, in the very act of trying to cover them up, the contradictions involved in clinging to an allegorical ontology and epistemology while trying to do away with the equivocating discourses it requires.[55]

Luther wants to preserve a two-world ontology with all its binaries intact (intelligible/sensible, substance/accidents, spirit/flesh), but he also wants to imagine that some language, the Word, can speak to both worlds with a single voice. Attempts either to resolve or to ignore this contradiction power much of Reformation thought. This is especially evident in its Puritan and sectarian manifestations, in which Christianity gradually deconstructs itself in the name of the single literal sense of Scripture. The Reformation's banner of literalism is the banner that often seems to cloak this deconstruction in denial.

I want to return for a brief meditation on the third thing that emerges from Luther's struggle over the twofold literal sense of Christ's begetting and his twofold nativity. It could be said that what keeps God's literal sense of "begotten" incomprehensible, even unhearable, to humans is "the flesh." If we were to imagine God begetting as men beget, we would have to imagine for God a woman. Christ would have to have a mother from all eternity. Not only would this render God twofold along the axis of gender, but it would also pave the way for the reintroduction of pagan notions about the continuity of substance between God and humans. As such notions knock against the door that holds them hidden, Luther both opens that door—"this Person born of the Virgin Mary is *at the same time* true man and true God"—and denies that he has opened it: "beware of debating more subtly how this was done or could have been done." The third thing always pushing against that door is woman, the unspoken, even unspeakable, and unspeaking place of begetting.

In order to hear God's literal sense, the sense he shares with his begotten Son, perhaps one must become that Son, occupy the place of that Son. This would require being "begotten" as Christ was (incomprehensibly and unsayably) "begotten," that is, without a mother—born again, "not of the flesh but of the Spirit." To be born again as really real is, perhaps, to be born again from no-woman. Woman, then, is, in a sense, the place of the hopelessly human literal and historical, the literal sense that is not God's literal sense and the history that will be replaced with God's eternity. "The wicked are estranged from the womb: they go astray as soon as they be born, speaking lies" (Psalm 58:3).

Three

"Which Things Are an Allegory": Being a Son of God

The ugly baboon backside of Christendom is racism.

Thomas Keneally, on "Fresh Air," National Public Radio, 24 March 1994

Among reformers, writes Lewalski, "a favorite biblical text for making the necessary distinctions" between allegory and typology was Galatians 4:22–31 (Lewalski, 120):

> For it is written that Abraham had two sons, the one by a bondmaid, the other by a freewoman. But he who was of the bondwoman was born after the flesh; but he of the freewoman was by the promise; which things are an allegory; for these are the two covenants: the one from the Mount Sinai which gendreth to bondage, who is Hagar. For as this Hagar is Mount Sinai in Arabia, and answereth to Jerusalem which now is, and is in bondage with her children. But Jerusalem which is above is free, which is the mother of us all. For it is written, Rejoice, thou barren that bearest not; break forth and cry, thou that travailest not; for the desolate hath many more children than she who hath an husband. Now we, brethren, as Isaac was, are the children of the promise. But as he that was born after the flesh persecuted him that was born after the Spirit, even so it is now. Nevertheless, what saith the scripture? Cast out the bondwoman and her son; for the son of the bondwoman shall not be heir with the son of the freewoman. So then, brethren, we are not children of the bondwoman, but of the free.

Paul's allegoresis of Genesis was indeed a much-cited passage among reformers eager to forge a new hermeneutics distinct from the scholastic allegorizing of the Roman Church. That it was invariably cited and even commented upon in detail may mean not that it was a "favorite" text, but that it was a text that generated a great deal of anxiety among reformers committed to the one true literal sense of Scripture. I suspect this was so for a number of reasons. First, no other passage in the New Testament appears so explicitly to draw an allegorical interpretation from so apparently unallegorically intended a text. Indeed, it seems quite clear that what Paul understands allegorically here is not so much a text, but a historical event. And the principal agents in that event—Abraham, Ishmael, Isaac, Sarah, and Hagar— are understood as allegorical signs of something else. This is most clearly so in the case of the two mothers. Hagar is taken here to signify "Jerusalem which now is," that is, the Jews and "Judaising Christians" like Peter and James. Sarah is understood as standing for "Jerusalem which is above," the mother that is not a mother in any fleshly sense. Paul quite freely (some have suggested midrashically[1]) appeals to otherwise unrelated passages of Scripture and obscure word-plays to identify Hagar with Mount Sinai and thus with "the Law" and "the flesh," while Sarah is identified with the paradoxically "barren" and once rejected, but now to be restored, "wife" of the Lord that figures in Isaiah's prophetic Zion poems.[2] Paul interprets Sarah, Abraham's aged and almost childless spouse, as Zion, or the heavenly Jerusalem whose children are born, not from copulation, conception, and "travail," but "after the Spirit." Ishmael, then, is a figure for all those "born after the flesh," and Isaac a figure for those born again as "the children of the promise." Implicitly in this allegoresis, Abraham occupies the place of God the Father.

It is difficult not to see Paul's exegesis as producing precisely the principal effect the Reformers alleged against medieval scholastic exegesis: the ancient Israelites are taken to be allegorical things, and Jews who read the history of Abraham as an authorizing precedent for determining who was a Jew (the descendants of Isaac) and who was not (the descendants of Ishmael) are simply "unaware that their whole history was an allegory" (Preus, 33). By reading their history literally, the Jews of Paul's day "mistake" themselves for sons of Isaac, and so legitimately of Abraham, thus literally and synecdochically Jerusalem. Paul's allegorical reading identifies these Jews, and the Jerusalem Christians who continue to prize their Jewishness, as spiritually (and therefore really) Ishmaelites, sons of the "bondwoman." According to his allegorical reading, then, the Scripture commands that these Jews, especially those who "persecute" the Spirit-born, be "cast out" as false sons of Abraham, sons "born after the flesh," rather than "children of the promise." Paul's allegoresis, in short, redefines Israel as precisely not Jews—indeed, not anyone who mistakes "carnal" genealogy or ritual substitutes for genealogy as having anything whatever to do with being a son of God.

It should not be hard to see, then, why it was so important to reformers to deny that what Paul is doing in this passage is anything so hermeneutically suspect as constructing an allegory upon the plain sense of Scripture. Paul's allegorical reading of Genesis history must be God's authorized meaning, not only because it installs the crucial distinction between Jews and God's "true Israel," but because it also authorizes a further reading of contemporary events whereby "Papists" are also understood as the "sons of the bondwoman" and Rome as "Jerusalem which now is." Bunyan's Mr. Legality and his "Village of Morality" similarly invite readers to identify the latitudinarian Church of England as a false Jerusalem, populated by sons of "the Bondwoman which now is" (*PP,* 23).[3] Rome to the Reformers and Canterbury to the English Puritans—these also, like Paul's Jews, are the real sons of Ishmael. If the Reformers feel they must condemn allegorical readings of the Scriptures, they must also save Paul's reading as legitimate, for it does the crucial work of defining who is the other to be cast out and condemned to destruction. This was done quite simply by denying that Paul's method is really allegory at all.

Traditional scholastic exegesis has no problem with Paul's allegory, since under that model, Paul's allegory of Abraham's family is simply a subset of the "typical sense," the sense intended by the Holy Spirit. The words of Genesis signify things, and Paul interprets those things as the Holy Spirit intended them to mean. But Luther and the Reformers want a God who speaks literally, whose words (not just the things signified by the words) literally mean what they say. If God promises things, and those promises are the ground of faith, they must be literally heard. They must not be held hostage to an interpreter's gnosis. When the Scriptures, in this case Genesis, appear to speak about what constitutes a true son of the promise or the covenant, they must be understood as speaking literally. Here, if anywhere, there can be no room for juggling, punning, and polysemous ambiguities.

William Tyndale carried Luther's campaign for the absolute literalness of Scripture to England. "The fayth," he announces in *The Obedience of a Christian Man,* "was loost thorow allegories."[4] Allegorizing exegetes, he charges, are in the service of the Pope:

> They devide the scripture into iii. senses, the litterall, tropologicall, allegoricall anagogicall. The literall sence is become nothinge at all. For the pope hath taken it clean awaye and hath made it his possession. He hath partly locked it up with the false and counterfayted keyes of his tradicions cerimonies and fayned lyes. And partly dryveth men from it with violence of swerde. For no man dare abyde by the litterall sense of the texte, but under a protestacion, if it shall please the pope. (129ʳ⁻ᵛ)

Tyndale imagines the leaders of the Roman Catholic Church as latter-day Pharisees who by rhetorical sleights of hand, spectacular ritual practices, and even threats of violence, have "locked" away the literal sense of God's word, the promises upon which every faithful Christian must stand. The Church has replaced God's literal promises with mysteries, teaching the lay-folk what they should believe by way of allegories, what they should do by tropologies, and what they should hope by anagoges. Tyndale, like Luther, wants a faith, a hope, and a morality based on a single literal sense, spoken by God to him:

> Thou shalte understonde therefore that the scripture hath but one sence which is the literall sence. And the literall sence is the rote and grounde of all and the ancre that never fayleth whereunto if thou cleve thou canst never erre or go out of the way. And if thou leve the litterall sence thou canst not but go out of the waye. (129ᵛ–30ʳ)

Reading the Scriptures in any but a literal way will be the first step "out of the way."

Tyndale sounds like the most absurd sort of literalist here, but he is not. He immediately stipulates that Scripture in many places speaks in "proverbes, similitudes, redels, or allegories," and so may require diligent searching and interpretation to arrive at its intended literal sense. The Song of Solomon, for example, was universally acknowledged to be this kind of Scripture passage. The Scottish Puritan James Durham, in his *Exposition of the Song of Solomon,* follows the Reformers' careful distinction between interpreting allegorical passages of Scripture and allegorically interpreting "plain Scriptures":

There is a great difference betwixt an Allegorick Exposition of Scripture, and an Exposition of Allegorick Scripture: The first is that, which
many Fathers, and School-men fail in, that is, when they Allegorize
plain Scriptures and Histories, seeking to draw out some secret meaning, other than appeareth in the words; and so will fasten many senses
upon one Scripture.[5]

Durham also shares Tyndale's antipathy for the "School-men" and
their secret meanings.

But Tyndale is also willing to allow the more homiletic exegetical
practice of borrowing "similitudes or allegories of the Scripture and
apply[ing] them to our purpose" (Tyndale, 130^r, 131^r). This is the sort
of thing a preacher might do when applying some Scripture passage to
contemporary events, or to one's personal experience, or to illustrate,
but not to authenticate, some point of doctrine. Such allegorical illustrations, or applications, warns Tyndale, "are no sence of the scripture:
but free thynges besydes the scripture and all together in the liberte of
the spirite" (131^r). He offers an example of this sort of homiletic allegoresis. In John 18:10, Simon Peter is reported to have cut off the right
ear of the high priest's servant, Malchus. Jesus rebukes Simon Peter.
Luke's gospel also reports that Jesus healed Malchus's ear. Tyndale's
commentary:

There hast thou in the playne texte greate lerninge, greate frute and
greate edifienge which I passe over because of tediousnes. Then come I,
when I preach of the law and the gospell, and borow this example to
expresse the nature of the law and of the Gospell and to paynte it unto
the before thine eyes. And of Peter and his swerde make I the law and of
Christ the Gospell sayenge, as Peters swerde cutteth off the eare so
doeth the law. . . . But Christ, that is to saye the Gospell, the promyses
and testamente that God hath made in Christe healeth the eare and conscience which the law hath hurte. (131^r–131^v)

"This allegory," says Tyndale, though it is very effective in rooting and
engraving a divine truth "moch deper in the wittes of a man then
doeth a playne speaking," "proveth no thinge nether can doo," for "it
is not the scripture, but an example or a similitude borowed of the
scripture" (132^r). The divine truth Tyndale has made this Scripture passage illustrate should not be mistaken for any sense, literal or figura-

tive, of that Scripture. If the doctrine Tyndale has made the story illustrate is true doctrine, it is true, not on the authority of this story, or Tyndale's allegoresis, but because that doctrine is stated plainly and literally somewhere else in the Scriptures. If the doctrine illustrated in this way cannot be found plainly stated elsewhere in Scripture, then such allegorizing would be a stepping "out of the way" of faith, just as the "chopological" Papists so often allegedly do.

Because such homiletic allegories, says Tyndale, "prove nothinge, therefore they are to be used soberly and seldom and only where the texte offereth an allegory." He cites Paul as a precedent for such homiletic allegories which "borow" Scripture's literal sense as an allegorical figure:

> And of this maner (as I above have done) doeth Paul borow a similitude, a figure, or an allegory of Genesis to express the nature of the law and the Gospell, and by Agar and hyr sonne declareth the property of the law and of hyr bonde childern which will [want to] be iustified by deades, and by Sara and hyr sonne and of hyr free childerne which are iustified by fayth. . . . And like wise doo we borow likenesses or allegories of the scripture, as of Pharao and Herod and of the scribes and pharises, to expresse oure miserable captivity and persecucion under Antichrist the Pope. (123ᵛ)

There is an important contradiction here between Tyndale's assertion that such allegories "prove nothinge" because they are "no sense of scripture, but free thinges besides the scripture" and his appeal to Pauline precedent. The Pauline precedent for such allegories is itself part of canonical Scripture. Paul's allegoresis of a perfectly "playne" passage of Genesis, which in itself offers no allegory, is itself Scripture. Thus, when Paul says of the Genesis story, "Now this is an allegory [*allēgoroumena*]" (Galatians 4:24), he cannot be understood by Tyndale or by any other Christian commentator as elaborating a "free thinge besides the scripture." If Paul's exegesis of Genesis is itself Scripture, then the allegorical sense he gathers from the Genesis story is God's literal sense and has the immediate authority of the Spirit. Tyndale pretends to be unaware of this difficulty as he allows the canonical authority of Paul's precedent to spill over onto his own interpretations of Pharaoh and Herod as figures of the Pope, allegorizations in support of which there are certainly no "playne" passages anywhere in Scripture. What began as Tyndale's attempt to distinguish between a preacher's witty "applications" of Scripture and the Scripture's own authoritatively literal voice winds up with a virtual conflation of the two.[6]

Luther, from whom Tyndale doubtless borrowed this distinction between illustrative allegories and Scripture's doctrinal authority, makes a much better job of it. Nevertheless, he succeeds only insofar as he covers his equivocations more subtly than Tyndale did. Luther had little patience with the "four-horse team" that powered scholastic hermeneutics, wherein the Holy Spirit was imagined to speak only by way of allegories, tropologies, and anagoges. "With these trifling and foolish fables they rent the Scriptures into so many and diverse senses, that silly poor consciences could receive no certain doctrine of any thing."[7] Luther wants a hermeneutic that can generate from Scripture a doctrine that can be grasped by the poor and unlearned, but he also recognizes the rhetorical and even aesthetic force of an allegory as an illustration. This, he argues, is what Paul's allegory of Abraham's family supplies:

> Allegories do not strongly persuade in divinity, but as certain pictures they beautify and set out the matter. For if Paul had not proved the righteousness of faith against the righteousness of works by strong and pithy arguments [that is, without resorting to allegoresis], he should have little prevailed by this allegory. But because he had fortified his cause before with invincible arguments, taken of experience, of the example of Abraham, the testimonies of Scripture, and similitudes,— now in the end of his disputations he addeth an allegory, to give a beauty to all the rest. For it is a seemly thing sometimes to add an allegory when the foundation is well laid and the matter thoroughly proved. For as painting is an ornament to set forth and garnish a house already builded, so is an allegory the light of a matter which is already otherwise proved and confirmed.[8]

Allegorical interpretations of otherwise plain passages of Scripture, even those produced by Paul, should not be used to prove or to confirm any points of doctrine or faith. The "school-men" taught that the Holy Ghost spoke *quid credas* precisely by such allegories. Luther denies this. Calvin echoes Luther, charging that "Origen, and many others along with him, have seized the occasion of torturing Scripture, in every possible manner, away from the true sense. They concluded that the literal sense is too mean and poor, and that, under the outer bark of the letter, there lurk deeper mysteries, which cannot be extracted but by beating out allegories" (*Commentaries on Galatians,* 135).

Origen and the "school-men" torture the Scriptures, ingeniously and satanically beating allegories out of the plainest-speaking passages, assuming that the Holy Spirit is incapable of speaking plainly and perspicuously. Paul, however, is never so charged. To Luther, Paul is merely appending a rhetorical ornament to his otherwise "strong and pithy arguments." Calvin admits that Paul advances here a "mystical interpretation" (*anagōgē*), but he tries to argue that Paul's interpretation is "not inconsistent with the true and literal meaning" of the passages from Genesis. "Let us know, then, that the true meaning of Scripture is the natural and obvious meaning; . . . Let us not only neglect as doubtful, but boldly set aside as deadly corruptions, those pretended expositions, which lead us away from the natural meaning." Paul's interpretation, argues Calvin, does not violate this principle, for it "does not involve a departure from the literal meaning" (136).

Getting Paul off the hook in this case finally proves to be impossible, for nothing could be clearer than that Paul's allegorical interpretation of Genesis here is specifically designed to make Torah speak the precise opposite of its literal sense—to identify the Jews as Ishmaelites and the gentile Galatian Christians as God's "true Israel." Paul has chosen to allegorize precisely the strongest proof-text in his "Judaising" opponents' arsenal—those passages of Torah that had always been interpreted as announcing the exclusion of Ishmael's progeny from any claim to be covenanted sons of Abraham.

Modern Protestant commentaries on Galatians share much the same anxiety over Paul's allegory as we have seen in the early Reformers. Some employ the same dodge as Luther, Calvin, and Tyndale, admitting that Paul's exegesis is allegorical, but denying it any doctrinal or argumentative force—it is merely a clever illustration, supplemental to his argument.[9] Most, however, admit that Paul's exegesis is central to, even the climax of, his argument against the "Judaisers," but deny that what Paul calls *allēgoroumena* is really an allegorical reading.[10] A few who are willing to admit the term *allegory* do so only by distinguishing, like Calvin, Paul's allegory from Philonic and Alexandrine allegory.[11] Virtually all modern Protestant commentators echo, whether deliberately or not, the early Reformers' warnings that Paul's allegorical exegesis is not "capricious" or "fanciful" like those of Philo and the Alexandrine school, since it preserves some sense of the historicity of Genesis's Abraham.[12] Among Protestant commentators, I have found none willing to take seriously the conclusion reached by H. J. Schoeps, who acknowledges that Paul's understanding of "saving history" "simply dissolves the facts of history" and evacuates the historical Abraham and the historical Israel from Scripture (Schoeps, 235).

Recent scholars who read Paul from an explicitly non-Christian position manage to see much more clearly, it seems to me, what Paul is doing in Galatians 4:21–31. Paul uses midrashic exegetical techniques specifically to turn Torah against itself, to make us hear Torah contradicting Torah. Though Daniel Boyarin and Gerald Bruns convincingly argue that midrash is properly understood as a largely nonallegorical, even antiallegorical, hermeneutic method, Paul's midrash is rooted in the context of a two-world apocalyptic dualism.[13] Such a context virtually guarantees that Paul's midrash will do what he wants it to do—produce an antinomian reading of the law.

Paul's midrash on Abraham's two sons is not, as Luther would have it, an ornamental appendix to otherwise "strong and pithy arguments." Paul introduces this midrash, not as an afterthought or as a supplemental illustration, but as a direct appeal to Torah in support of his case: "Tell me, ye that desire to be under the law, do ye not hear the law? For it is written . . ." (Galatians 4:21–22a). From a rabbinic perspective, then, this should introduce the clinching argument, and is not, as Luther wants to see it, merely a clever illustration directed "especially [to] the simple and ignorant" who, finding it difficult to follow doctrinal arguments, are "greatly delighted with allegories and similitudes" and so more effectively persuaded by "pictures" than by arguments (*Luther's Works*, 27:422–23). Galatians 4:21–31 concludes Paul's argument against the "Judaisers" who have apparently been troubling Paul's Galatian gentile converts, insisting that they be circumcised and keep the law or they cannot be real Christians, part of God's "true Israel." The "Judaisers" may, in fact, as C. K. Barrett has suggested, have built their arguments against Paul precisely from the same passages of Torah (Genesis 15–21) out of which Paul constructs his antinomian midrash.[14] Presumably Paul's opponents have read in

Genesis the Torah's announcement that only those born of Abraham's seed or adopted into his family and (in any case) made part of the covenant by circumcision can have any claim to be God's covenanted people. Paul boldly claims that precisely the same Torah supports his case for a spiritual, as opposed to a carnal, understanding of what it means to be a "son of Abraham." The argument shows all the signs of being directed specifically to an audience familiar with Torah and traditional midrash upon Torah, that is to say, a rabbinically trained audience.

Paul's clinching argument also follows another midrashic tradition by insisting that his interpretation yields an explicit imperative directly relevant to the Galatians in their particular situation: " . . . what saith the scripture [to you Galatians, here and now]? Cast out the bondwoman and her son; for the son of the bondwoman shall not be heir with the son of the freewoman. So then, brethren, we are not children of the bondwoman, but of the free" (Galatians 4:30–31). Since Paul's midrash upon Genesis has proved that gentile Christians, "as Isaac was, are the children of promise," the law, as Paul interprets it, commands that the "children of the bondwoman," that is, those who trust in the Sinaitic law and identify themselves with the "Jerusalem which now is" (Galatians 4:25), must be "cast out," just as Ishmael was cast out from Abraham's family and from the special covenant in spite of the fact that he was circumcised. Like traditional rabbinic midrash, Paul interprets the Torah in a manner "oriented towards the time and circumstances of the interpreter," as a "decree issued this very day."[15] The law, insists Paul, specifically commands the gentile Christians at Galatia to reject the "Judaisers" and to reject the *halakhah* they and the Jerusalem Jewish Christians observed. In short, says Paul, the law says, cast out those who appeal to the law, for the true law is spiritually oriented, not materially oriented. Paul's midrash is not only offered as proof and confirmation of his doctrine—who is really a son of Abraham—but it also issues a specific imperative directed at the Galatians, telling them what they must do: "cast out" the Jews and the false-Christian "Judaisers." Paul makes it clear just how violent a casting out he imagines the Torah calls for when he says in 5:12, "as for these agitators [the Jews and "Judaisers" advocating circumcision], they had better go the whole way and make eunuchs of themselves."[16] Paul's midrashic argument ends with a bloody and violently anti-

Jewish slur, suggesting that those who misread the Torah as enjoining circumcision upon the "sons of Abraham" might just as well castrate themselves, for they are, after all, not only not the real "sons of Abraham," but not real men at all.[17]

Paul's midrash, then, is not only clearly intended as a doctrinal interpretation of Genesis, it is also intended as a violent insult to Jews and Jewish Christians. The Torah, claims Paul, says that unconverted Jews are hopelessly, disgustingly, and even ridiculously "carnal"; they are literally the hated Ishmaelites, sons of a slave-woman and wicked from birth. Rabbinic midrash accounted for Ishmael's exclusion from the special category of "son of Abraham" on a variety of grounds: that he did wicked things like ravishing maidens, seducing married women, practicing idolatry, attempting to kill Isaac under the pretense of "sport";[18] that he was born a slave and so could not inherit along with Isaac;[19] and that Isaac's birth from the proverbially "barren" Sarah was a special miracle that manifestly superseded the more mundane birth of Ishmael. Insofar as recorded midrash preserves a long oral tradition, Paul may be drawing upon such midrashim in his exegesis. Paul's Ishmael represents the most insistently carnal of dispositions, satisfying the lusts of "the flesh" without regard to the spirit. Paul's list of the "works of the flesh" in the next chapter (Galatians 5:19–21) includes all of the charges traditional midrashim leveled against Ishmael: adultery, fornication, idolatry, envyings, murders, and reveling (another rabbinic sense of "sport"). Ishmael was traditionally understood as particularly solicitous about the material inheritance he felt due as the eldest son and quite unmindful of the "spiritual" and nationalistically future-oriented nature of the covenant. Such traditions play nicely into Paul's identification of the legalistic-minded "Judaisers" with Ishmael, the son born into "bondage under the elements of this world" (Galatians 4:3).

Paul's midrash, insulting and violent as it is, is thus not entirely without precedent in rabbinic tradition. Violent hatred of Ishmael was already in place; Paul merely reinterprets the Torah as recommending violent hatred of Jews and "Judaisers" who, says Paul, inhabit the place of Ishmael and Hagar. In fact, one rabbinic tradition quite explicitly identifies Ishmael, and those like him, as cut off from Abraham's "seed" precisely because they reject "belief in two worlds," neglecting the age to come and its rewards by concentrating exclusively on this world and its material rewards. According to this midrash, God says, "I have given a sign [whereby the true descendants of Abraham can be known], viz. he who expressly recognizes [God's judgments]: thus whoever believes in the two worlds shall be called 'thy seed.'"[20] Presumably this midrash was meant to be helpful in explaining how circumcised sons of Abraham like Ishmael and Esau were excluded from the covenant of true sons, but this, along with other elements of midrashic tradition, might well have contributed to Paul's radical turning of the law against the law—"Tell me, ye that desire to be under the law, do ye not hear the law?"—by identifying the Jews of his day as virtual Ishmaelites because of their "carnal" understanding of and appeal to the law. Paul's radical reinterpretation of the value of the law (and of Israelite genealogy, history, and ritual practice generally) is really just a step beyond what midrashic tradition already offered. This crucial step is the move from distinguishing between materiality and spirituality in ritual practice to opposing materiality to spirituality across the board: "For the flesh lusteth against the Spirit, and the Spirit against the flesh; and these are contrary the one to the other, so that ye cannot do the things that ye would" (Galatians 5:17).[21] "Judaising" Christians and Jews simply cannot keep the law in both the spirit and the flesh; ritual practice in the flesh is in fact, by its very nature, opposed to spiritual practice. Torah itself, claims Paul, makes this clear.

There is in this ontological opposing of spirit and flesh an analogy to hermeneutic practice. The historical or literal meaning of Abraham's family cannot be fully integrated with the spiritual meaning; they are also opposed to each other as is flesh to spirit, this world to the next. Nothing illustrates this principle as sharply as Paul's identification of Jewish ritual practice of the law with Hagar and Ishmael, those "cast out" from Abraham's covenant with God, and his corresponding identification of the uncircumcised gentiles with Isaac, the miraculously produced son of Sarah. Perhaps no other allegory so monumentally says one thing and means another.

One more traditionally midrashic feature of Paul's exegesis must be noted before we return to the Reformers' commentaries upon it, for this feature is one that particularly fascinates Calvin and Luther. This is Paul's quotation in the midst of his exegesis of Isaiah 54:1: "For it is written, Rejoice, thou barren that bearest not; break forth and cry, thou that travailest not; for the desolate hath many more children than she who hath an husband" (Galatians 4:27). This practice of linking one Scripture passage to another by way of mutual explication is an oft-noted feature of midrash.[22] The principle, simply stated, is that Scripture interprets Scripture; in particular, the Prophets and the wisdom books interpret the law, and vice versa. Paul quotes Isaiah here specifically because of the traditional identification of Sarah as the "barren" one. God's miraculous power and his special favor toward Isaac and Abraham was thought to be especially evident in his bringing Israel from out of the womb of one assumed to be incapable of giving birth, "barren." This became a kind of emblem of many of God's special providences with regard to his people: bringing them up out of the idolatrously "barren" land of the dead (Egypt), out of the wilderness, and out of numerous episodes of exile and apostasy. The children of Israel and of Abraham are, quite paradoxically, identified as the remarkable children of one incapable of childbearing.

The *Midrash Rabbah* on Genesis states that this miracle was accomplished quite literally by God fashioning for Sarah the ovary she apparently lacked from birth.[23] But Paul's midrash explicitly avoids any such materialistic ("fleshly") account. He insists that the true birth of any "son of Abraham" is not really a material birth, but a spiritual one. True birth is birth from the one with no ovaries, the "desolate one," the unmarried one; it is analogous to but ontologically opposed to material birth. The Galatians, asserts Paul, had their true birth from him and from Christ, or more precisely, from him as Christ. We recall that he closed the last section before the allegory with the intimate, almost motherly, address, "My little children, of whom I travail in birth again until Christ be formed in you, . . ." (Galatians 4:19). Material motherhood, just like fleshly generation, is of this world, and as such, is carnal, the opposite of (though analogous to) the spiritual. True motherhood, like true birth, is spiritual. In the context of what Paul sees as "the apocalyptic antinomy between cosmos on the one hand (which includes both law and 'unlaw') and the New Creation ushered in by Jesus Christ on the other," Paul-Christ is the true mother of any and all true "sons of Abraham."[24] True "travail" is metaphysical and doctrinal work, Paul's labor, Christ's labor. Furthermore, the true child of this mother is also Christ: "till Christ be formed in you." Christ-Paul is begetter and laborer in this birth of Christ in the believer-as-womb. The womb is the self as flesh, the material ovary given by God in material creation as the site wherein Christ is conceived and from which the redeemed self is born, releasing the spiritual Christ from out of the bondage constituted by material existence, that is, the transformation from flesh-being (false being) to spirit-being accomplished by conversion. Paul's analogy between fleshly birth and spiritual birth does not exactly "work"—Paul-Christ is mother, but also fetus—yet the very sign of these spiritual roles is the fleshly "barrenness" or "desolation" of both the fleshly Paul and the material Jesus. The analogy plays on these aporias precisely to point out how material ontology is only roughly analogous to spiritual ontology and is always, finally, the opposite of fleshly ontology. In spiritual ontology, of course, there is only one real thing, whether it be mother, son, father, or fetus, and that is Christ. All other things, (including words) are merely signs—and inadequate ones at that—of the one true thing.

It is not difficult to show that the Protestant Reformers understood Paul's exegetical methods and his results far better than they let on. Luther and Calvin are both eager to apply Paul's imperative to "cast out" the "sons of the bondwoman" to the "Papists," the Anabaptists, indeed, to anyone with whom they disagree. And both implicitly acknowledge that what is at stake here is precisely a point of doctrine, one might almost say *the* point of doctrine—that is, who is a true son of God and who is a false pilgrim, or a mere poseur. Just as the first-century politics of the early Christian sects drove Paul's allegoresis, so Reformation politics drives Luther's and Calvin's. They want Scripture to announce plainly the illegitimacy of misbelievers, for this is crucial to the self-identification of the truly "saved." For Paul, the misbelievers were the Christians who insisted on remaining Jews; for the Reformers, the misbelievers or false Christians are the "Papists" on the one hand and the radical Anabaptists on the other; for English Puritans, they are the established church or whatever sectarians oppose them. Thus, the category of "the Jew," derived in part from the Jewish category of the "cast-out" bondwoman and her son, is an ever-expanding version of the other.

Luther reads Paul's allegory at first as "the light of a matter which is already otherwise proved and confirmed," treating it as a "wonderful" illustration of the difference between law and grace, the "Old Testament" and "the New":

> Abraham is a figure of God, which hath two sons, that is to say, two
> sorts of people, who are represented by Ishmael and Isaac. These two
> are born unto him by Agar and Sarah, the which signifieth the two Tes-
> taments, the Old and the New. The Old is of Mount Sinai, begetting
> unto bondage, which is Agar. (*Luther's Works,* 27:426)

Luther's reading proceeds with care, maintaining a rhetoric of analogy
proper to an illustration that is to be taken as the product of Paul's
homiletic wit, not the Holy Spirit's literally intended sense of Genesis:

> Likewise then as Agar the bondmaid brought forth to Abraham a son,
> and yet not an heir but a servant; so Sinai, the allegorical Agar, brought
> forth to God a son, that is to say, a carnal people. Again, as Ishmael was
> the true son of Abraham, so the people of Israel had the true God to be
> their father, which gave them his law, his oracles, religion, and true ser-
> vice, and the temple. . . . Notwithstanding this only was the difference;
> Ishmael was born of a bondmaid after the flesh, that is to say, without
> the promise, and could not therefore be the heir. So the mystical Agar,
> that is to say, Mount Sinai, where the law was given and the Old Testa-
> ment ordained, brought forth to God, the great Abraham, a people, but
> without the promise, that is to say, a carnal and servile people, and not
> the heir of God. (426–27)

Luther gradually, almost imperceptibly, slips from treating Paul's allegory as a mere illustration or "ornament" into treating it as doctrinal.
We can trace this slippage in the shift from taking Sinai as "the allegorical Agar" to Sinai as the "mystical Agar." An allegory would be
nothing more than Paul's clever analogy; a mystical sense, however,
carries theological and doctrinal value, for anyone can spin out an allegorical sense, but only the Spirit can intend a mystical sense. Paul's
witty illustration begins to be treated as the Holy Spirit's mystically
intended sense of Genesis. Literally understood, Israel is the children
of Sarah; mystically understood, Israel is the illegitimate offspring of
Mount Sinai, the "mystical Agar." The "sons of Abraham" are not the
sons of "the great Abraham," and the true mystical sense of the Torah
itself proves this.

 Sarah must also be mystically or spiritually understood. Paul's "illustration" compares Sarah to "Jerusalem which is above" and is "the
mother of us all." Here Luther condemns the "trifling" allegories and

anagoges of the "school-men" who understand this "Jerusalem" in four different senses (430). For Luther, there is only one spiritual sense to the "heavenly Jerusalem"; she is the true Church of God's true sons on earth:

> Wherefore Sarah or Jerusalem, our free mother, is the church itself, the spouse of Christ, of whom we all are gendered. This mother gendereth free children, without ceasing, to the end of the world, as long as she exerciseth the ministry of the word, that is to say, as long as she preacheth and publisheth the Gospel, for this is truly to gender. (431)

"This is truly to gender." Paul's allegory, it turns out, squeezes from a story about two mothers and two sons a teaching about what is true motherhood and true gendering. Neither Sarah nor Hagar, it turns out, are true mothers after all, for true birthing is a spiritual, mystical matter. Isaac's literal birth is but a figure for the truly literal birth that is the birth of the church "in earth among men":

> even so we are born through the Gospel of that free-woman, Sarah; that is to say, the church, true heirs of the promise. She instructeth us, nourisheth us, and carrieth us in her womb, in her lap, and in her arms; she formeth and fashioneth us to the image of Christ, until we grow up to a perfect man, &c. So all things are done by the ministry of the word. Wherefore the office of the free-woman is to gender children to God, her husband, without ceasing and without end. (431–32)

The truly literal sense of the Genesis story, it turns out, is Paul's allegorically derived sense, the sense intended by the Holy Spirit.

And the labor of gendering, birthing, and mothering, according to this sense, is gendered labor—it is gendered masculine. "Truly to gender" is preaching and publishing the Gospel, bringing to new birth those still tainted by old birth. Just as the Jews are rendered in this hermeneutic "a carnal and servile people, and not the heir of God," so maternal labor, birthing and mothering in the flesh, is rendered a carnal allegory of "true" maternity and "true" spousehood. In short, Israel is not truly Israel and mothers are not truly mothers. Mothers, like the synagogue, the old self, and all shadowy types must, in the end, "be cast out." They are all servants to the truth rather than the truth itself. When William Franklin and his chiliastic followers rejected all "types and shadows" as not only no longer necessary but dangerously misleading now that Christ was theirs "in substance," they simply repeated the Reformation's characteristic gesture of relocating the "carnal." For them, Puritan orthodoxy, Parliament, "ordinances," and Scripture are now carnal "types and shadows." This gesture is peculiarly poignant, even pathetically painful, in the case of Mary Gadbury, a woman who cannot herself tell—and no one else seems to know for certain—whether she gave birth carnally or spiritually, whether her "child" was a monster, a "Dragon," a Christ, or a metaphor. Was she the vessel of a "spirituall" or a "naturall birth" (see above, chap. 1)? In her experience both as a woman and as the literal "Spouse of Christ"—which only men can truly be—all of these contradictions face each other in the fulness of their irreconcilability. She must have gone mad. Perhaps this is why she was committed to Bridewell and beaten so severely for so long. Her recantation seemed crucial to the project of re-suppressing these contradictions.

When Luther's commentary comes to consider Paul's quotation from Isaiah 54:1, a passage Luther calls "altogether allegorical," he quite freely adopts the language of proof, confirmation, and doctrine. The literal, Spirit-intended, sense of Isaiah's prophecy is simply "the difference which is between Agar and Sarah, that is to say, between the synagogue and the church, or between the law and the Gospel" (432). It has no other sense. By quoting Isaiah, then, Paul turns what would otherwise be no more than a clever allegorical illustration (like Tyndale's allegory of Malchus's ear) into prophetic testimony:

> Paul then by this testimony of Isaiah hath proved that Sarah, that is to say, the church, is the true mother which bringeth forth free children and heirs; contrariwise, that Agar, that is to say, the synagogue, gendereth many children indeed, but they are servants, and must be cast out. (435)

"This place" in Galatians, says Luther, "ought to be diligently considered," for it articulates "the most principal and special article of Christian doctrine, to know that we are justified and saved by Christ" (436). By proving that the Church, not the synagogue, is the true mother of God's true sons, Paul's allegory has become not a mere afterthought or appended "ornament," but crucial to Christian doctrine. Luther goes on to use this crucial passage to prove that "the Papists," like Ishmael, are the persecutors of the true church, the real sons of the mystically literal Abraham—God (444–45).

Calvin's reading of Paul's allegory follows a somewhat different tack. Paul's allegory, he claims, does not draw out of Scripture a multiplicity of meanings. The meaning Paul draws allegorically is perfectly consistent with the literal meaning of the Genesis story. Therefore, says Calvin, it is not really an allegorical reading at all, but a typological reading in which the "natural and obvious meaning" of the passage is perfectly consistent with the "mystical interpretation" Paul offers. There are not two meanings, then, but simply one meaning, variously "applied."

> But what reply shall we make to Paul's assertion, that these things *are allegorical?* Paul certainly does not mean that Moses wrote the history for the purpose of being turned into an allegory, but points out in what way the history may be made to answer the present subject. (*Commentaries on Galatians,* 136)

This echoes Tyndale's argument. Genesis is not an allegorical text; Paul simply uses the elements of a historical narrative to illustrate "the present subject," which is the doctrine of grace and law. "This is done by observing a figurative representation of the church there delineated" (136). Delineated by whom? Does Paul forge a figurative representation out of the story, or does he merely observe one that is already in place, in history? Calvin assumes the latter:

> As the house of Abraham was then a true Church, so it is beyond all doubt that the principal and most memorable events which happened in it are so many types to us. As in circumcision, in sacrifices, in the whole Levitical priesthood, there was an allegory, as there is an allegory at the present day in our sacraments,—so was there likewise in the house of Abraham; but this does not involve a departure from the literal meaning. (136)

This astonishing passage may be read as one of the most succinct examples of how typological interpretation springs with such apparent effortlessness from contradiction and denial. Moses didn't intend his story to be read allegorically, but the history he records is, nevertheless, an allegory of the Christian church. This is because, as we have

seen already, Calvin understands history—"God's continual government of the world"—as an allegory. Even the Christian church itself,
in its sacramental life, is an allegory of God's reality. The "true meaning of Scripture," then, its "natural and obvious meaning," is always
gathered allegorically. Only allegorical reading can produce God's literal sense.

But Calvin agrees with Chrysostom that this "present application" produced by Paul's allegory of Genesis history is "different from
the natural meaning" of that history. Paul's reading is a "catachresis" of
the meaning intended by Moses (136–37). The *Oxford English Dictionary* defines *catachresis* as an "improper use of words" or "application
of a term to a thing which it does not properly denote." The issue in
both the story and Paul's interpretation of the story is precisely who
can be properly called a "son of Abraham." The point of the story is to
identify Isaac as Abraham's only true son, and Ishmael as a "son" quite
improperly so-called. It indicates that only Isaac and his progeny can
be legitimately called "sons of Abraham." To call Ishmael a "son" is,
legally speaking, a catachresis. Ishmael is the perverse son, a son by
birth, but not by covenant, and covenant is a truer birth than birth.
According to Calvin, Paul offers no new sense, but simply extends the
sense offered by Genesis by applying the distinction between birth
"according to the flesh" and birth by "the promise of grace" (137) even
more broadly. This mystical sense is perfectly in keeping with the natural literal sense.

That this broader application of the "natural" sense of the story
results in the condemnation of the Jews as perverse sons of Abraham
who "are not God's children, but are degenerate and spurious, and are
disclaimed by God, whom they falsely call their Father," does not
trouble Calvin at all (139). This is because the catachresis, according to
Calvin, is not in Paul's interpretation, but in any interpretation that
fails to see that the original Genesis story, even in its most plain and
"natural" sense, is itself a condemnation of the Jews: "This is a heavy
reproach against the Jews, whose real mother was not Sarah, but the
spurious Jerusalem, twin sister of Hagar; who were therefore slaves
born of a slave, though they haughtily boasted that they were the sons
of Abraham" (140). The catachresis or perverse application of the term
"son" was always, says Calvin, the Jews' own misreading. The "pious
fathers" who, like Moses and Abraham, "lived under the Old Testa-

ment" for a time as Ishmael-like "sons" according to the flesh, eventually also became real sons of God through Christ, "for their slavish birth by the law did not hinder them from having Jerusalem for their mother in spirit" (138). All of God's sons are first born of flesh and the law and then again by the spirit. It was precisely to signify this double birth that Abraham had two wives and two sons.

Paul's interpretation, then, is not allegorical. There is no catachresis or misapplication of the story's sense. What Paul calls an allegory is nothing but the true literal sense of the passage applied as the Spirit intended it to be applied, so that the catachresis or perverse sense of "son" promulgated by both the Jews and the Roman Church might be exposed—"because for a time they presume to occupy that place, and impose on men by the disguise which they wear" (139). "The design of the apostle," says Calvin, is nothing but to explain the true and "natural sense" of all the Hebrew scriptures, both Torah and the Prophets:

> to deprive the Jews of all claim to that spiritual Jerusalem to which the prophecy relates. Isaiah proclaims, that her children shall be gathered out of all the nations of the earth, and not by any preparation of hers, but by the free grace and blessing of God. (142)

The Genesis story shows that "God employed the services of Sarah for confirming his own promise" (145)—that is, the casting out of both Jews and Catholics from amongst the true children of God: "If we shall call the Papists, Ishmaelites and Hagarites, and boast that we are the lawful children, they will smile at us; but if the two subjects in dispute be fairly compared, the most ignorant person will be at no loss to decide" (145). Paul's interpretation is clear, literal, and true; even "the most ignorant person" can see this.

If the history of ancient Israel was intended by God as an allegory, then of course reading it allegorically produces the literal sense God intended. Is this, then, what is meant by typology—a method that authorizes as literal and claims to make perfectly perspicuous to even "the most ignorant person" meanings that might appear to many to be quite flagrant perversions, even inversions, of the text? Anyone who cannot grasp these literal senses must be worse than "the most ignorant person," indeed, must be deliberately self-deceived and perverse, a living breathing catachresis of God's design—one of the damned.

"The Full and Perfect Meaning"

WILLIAM WHITAKER, WRITES LEWALSKI, "supplies perhaps the most cogent formulation of the conception towards which many of the reformers seemed to be groping—the identification of the typological-anagogical meaning as the symbolic dimension of the literal text" (Lewalski, 120). This simply means that in Whitaker's formulation, typological interpretation identifies meanings that are understood as already literally "there" in the text as the literal text's "symbolic dimension." When Paul reads Genesis "typologically," then, he does not take the two steps identified by medieval scholasticism as first, determining the things signified by the words and second, the things further signified by those things. For Whitaker, as for Luther and Calvin, the meanings medieval scholasticism identified as the mystical sense, an allegory of things signified by words, are meanings in the literal text itself.

> The apostle . . . interprets the history of Abraham's two wives allegorically, or rather typically, of the two Testaments; for he says in express words, ἅτινά ἐστιν ἀλληγορούμενα, allegorically interpreted to his purpose, and the illustration of the subject which he hath in hand. Indeed, there is a certain catachresis in the word ἀλληγορούμενα, for that history is not accommodated by Paul in that place allegorically, but typically; and a type is a different thing from an allegory. The sense, therefore, of that scripture is one only, the literal or grammatical. However, the whole entire sense is not in the words taken strictly, but part in the type, part in the transaction itself. In either of these considered separately and by itself, part only of the meaning is contained; and by both taken together the full and perfect meaning is completed. . . . When we proceed from the sign to the thing signified, we bring no new sense, but only bring out into the light what was before concealed in the sign. . . . For although this sense be spiritual, yet it is not a different one, but really literal; since the letter itself affords it to us in the way of similitude or argument. . . . By expounding a similitude, we compare the sign with the thing signified, and so bring out the true and entire sense of the words.[25]

The typological sense is the "true and entire sense of the words," not some sense gathered allegorically from the things signified by the words as scholastic theory stipulated. This means that the ancient Israelites not only failed to grasp the significance of the things signified by the words, but failed to read the words themselves. Where scholastic hermeneutics charged "the Jews" with being hopelessly literal-minded, ignoring the mystical senses figured by their own history, Protestant typologists level a far more damning charge: deliberately misreading the literal sense of their own scriptures. There is no catachresis, says Whitaker, between the so-called literal or historical sense and the typical or spiritual senses. It is all one "true and entire sense," the "full literal sense" of the original words. If there is any catachresis, it is in calling this "full and perfect sense" allegorical.

Whitaker echoes the familiar warning that "it is only from the literal sense that strong, valid, and efficacious arguments can be derived" (Whitaker, 409). Since Paul so clearly derives strong arguments from his interpretation of Abraham's two sons,

> It follows, therefore, that this and no other is the genuine sense of scripture [the literal sense]. For a firm argument may always be derived from the genuine and proper sense. Since, therefore, firm inferences cannot be made from those other senses, it is evident that they are not true and genuine meanings. Therefore, tropology, allegory, and anagoge, if they are real meanings, are literal ones. (Whitaker, 409)

Whitaker's bold tautology makes explicit the dissolution of those distinctions upon which medieval exegetes had built their dualistic hermeneutic theories, a dissolution that is implicit in Protestant exegetical practice at least since Luther. Whitaker's theme, reiterated throughout his *Disputation on Scripture Against the Papists,* is that the Holy Spirit, speaking to the individual believer's heart through Scripture, is the final authority in all matters of Scripture's interpretation—the Protestant hermeneutic circle.

Appealing to the Thomistic syllogism that "Since the literal sense is that which the author intends, and the author of holy scripture is God," any sense that can be construed as authorized by the Holy Spirit is the literal sense: "Since then that is the sense of scripture, and the literal sense, which the Holy Spirit intends, however it may be gathered; certainly if the Holy Spirit intended the tropologic, anagogic, or allegoric sense of any place, these senses are not different from the literal" (Whitaker, 408–9). Therefore, Paul's allegorization of Abraham's "two sons" renders the Holy Spirit's literal intentions in Genesis clear, since Paul, it must be allowed, is a Spirit-inspired author of canonical Scripture. Whitaker's typical sense serves here as a euphemism for the allegorical, permitting him to accord allegorical interpretations all the authority of the Spirit's literal intention.

William Perkins' formulation is virtually identical to Whitaker's:

> There is but one full and intire sense of every place of scripture, and that is also the literal sense. . . . To make many senses of scripture is to overturne all sense, and to make nothing certen. . . . It may be said, that the historie of Abrahams familie here propounded, hath beside his proper and literal sense, a spiritual or mysticall sense. I answer, they are not two senses, but two parts of one full and intire sense. For not onely the bare historie, but also that which is thereby signified, is the full sense of the h[oly] G[host].[26]

The "full and intire" literal sense, as Perkins puts it, is the sense that combines "the sign with the thing signified," suppressing the very distinction crucial to traditional theories of representation whereby the sign is specifically not the thing signified.

I have argued above not only that the literal sense of the Genesis story is different from Paul's allegorical interpretation, but that the two senses are mutually exclusive of each other. Paul's sons of Ishmael are Genesis's sons of Isaac and Genesis's Israel are Paul's "sons of the bondwoman." What Whitaker calls "the sign" (the story of Abraham's two sons in Genesis) and "the thing signified" (Paul's interpretation of that story) are not simply two different things, but two mutually exclusive things. How can one then formulate "the mutual relation between the sign and the thing signified" and so arrive at the "whole complete" literal sense of the Scripture? One can do this, of course, only by emptying the Genesis story of any significance, that is, of any literal meaning apart from that supplied by Paul's allegory of it. Medieval scholastic typology, following Augustine and Aquinas, insisted that words signify things and that things, in turn, are employed by God (and God alone) to signify other things. But Whitaker has recast typology in such a way as to elide the first-step signification, denying the status of "thing signified" to the sense of "the words taken strictly," and transferring this status to the "thing signified" by Paul's allegorical exegesis. By conflating, so to speak, the allegory of the poets (signifying things by words) and the allegory of God (signifying things by things), Whitaker has accomplished the very thing that Protestants characteristically accused Catholics of doing—treating the Bible as "a unified poetic text . . . a complex literary work," virtually an allegorical fiction.[27] Once such a conflation is accomplished, any insistence on the historicity of the events recorded in the Scriptures (especially in the "Old Testament") can only have the effect of endowing historical events themselves with much the same ontological status as fictions. The key distinction can no longer be that between fiction and history, but rather must be between human fictions and God's fiction.

This accounts for what Lewalski takes to be the characteristically Protestant practice of "viewing [oneself] as a correlative type with the Old Testament Israelites, located on the same spiritual plane and waiting like them for the fulfillment of all the signs in Christ at the end of time" (Lewalski, 132). For "spiritual plane," we may read ontological status, since the Protestant believer here has made a type, not only of the Israelites, thereby displacing them from the status of a thing signified, but also of herself. The Protestant Christian "recapitulates the spiritual essence of the Old Testament experiences in himself, thereby bringing his own life close to the province of typology." When John Donne, for example, declares to his congregation that "All God's *Prophecies,* are thy *Histories:* whatsoever he hath promised to others, he hath done in his purpose for thee: And all Gods *Histories* are thy *Prophesies;* all that he hath done for others, he owes to thee," he betrays the same conflation of the literary and the historical articulated by Whitaker. Lewalski concludes: "His assumption seems to be that God's Word and his World are to be explicated in much the same fashion."[28]

The distinction between word-signs and thing-signs has vanished under the pressure of a now extremely privileged ontological binary— this world and the world to come. The American Puritan poet Jonathan Edwards put it quite simply:

> This may be observed concerning types in general, that not only the things of the Old Testament are typical; for this is but one part of the typical world; the system of created beings may be divided into two parts, the typical world, and the antitypical world. . . . The material and natural world is typical of the moral, spiritual, and intelligent world, or the city of God.[29]

Lewalski has argued that Edwards here extends "typological symbolism beyond recognition by using its terminology to describe a Platonic *allegoresis,*" but, as I have argued, Protestant typology has from the beginning been such an allegoresis simply rendered deniable as such by the euphemism typology. I can agree with Lewalski's claim that Donne (and Protestant and Puritan poets generally) "does not relinquish the historical ground of typological symbolism" only by recognizing that this "historical ground" has itself been rendered ontologically commensurate with the fictional and the literary.[30]

When John Bunyan writes the history of his own life and his experience of "New-birth," he calls it "a Relation of the work of God upon my own soul," and invites his "readers" to "be put in remembrance" of God's grace to them "by reading his work upon me." Reading Bunyan's words and reading God's work, reading Bunyan himself, are all parts of reading the "full and intire" literal sense. Bunyan offers himself, even reads himself, as God's work, as if he were himself textual to begin with, and his autobiography but a further text upon the text; both the text of the Word and the text of his being, and all such texts combined, constitute nothing but the full literal sense of God's great allegory.

Four

Reading the Self: Biblical and Pauline Stories of Identity

Wouldest thou loose thy self, and catch no harm?
And find thy self again without a charm?
Would'st read thy self, and read thou know'st not what?

Bunyan, "The Author's Apology"

It has long been widely recognized that Protestants and Puritans most commonly understood self-knowledge as something achieved by reading and exegesis. The Bible, the natural order, contemporary events, and one's own personal experiences were all regarded as various books in God's multivolume allegory. And to read these various books correctly was to read them intertextually. In *Devotions Upon Emergent Occasions,* John Donne imagines his own experience of illness as a book, the proper reading of which prompts him to "a new reading" of all the other "books" God requires his elect to read and reread with unremitting diligence. For God, insists Donne, "hast proceeded openly, intelligibly, manifestly by the book," where "the book" is understood as a grand intertextual treatise, a kind of multivolume anatomy of many smaller books:

> From thy first book, the book of life, never shut to thee, but never thoroughly open to us; from thy second book, the book of nature, where, though subobscurely and in shadows, thou hast expressed thine own image; from thy third book, the Scriptures, where thou hadst written all in the Old, and then lightedst a candle to read it by, in the New, Testament; to these thou hadst added the book of just and useful laws, established by them to whom thou hast committed thy people; to those, the manuals, the pocket, the bosom books of our own consciences; to those thy particular books of all our particular sins; and to those, the books with seven seals, which only *the Lamb which was slain, was found worthy*

to open; which, I hope, it shall not disagree with the meaning of thy blessed Spirit to interpret the promulgation of their pardon and righteousness who are washed in the blood of that Lamb.[1]

The Protestant self is both reader and text; the Protestant's God is both author and exegesis: "all mankind is of one author, and is one volume; when one man dies, one chapter is not torn out of the book, but translated into a better language" (17. Meditation, 108). The self that is imagined as finally emerging from the correct exegesis of all these texts, understood intertextually, is, of course, the self that is God.

But this result is perpetually deferred, for however "openly, intelligibly, manifestly" God proceeds in this grand exposition of himself, he does so not directly, but "by the book." And this book is "never thoroughly open to us;" its meanings are expressed "subobscurely and in shadows;" the full opening or exposition of these books, understood in their comprehensive and "full literal sense," is reserved exclusively to *"the Lamb which was slain."* Thus God is both author and meaning, and the only fully capable exegete is also God, the Son or the Spirit. The elect are those who by unremitting practice in reading and interpretation, or perhaps in spite of such practice, somehow are transformed into the one exegete capable of opening the seals of shadow and obscurity that shroud this worldly text we variously—and mistakenly—call life, or self, or history, or experience.

The Protestant self, insofar as it was (as Lewalski puts it), "close to the province of typology," was considered a kind of "Old Testament" that required interpretation to understand correctly. But Christianity also spoke enthusiastically about the new self, the self produced by such interpretation or translation, and this new self was imagined as no longer a type, but the antitype, the Christ only dimly shadowed in the type. The typical self, the self as Israelite, was taken to be an allegory of the new self promised by and as Christ. Insofar as this allegorical self prefigured the new self in Christ, it was thought to deserve the positive term Israelite, but insofar as it also obscured and deferred the new self, it was simply the Jew.

Another way of putting this matter is to say that self-knowledge and identity in Protestant discourses are figured almost exclusively as hermeneutically based—"reading," as Bunyan puts it in his autobiography, "the work of God upon my own Soul." This reading must, according to Bunyan, jibe perfectly with what is "written in the scripture" (*GA*, 1–2), to the point where the reading of experience and the experience of reading Scripture become indistinguishable from each other. Bunyan's struggle to reach such a point forms one plot of *Grace Abounding*, an autobiography often thought to be strangely plotless. That book is the subject of the next chapter. There we shall see that Puritan literalism, doggedly pursued to extremes, does not arrive at the desired country of transparent language and unmediated reading without first looking squarely into the abyss of infinitely deferred meaning and the threat of meaninglessness. Reading the self correctly, as it turns out, is also a process of reading an old self out of existence; and the new self, the only one who can read/experience things correctly—in a "gospel sense"—is a self perpetually deferred, a self that has its being elsewhere.

Reading and interpretation are, of course, notoriously problematic processes. As Protestants try to ground self-definition and a collective "redeemed" identity ("the Church") in hermeneutics rather than in ritual practices or genealogy, two contradictory tendencies inevitably appear. On the one hand is a herculean effort to establish a univocal hermeneutic that can guarantee a single literal sense whether the text being read is history, experience, or the Scriptures. Late medieval scholastic hermeneutics with its multiple levels of meaning, its allegories and tropologies and mystical senses, appeared frightfully unsuitable to the Protestant project of reading the self correctly. Typology, as it was articulated by the Reformers discussed in chapter 3, tried hard to reconcile "catching the sense at two removes" with the literalism Protestantism required.[2] On the other hand is the tendency, almost universally lamented and decried, of Protestantism to splinter into dozens, even hundreds, of ever smaller collective identities. It seems that the more energetically Puritans pursued the goal of grounding self and collective identities in a simple and literal hermeneutics, the more such a hermeneutics produced a plethora of "true" churches. In extreme cases, like those of William Franklin, James Nayler, Lodowick Muggleton, or Thomas Tany, this tendency produced nearly idiosyncratic hermeneutics and a radically idiolectic discourse of the self.

These two contradictory tendencies are coarticulated in the Protestant and Puritan emphasis on the Pauline concept of new birth.

Daniel and Jonathan Boyarin call attention to the allegorical dynamic of new birth as Paul articulates it in Galatians: "new birth . . . is understood as substituting an allegorical genealogy for a literal one."[3] It would seem, then, that at the heart of Puritan literalism lies a hard kernel of allegory that both enables unmediated literal reading—only the redeemed can read "the gospel sense" of Scripture or experience—and marks the literalist ideology as radically dependent upon an allegorical conception of self and identity. The Boyarins elaborate:

> Accordingly, if one belongs to Christ, then one participates in the allegorical meaning of the promise to "the seed of Abraham," an allegorical meaning of genealogy that is already hinted at in the biblical text itself, when it is said that in "Abraham all nations would be blessed" (Gen. 12:3) and even more when it interpreted his name as "Father to many nations" (Gen. 17:5). The individual body itself is replaced by its allegorical referent, the body of Christ of which all the baptized are part.

As Daniel and Jonathan Boyarin argue, Paul's allegorization of genealogy and the body may indeed have been motivated by an "authentic" and even "progressive" passion "to find a place for the Gentiles in the Torah's scheme of things," but the literalizing force of Protestant typology manages to grow something violently exclusivist from Paul's "radically dualist and allegorical hermeneutic."[4] As we have already seen, Protestant and Puritan typology shifts the designations *literal* and *real* to the far side of the *parousia,* claiming that what the Boyarins call the "allegorical meaning" is fully or completely literal and thus exclusively real. As the "allegorical referent"—what the scholastics called the mystical sense—is revalued as the real and the literal, then of course the "individual body itself," along with its history and experience, must be allegorical, pseudo-real, a signifying text or drama rather than the something signified. Anyone who rejects the experience of new birth, or who can be shown to have experienced it incorrectly or inadequately, is liable to be considered less than fully or really real. For Western Christianity, the archetypally "carnal" person, the one who refuses to experience new birth and persists in understanding Israel genealogically and/or ritually, is the Jew. After Paul, the Boyarins suggest, "the place of difference increasingly became the Jewish place, and thus the Jew becomes the very sign of discord and disorder in the Christian polity."[5] Nevertheless, we must not forget that in

Protestant and Puritan typology, the Jew—the Israelite of the Hebrew scriptures—is also a signifier of membership in the one body of Christ, the only literally real body. Thus, to be really real is, in one sense, to be really Jewish, where "really Jewish" is understood as being spiritually reborn into Christ's body. Any appeal to a sense of self grounded in this world—genealogy, ritual practice, ethnicity, sexual difference—marked one as carnal, a mere signifier of true being. I suspect that this understanding of self and group identity underlies more modern and secularized versions of liberal identity politics—we are all somehow deeply the same—but in the early modern period it could also underwrite a politics that could assign Catholics, Episcopalians, royalists, aristocrats, and misbelievers of whatever stripe to "the Jewish place" of pseudo-being.

Though Boyarin and Boyarin are committed to understanding Paul's new-birth allegory as progressive and universalist both in its intent and its effects,[6] Slavoj Žižek offers a somewhat less sanguine interpretation. For Žižek, the image of "society as a Corporate Body"— "an organic Whole, a Social Body in which the different classes are like extremities, members each contributing to the Whole according to its function"—is the "fundamental ideological fantasy," common to virtually all ideological formations.[7] Paul's image of all people—"Jew or Greek," "bond or free," male or female—as members of one body in Christ may be taken, as the Boyarins suggest, as the "moral center of Paul's work."[8] As such, it is easy to see how such a vision encourages a kind of universalism, but however universalist Paul's intent may have been, it remains a spiritualist universalism that clearly devalues particular bodies and their particular differences, and excludes as "fleshly" anyone who overvalues either those bodies or their differences. Paul explicitly directs that the pro-circumcision "Judaisers" be "cast out" and "cut off" (Galatians 4:30, 5:12). Luther's 1519 translation of Galatians 5:12, as we noted before, is a more literal rendering of Paul's violent attitude than the Authorized Version: "Tell those who are disturbing you I would like to see the knife slip."[9] In 1 Corinthians 4:1–5, Paul appears to recommend the "destruction" of a fornicator's "flesh" so that his spirit "may be saved." Difference has positive value only within an overarching context of sameness—one body—but those who persist in grounding identity in "carnal" differences must be "cast out" as unredeemably other.[10] Christianity typically offers to absorb difference, but not to coexist with it.

Žižek argues that this fundamental ideological fantasy of society as a corporate body typically requires a fetishized other. Thus Žižek accounts for "the Jew" as "a fetish which simultaneously denies and embodies the structural impossibility" of such a corporate society, a "fetishistic embodiment of a certain fundamental blockage," the always already known—and, in a way, even acknowledged—impossibility of the ideological fantasy. The Jew as fetish serves to mask the knowledge that the realization of Christ's kingdom on earth is structurally impossible in Christianity's own terms, terms whose meanings depend upon a set of binary oppositions that constitute God as not-man, flesh as not-spirit, this world as not "That which is to Come."[11] The figure of the Jew is deployed to embody this impossibility, thereby masking the ideological fantasy's own immanent structural impossibility.

For Paul, and in the Reformation thought that foregrounds Paul, however, the trope of Israel cuts two ways. Paul, "crucified" to the world and yet living still in a world "crucified" to him, fancied himself, like all true Christians, a member of "the Israel of God," as opposed to the shadowy allegorical Israel of the flesh (Galatians 6:14–16). The Christian who, as Lewalski puts it, "view[s] himself as a correlative type with the Old Testament Israelites, located on the same spiritual plane and waiting . . ." occupies the position of deferred fulfillment. Israel marks the place of deferment, the "not yet" of those who claim their destiny is to be made one with Christ.[12] The Israel fetish, then, is Žižek's Jew fetish with a crucially different spin: where the figure of the Jew "simultaneously denies and embodies the structural impossibility" of the "Kingdom come," the figure of Israel signifies the displacement by deferral of the Christian self from itself, the condition of being ever a type of one's new self, being a not-yet-self.

Realizing the fantasy of a fulfilled self would of course mean the absolute abolition of this place of displacement. Israel would not just pass out of existence but would turn out never really to have existed at all. Meanwhile the Israel fetish that is so much a feature of Protestant, and especially Puritan, Christianity masks the knowledge that the self that is not-yet-self is foundational to Pauline and neo-Pauline Christianity. The deferred self, the citizen of the kingdom not yet endowed with a citizen's rights, is passed off as the condition of being Israel rather than the inevitable condition of being Christian.

Chiliastic and millenarian Puritans of the revolutionary period in England had, as we have seen, lost patience with deferral and the allegorical structures that rationalized it. Chiliasts discarded the notion of two Israels, one carnal and the other spiritual, just as they discarded the notion of a God without a body. Millenarians announced the imminent arrival of the apocalypse, the end of allegorical ontologies. Luther's and Calvin's abortive attempts to rehabilitate the Israel of Scripture as the "faithful synagogue" or the earliest "Church" were re-energized by the likes of Muggleton, John Robins, Thomas Tany, and many others. Some of these, notably John Traske, Hamlet Jackson, and their followers, actually identified themselves as Jews, and took to keeping the Jewish Sabbath and practicing Jewish ritual (Katz, 18–42). Thomas (ThoreauJohn) Tany announced himself as literally "High Priest to the Jewes" and prophet of *"Jesus, Jehovah, Adoniel, L, Jah, Eloah, Aove, Iele, Throon, God the Same."*[13] He was reported to have circumcised himself. John Robins identified his redeemed self as John the Baptist and Christ, and took to raising the dead, especially Hebrew prophets.[14] If the Jews were God's Israel in the flesh, Tany reasoned, then they must be returned to England, and all Christians must reidentify themselves with the Jews in body and in ritual practice as well as in the spirit. Only then would the world be prepared for messianic rapture. No longer would there be two Israels, one of the flesh and one of the spirit, but all would be one. Whatever universalism might have motivated Paul's allegory of new birth bears fruit among these radical sectarians, but it does so only insofar as allegory is abandoned; God's Israel is both flesh and spirit.

The frantic search for an Ur-language was also part of this unorthodox movement. Many thought Hebrew, or some prelapsarian or pre-Babel form of Hebrew, was God's own language, and the attempt to recover, or reconstruct, the original *lingua humana* (or *lingua dei*) reached a fevered peak by midcentury. For some, the idea was to recover not only an originary universal language, but also a radical language, especially a system of writing "Real characters" so radically fitting to the essences of the things they named that figural language would be rendered unnecessary.[15] With such a language, metaphor and allegory would become indeed what Tyndale, Luther, and Calvin wanted to believe they were—mere "ornament." Language, especially the language of the Scripture, would become utterly transparent, absolutely and unmediatedly literal. So would all of the "books" Donne imagines. God's revelation of self and identity would no longer be obscure or "subobscure," but entirely open and clear. Reading and interpretation would no longer be necessary; all would simply, as Sedgwick believed, "see it."

Widespread fascination with the Jews, the Hebrew language, and Jewish ritual and mysticism combined with Puritan millenarianism to bring about the Whitehall Conference of 1655, which debated the repeal of Edward I's decree of 1290 that had formally expelled Jews from England. Protestant, and especially Puritan, philo-Semitism—or what many mistook for philo-Semitism—became prominent enough in England to allow Rabbi Menasseh ben Israel, "the Jewish advocate of readmission, to write that 'today the English nation is no longer our ancient enemy, but has changed the Papistical religion and become excellently affected to our nation, as an oppressed people whereof it has good hope'" (Katz, 8). The Whitehall conference effectively repealed the medieval ban on Jews, but stopped short of any formal public declaration to that effect. After 1655, it became clear that orthodoxy was more interested in the Israelite and the Jew as two alternating fantasies instrumental to the Protestant work of self-reading than it was in any actual Jews, especially Rabbi Menasseh ben Israel, who died debt-ridden and disappointed.[16] Tany perished at sea on his way to Jerusalem. Orthodox Puritanism retreats from hyperliteralism, preferring to preserve the allegory at the heart of its literalism, the allegory of new birth and the discourses of deferral. In the last two chapters of this book, I will argue that Bunyan, though he may have come to Puritanism through the radical channels of congregationalism and Army preachers, follows the orthodox path of a return to allegory. This orthodox path is firmly charted by Calvin's understanding of self and God as two poles of an absolute binary.

Calvin's God/Self Binary

CALVIN OPENS HIS *Institutes of the Christian Religion* with a meditation on what knowledge of God and knowledge of self must have been like for those who lived without benefit of the law, the prophets, or the

Gospels. Calvin understands his project in Book 1 as offering a pre-Christian, even pre-Jewish, account of the knowledge of God—"The Knowledge of God the Creator" as opposed to "The Knowledge of God the Redeemer, as First Manifested Under the Law, and Thereafter to Us Under the Gospel," which is the topic of Book 2. In other words, Calvin opens his *Institutes* with what he takes to be a paradigm of God-knowledge and self-knowledge that is independent of God's revelation of himself in the Law and in Christ. As such, this is Calvin's attempt to imagine what God-knowledge and self-knowledge must have been like for the most ancient Israelites, even the pre-Israelites of Genesis, who presumably had, as yet, no Torah.

> Our wisdom, in so far as it ought to be deemed true and solid wisdom, consists almost entirely of two parts: the knowledge of God and of ourselves. But as these are connected together by many ties, it is not easy to determine which of the two precedes, and gives birth to the other.[17]

Calvin goes on to explain that the knowledge of God comes by way of a knowledge of self and the knowledge of self by way of the knowledge of God, that is to say, the self is known as not-God, and God as not-self. The "many ties" that connect these two "parts" of knowledge are familiar—a human is an image or likeness of God, and God reveals himself to humans by anthropomorphic accommodations. One resembles the other. But Calvin is even more insistent on the radical difference between God and self. It is contemplation of the self's utter "depravity and corruption" that gives rise to the first thoughts of God; conversely, contemplation of the "face of God" is what convinces one of the self's "false show of righteousness" and "miserable impotence" (*Institutes*, 1.1.1–2). The self is God's otherspeak—one might say, God's allegory. Or God is the self's other, the self's allegory. Without benefit of revelation, one cannot say for sure "which of the two precedes and gives birth to the other."[18]

The metaphor of giving birth is used here to mark the as yet undecidable (without revelation) question of originary precedence—which element in the binary is privileged as origin of the other. Do we know about God indirectly by analogy with and in contrast to what we know about ourselves, or do we know about ourselves by analogy with and in contrast to God? The issues of precedence and origin are bracketed in a metaphor so that the self/God binary is preserved as a binary. The binary polarity combines with the question of relation to forge the allegorical kernel of Calvin's thought. If these questions could be settled, suggests Calvin, the self/God relation would no longer be truly a binary, but a birth story.

In an important sense, a birth story is precisely the wrong figure for thinking about the relations between the self and God according to orthodox monotheism, whether it be early Yahwism or Christianity. The God of Abraham, Isaac, and Jacob is insistently figured as distinct from the Egyptian, Canaanite, and Babylonian gods in that he created rather than birthed or engendered human beings. "The Father" of Yahwism and of Christianity is a metaphorical rather than a biological father. He adopts rather than begets his children, not to mention the highly inappropriate—because feminine—images of conception and birthing. There is no continuity of substance between the God of Israel and the children of Israel.[19]

Nevertheless, birth, genealogy, and primogeniture remain significant values throughout biblical narratives and become ambivalently crucial in the Gospels. Abraham, for example, is called and chosen to be a "Father of nations," oddly enough, by the command to separate himself from his own father and kin: "Go from your country and your kindred and your father's house to the land that I will show you" (Genesis 12:1). This would seem to suggest that a new understanding of fatherhood, in contradistinction to genealogy and kinship, is being forged. But it is not at all that simple. The promise of a place in this new land is specifically directed toward Abraham's descendants, his "seed" (12:7), as if genealogy and generation are to continue to play crucially significant roles in determining who inherits the promise and who does not. The apparent choice of Isaac over Ishmael as heir to the promise does not simply suggest a departure from the principle of primogeniture, but also registers a deep ambivalence about the competing claims of an identity grounded in genealogy and an identity grounded in God's inexplicable will. It is possible to read Isaac's position as privileged by virtue of his mother; Sarah was Abraham's wife, while Ishmael's mother, Hagar, was a "handmaid," a surrogate. There is even a suggestion of racial significance in the tradition that Hagar was Egyptian, thus incapable of transmitting the inheritance of God's promise. But the story is also full of suggestions that Isaac's peculiar legitimacy is grounded not so much in genealogy and racial purity as in something miraculous operating outside and above normal human generation. Sarah is very old, well past childbearing years. Her "barrenness," she believes, is God's doing (Genesis 16:2). Likewise, Isaac's birth is related as more an act of God than an act of human generation: "The Lord visited Sarah as he had said, and the Lord did to Sarah as he had promised. And Sarah conceived and bore Abraham a son" (21:1–2). "The Lord," the same One who initiated his promise to Abraham by calling him out from father and kin and offering him a new identity apart from genealogy, is presented here as both a closer and an opener of wombs (20:17–18). Ishmael, "because he is [Abraham's] offspring" (12:3), inherits a blessing and a promise, but not *the* blessing and *the* promise. Isaac inherits because he is something more than merely an "offspring"; his identity as a patriarch is grounded in something grander than genealogy.[20] God's role as a kind of (non)begetting father to Isaac is figured as a calling and a naming that somehow supersedes genealogy. He names Isaac, and in anticipation of Isaac's birth, he renames Abram and Sarai. Etymologically, Abraham is not quite a replacement of Abram, but the insertion of a "medial -*ha*- . . . in a manner common in Aramaic."[21] Abram remains "the underlying form." The addition -*ha*- registers the difference between "the exalted father" and the "father of multitudes." Since Abram is called "exalted" only in a childless condition, it is difficult not to see here some intimation of the competing and displacing claims of God as father and Abraham as father. Does Isaac's apparently miraculous birth, as opposed to Ishmael's perfectly explicable birth, mark God as "the true Father," displacing not just Abram's name but his promised role? The requirement that Abraham be willing to sacrifice Isaac, his only son, to God underscores this suggestion of an identity for which genealogy, in and of itself, is an insufficient ground.

Jacob's (Israel's) favorite wife, Rachel, is also represented as "barren." In what could be read as an instance of God's annoying habit of disappointing Jacob's patriarchal ambitions, he closes Rachel's womb and makes the "hated" Leah fruitful (29:31). When God finally does open Rachel's womb with the birth of Joseph, both she and Jacob recognize the birth as principally an act of God (30:23–24). Jacob's recognition that God, rather than he, is the "opener of wombs" and the "Father" of nations is expressed with anger, irony, and resentment:

> When Rachel saw that she bore Jacob no children, she envied her sister; and she said to Jacob, "Give me children, or I shall die!" Jacob's anger was kindled against Rachel, and he said, "Am I in the place of God, who has withheld from you the fruit of the womb?" (30:1–2)

By insinuating a negative response within his rhetorical question, "Am I in the place of God," Jacob angrily and frustratedly acknowledges Yahweh's overarching control of the special Fatherhood promised to Abraham, Isaac, and himself in the covenant: "Be fruitful and multiply; a nation and a company of nations shall come from you, and kings shall spring from you" (35:11). God, admits Jacob, is the ultimate opener of wombs, and as such, God, in effect, displaces Jacob from the promised place of father of nations and kings. The implied answer to Jacob's sarcastic question is more than a simple "No"; the answer implies that God is in the place of Jacob, the place promised him as Israel, father of nations. In his anxious pursuit of the promised place of father of kings, Jacob had favored Rachel, but God seems to have chosen instead the displacing wife, the unfavored Leah, blessing her with amazing fecundity. And, to complicate the ambiguity between genealogy and inexplicable chosenness still further, Leah's fourth son, Judah—not Israel's favorite, Joseph—is destined to be the father of kings, the genealogical root from which springs King David and the promise of the messiah.

Even the Gospels, however much they announce themselves as a story of birth as the ground of relatedness between God and his "children," and however much they focus on the Son's place in a documented line of descent from David, cannot help registering a deep ambivalence about the significance of genealogy and birth to identity. Matthew's gospel opens with a very strange genealogy of Jesus Christ. It is, in a very important sense, a non- or anti-genealogy. Though it announces itself at the start as "the genealogy of Jesus Christ, the son of David, the son of Abraham" in an attempt to establish Jesus' genealogical and prophetic *bona fides* as messiah, its established formula for genealogical consistency—"the father of"—is startlingly abandoned at the crucial juncture: " . . . and Matthan the father of

Jacob, and Jacob the father of Joseph the *husband* of Mary, of whom Jesus was born, who is called Christ" (Matthew 1:1–16, italics added). Something similar appears in Luke's genealogy (Luke 3:23–38), which traces Jesus' descent backward all the way to Adam and to God. Luke's repetitive formula is "the son of," but he begins by announcing Jesus as "being the son (as was supposed) of Joseph," and ends with the string: "Seth, the son of Adam, the son of God." The apparently seamless transition from biological sonship—"Seth, the son of Adam"—to what monotheism has always insisted is an ontologically different, nonbiological, sort of sonship—"Adam, the son of God"—is called into question from the start by the disruptively parenthetical "as was supposed." Is Jesus the son of God the way Adam was the son of God, or the way Seth was the son of Adam? This question, however, is rendered impertinent by the parenthetical suggestion that all this detail of patrilineal descent is really somehow beside the point. Jesus was only (mistakenly?) supposed to be the son of Joseph, but was really the son of God. If this preserves a distinction between being a son of man (Joseph) and a son of God, then why do the closing phrases of the genealogy pass over precisely that distinction so glibly—"the son of Adam, the son of God"? Similarly, Matthew's abrupt shift from "the father of" to "the husband of Mary" where we were led to expect "the father of Jesus" signals the messiah's identity as something more than and radically different from a genealogical matter—something more than and different from birth, since "Jesus was born" of Mary, but is "*called* Christ." Is Christ's identity as messiah grounded in genealogy, prophecy, or special calling beyond and in contradistinction to both? The Gospels seem to say two different things at once—that all of these taken together, even though they appear to contradict each other, form the grounds of legitimate identity. In short, the question remains a question, even a question about the possibility of asking the question properly. Who is a son and who is not? What is a son of God? How do we know? These are questions to which the Hebrew scriptures offer competing answers, and taken all together, they refuse to settle the matter. Even the Gospels' anxious focus on fulfillment does not settle the matter clearly. This is the problem Paul's allegorical midrash on new birth tries to solve once and for all.

For Christianity, Christ's identity and his self-knowledge are taken to be paradigmatic for identity and self-knowledge generally. Either one is a son of God, a son of Abraham, and so is heir to the promise, or one is not. But is this sonship to be understood genealogically, vocationally, juridically, metaphorically, or metaphysically? Is it literal or figurative? How do sex and gender fit in? Can a woman be called to be metaphorically a son? Is this legitimate? Are womanness and motherhood purely carnal matters? The Hebrew scriptures, particularly Genesis and Exodus, may be read as challenging the very legitimacy of any attempt to settle this question. Not that the question is not asked: it is repeatedly asked, usually implicitly, but it appears to be treated as a radically undecidable question, one Jacques Derrida insists "must be maintained. As a question."[22] The question must be maintained as a question because if God is omniscient and his Scriptures repeatedly pose the question with an answer "already initiated . . . beneath the mask of the question," then it is not a real question at all, but merely a rhetorical question. Maintained as a question, forever deeply undecidable—even, in a sense, never properly asked—it has the power, suggests Derrida, to found a "community of the question about the possibility of the question." In such a community, the grounds of identity and membership can never be fully and finally decided. This means that no determination of otherness—who should be "cast out"—can ever be definitive. Ishmael, too, is somehow part of God's covenant. So is Ruth the Moabite and Tamar the Canaanite who tricks her father-in-law into incest and so initiates the Davidic line. Jacob the cheat and Joseph the snitch are not "cast out." Something like this undecidability underlies Daniel and Jonathan Boyarin's idea of a "diasporic" and "disaggregated identity," which they claim characterizes Jewishness in its best sense: "Jewishness disrupts the very categories of identity because it is not national, not genealogical, not religious, but all of these in dialectical [I would add, dialogic] tension with each other."[23]

The question of how one is and knows one's self to be a child of God—that is, how the self/God binary Calvin imagines as fundamental comes to be refigured as a Father-son relation or a birth story—remains very much a question until Paul attempts an answer. Paul appears peculiarly alert to the highly problematic place of motherhood in the history of this question. Motherhood, specifically the material body of the mother, comes to Paul from the Hebrew scriptures and the Gospels as the troublingly disruptive, because mediating, link in

the relations between God and his sons—are sons born, made, chosen, called? The clearest evidence that Adam was made rather than
born is his motherlessness. Jesus was indeed born, but was the Son of
God born—"Truly, truly, I say to you, before Abraham was, I am"
(John 8:58)—or simply "begotten"? In Matthew's genealogy, all the
mothers listed are genealogically or ethically disturbing: Tamar (a Canaanite who "played the harlot" with her father-in-law), Rahab (the
name, at least, of a notorious harlot), Ruth (a Moabite), and "the wife
of Uriah" (presumably a Hittite and David's adulterous paramour). Is
this list meant to highlight by contrast Mary's ethical purity? It is impossible to say. Perhaps the notion of immaculate conception itself
registers a certain ambivalence about motherhood, not unlike the ambivalence surrounding the "opening" of "barren" wombs in Genesis.
On the other hand, biological fatherhood is only hardly more of a reliable link between God and his "children." Is Abraham or God understood to be the "father" of Isaac? Is the chaste and gifted Joseph
Jacob's work or God's? Paul read in the Hebrew scriptures a record of
ambivalence about how the flesh—material bodies, seed, mothers—
participates in, mediates, or qualifies the fundamental relationship of
God to human beings.

Perhaps, as is often suggested, Paul's Hellenism prompts his attempt to settle the question, to slice the Gordian knot by opposing
spirit to flesh and figuring one as an allegory of the other. No longer
dialectical or dialogic, the relation between God and his children will
be figured as one of binary opposition held together by allegorical
analogy. Genealogical or ritual sons of Abraham are allegories of true
sons; the first figures or shadows forth the other, but is decidedly not
real or true. Thus, Paul warns the Galatians not to be led astray by
Peter and James and the "Judaisers," who appear to have insisted that
Gentiles must first become Jews before they can become proper Christians, that is, that they must be circumcised and keep the law, thereby
indicating in their flesh their adoption as sons of Abraham and so heirs
to the covenant. Against the "Judaisers" Paul argues that being a son
of Abraham is entirely a matter of the spirit, a matter in which the flesh
plays no part: "Are you so foolish? Having begun with the Spirit, are
you now ending with the flesh?" (3:3). Paul effectively characterizes
the "Judaisers" and Judaism as perversely bound to unspiritual
(fleshly) concepts of identity and selfhood. Being a son of God, even a

son of Abraham, he seems to say, has nothing whatever to do with genealogy or its fleshly marks, nothing to do with community and its laws, indeed, nothing really to do with paternity and filiation, understood biologically or legally.

Paul's announcement in Galatians 2:20—"It is no longer I who live, but Christ who lives in me"—offers to solve the problematic relations between self and God by deciding the undecidable question. God is not so much related to the self, but replaces the self. This appears to underwrite the self/God binary Calvin imagined as fundamental to being and to knowledge of being. The *I* must perish and be replaced by Christ. Unlike Jacob (and later Joseph [Genesis 50:19]) asking his poignant question, "Am I in the place of God"—and Hebrew narratives can ring many variations of the sense of "place": place of the father, genealogical place, ritual place, even geographical place—Paul attempts to make an announcement: in new birth the self is replaced by a Christ-self. The Puritan Edmund Calamy, in *The Monster of Sinful Self-Seeking, Anatomized*, describes "blessed" self-seeking, as opposed to "cursed" self-seeking: "the more we seek the things of Christ, the more we seek our selves. . . . A Christ seeker, and a true selfe-seeker are termes convertible" (8). He "that beates downe his Body, and brings it into subjection . . . that weares and fires out his body in the service of God, . . . this is the true . . . and blessed selfe-seeker" (8–9). "Sinful and Monstrous" self-seeking is "when a Man makes *himself his* God" (13), and since "The Soule of man is the Man of Man" (8), the blessed self-seeker is he whose soul is replaced by Christ, whose self is God.

But Paul's effort to solve the question of identity is not as successful as its neo-Pauline versions. In Paul's version the self is indeed replaced by Christ, but the new Christ-self "lives in me," where the "me," what remains of the old self after conversion, is a kind of abjected self, no longer really a self, but a place occupied by the new self that is Christ.[24] Susan Handelman, drawing on Lyotard and Derrida, draws a sharp distinction between what she takes to be Jewish ("Rabbinic and Derridean") and Christian (Pauline) modes of thinking about identity. Christianity, as she would have it, writes the story of the self in terms of fulfillment, replacement, and "an erotic drive to bring the Other back to the Same." Jewish thought, by contrast, meditates without answers on "interpretation, mediation, displacement, deferment, exile, absence, equivocal meaning. . . . In Jewish thought, the difference between the father and the son is irrevocable. There is no 'fulfillment' of the word in an ontological return to the sameness of son and father as in Christianity."²⁵ Handelman's distinction is serviceable as a sort of rule of thumb, but it is entirely too sharp to account for all the evidence. For all his Hellenistic dualism of spirit and flesh, Paul's favorite image for conversion is new birth, rather than some kind of annihilation of the self and absolute replacement by Christ. The rhetoric of death to self must coexist, paradoxically, with the rhetoric of a new self born from the old self. The old self cannot die before the new self is fully born, and this birth is never complete in this world. "Christ lives," says Paul, "in me," figuring the new self as conceived in and struggling to be born out of the remainder old self, the *me*. The old self is a metaphorical womb that, to borrow Sibbes's term, "carries" Christ in this world until new birth is fully realized in the next. As I have already argued, this is all part and parcel of Paul's claim that only spiritual birth is true birth and that fleshly birth is but a dim shadow of the real. Paul insists that true motherhood, like true fatherhood, is spiritual, not carnal. Nevertheless, however much he metaphorizes birth and motherhood, he also insists that the "body of this flesh" from which he longs to be parted is the "kernel" out of whose death a "spiritual body" will be raised (1 Corinthians 15:37–44). All ideologies, says Žižek, include within themselves "some unsupportable, real, impossible kernel" around which the ideology grows like a pearl around a bit of aggravating sand, and this kernel betrays the ideology as impossible to realize. Perhaps the doctrines of incarnation and resurrection of the body together form the impossible kernel at the center of Paul's ideology of new birth into Christ's spiritual body. This is what we should expect, for conversely, the Hebrew scriptures, *pace* Handelman, also play with the notion of a son who becomes a father, and a human being who invites others to see him as "in the place of God."

I refer to the story of Joseph in Genesis 37–50, a story that poses questions of identity in dozens of different ways and comes to a dramatic close as Joseph asks his brothers the same apparently rhetorical question Jacob once angrily addressed to the "barren" Rachel. As his brothers, the patriarchal sons of Israel, prostrate themselves before him for the umpteenth time and offer to become his slaves, Joseph responds, "Fear not, for am I in the place of God?" (Genesis 50:19). Paul and the neo-Pauline exegetes of the Reformation focus chiefly on the stories of Abraham, Isaac, and Jacob in their attempts to forge a new discourse of identity. These stories offer obvious handles for arguing that one is called or chosen to be a son of God, rather than born to it. Abraham is called into covenant, not born to it; Isaac's birth is semi-miraculous and the story of his near-sacrifice can be read as foreshadowing Christian models of redemption and transformation; Sarah can be allegorized, as Paul demonstrates so boldly; and Jacob must wrestle with an angel and submit to being renamed, given a new identity. True, reading out of these stories a clear case for true identity as a redemption/transformation experience requires that many of their details be ignored or allegorized, but the Joseph story presents even harder problems. Taken as a whole, it is too willing to meditate on the contradictions, ironies, and contingencies of identity and the self's relation to God. Perhaps this is why Protestantism never adopts it as a model for the redeemed self as it did the others. Joseph, at so many points, is both self and other—Hebrew patriarch and Egyptian master, a son of Abraham and adoptively a son of Ishmael, both a Jacob (an ambitious younger son) and an Esau (excluded from the messianic line). Nevertheless it is Joseph who articulates most poignantly the question—"Am I in the place of God?"—which the Pauline announcement—"Not I, but Christ"—tries to answer.

Following Handelman's distinction, it would be easy to see Joseph as thinking identity interrogatively and Paul declaratively, but as I argued above, it is not that simple. If the yang of Paul's confident announcement contains at its center yin-like traces of a question—what is spiritual birth? what is a spiritual body? what is this *me* that God loves, chooses as his point of entry into the world, and promises to resurrect?—so the yin of Joseph's question has about it some of the yang of Paul's announcement. To his brothers Joseph's question must have sounded rhetorical, the obvious answer being "Yes." After all, Joseph's boyhood dreams, predicting that his brothers, even his father and mother (the sun, moon, and stars), would bow down to him (Genesis 37:5–11), seem to have come true. All the weird things the brothers experienced in Egypt—money and silver cups mysteriously appearing in their sacks (44:2–5, 9–12, 15), an Egyptian vizier/wizard who holds the older son hostage for the younger (42:15–21), who mysteriously seats them all by order of their birth (43:32–34), and accuses them of spying (as they thought Joseph once spied on them)—all these events, choreographed by Joseph, the brothers have long been convinced add up to evidence of the hand of God threatening them with retribution for selling Joseph into slavery and reporting him to Jacob as dead. "Therefore is this distress come upon us. . . . So now there comes a reckoning for his blood" (42:21–22). "What is this God has done to us?" they ask themselves (42:28). Even after Joseph reveals himself to them and they realize that he has done all these things, they are not convinced that God has not in some weird way done them too, that their brother is not some kind of god, just as he once dreamed he would be. Even Joseph's form of address here—"Fear not, for am I in the place of God?"—echoes the familiar formula by which the God of Genesis and Exodus addresses mortals.[26] Joseph's words of comfort—"I will provide for you and your little ones"—follow the formula of providential comfort so closely that his identification of God as the overarching agency behind all that has taken place does not settle the question securely in the negative. When Joseph's brothers hear him ask, "Am I in the place of God?" they have every reason to answer "Yes" as they prostrate themselves before the favorite brother once again, the younger brother who—instead of the eldest—has presided over old Jacob's embalming and burial, the brother whose dreams of universal dominion appear to have come true, the brother they fear will pursue apparently divine retribution even further. The brothers read in all Joseph's mystifying displacements the hand of God. And Judah, for one, sees them as virtually equivalent to God's actions: "God has found out the guilt of your servants; behold we are my lord's slaves" (44:16).

It is even hard for the orthodox reader (one who holds God to be utterly transcendent, having no specific place, but inhabiting every place) to answer Joseph's question firmly in the negative. From the story's beginning, we are encouraged to read Joseph's displacement from father and family as his special placement into the unwavering favor of Yahweh. Egyptianized though he is, the narrator reminds us repeatedly, "The Lord was with Joseph, and he became a successful man" (39:2, repeated at 39:23). Every displacement he suffers becomes an occasion for the narrator to remind us that the Lord is "with him." It is as if displacement from father, family, home, language, and heritage were a condition of Yahweh's being "with him." (We remember that God's call to Abram was explicitly a call to displacement, to come out from his "father's house.") In his progress from slave to overseer, from disgrace to prison to trusty to grand vizier, Joseph's unfailing success is represented as his heavenly Father's special favor. When he stands before his prostrate brothers and asks, "Am I in the place of God?" it is hard, even for readers, to answer in the negative.

So, then, may we read Joseph's question as thoroughly rhetorical, that is, not really a question at all, but what Jacques Derrida calls a question "determined enough for the hypocrisy of an answer to have already initiated itself beneath the mask of the question?" Does Joseph's question anticipate Paul's announcement of a virtual equivalence of self and God? Or is it even bolder than Paul's, suggesting that the self has replaced God rather than God replacing him? Our provisional answer must be "No," for Joseph's question, placed as it is at the very end of Genesis, invites its readers to a broader range of interpretive efforts than those it imposes on the brothers.

Genesis, the book of beginnings, has long been read as a narrative of the beginning of God's covenant with a specially chosen, specially favored people. From Abraham on, the promise made and reiterated by God from one generation to the next has two principal parts—that the promisee will be the father of a great and privileged nation, and that this nation will inherit a special place, the promised land. The place of God is, in one important sense, then, always the place of the patriarch. The patriarch is defined as one who is in the process of being placed by God—placed in history, in genealogy, in power, and also, of course, placed in the land, the geographic place of promise. But another persistent theme of Genesis and its narrative of the covenant is displacement. If the place of the patriarch is the place of the promise (the promise of a place in the genealogical chain that "inherits" the promise of a homeland), it is also the place of interminable displacement. The story of the promise of a place is a story riddled with crucial displacements as the ideology of a genealogical place in the covenant wrestles with the ideology of inexplicable chosenness: Isaac, not Ishmael; Jacob, not Esau; Judah, not Simeon or Joseph. Even the story of Joseph, the longest and arguably most complex narrative entity in Genesis, the story of a displaced favorite son, is itself a kind of displaced story, tracing in detail the life of one *not* destined to be the father of kings. When chapter 38 interrupts Joseph's otherwise integral story to tell us about Judah's dramatic attempts at becoming a father of kings, it is really an interruption of an interruption, a displacement of a displacing story, for Judah's story traces the genealogical line of King David and the messiah, interrupting Joseph's story of God's inexplicable favor, the counter-story to genealogy.

It is worth remembering that the story of Joseph is a story of how Israel came to be in the originary place of displacement: Egypt. It is the story of how Joseph, Israel's favorite son, and specially favored by God, becomes an Egyptian, an Ishmaelite, marries into the Egyptian priestly family, takes for himself an Egyptian name, and names his first son Manasseh, meaning "God has made me forget . . . all my father's house" (41:51). It is the story of how Joseph makes himself a place in displacement—he names his second son Ephraim: "God has made me fruitful in the land of my affliction" (41:52).

Gerhard von Rad identifies the exodus from Egypt as a kind of narrative *credo,* and, as such, a root of Jewish identity.[27] The Deuteronomist instructs the Israelites, upon taking possession of the promised land, to go before the priest and recite the following:

> And you shall make response before the Lord your God, "A wandering Aramean was my father; and he went down into Egypt and sojourned there, few in number; and there he became a nation, great, mighty, and populous. And the Egyptians treated us harshly, and afflicted us, and laid upon us hard bondage. Then we cried to the Lord the God of our fathers, and the Lord heard our voice, and saw our affliction, our toil, and our oppression; and the Lord brought us out of Egypt with a mighty hand and an outstretched arm, with great terror, with signs and wonders; and he brought us into this place, and gave us this land, a land flowing with milk and honey. (Deuteronomy 26:1–9)

Being one of the chosen here is more than being one who is free; it is defined as being one of those "brought . . . out" of Egypt and "brought . . . out" of slavery. The freedom promised is defined specifically as freedom from Egyptian bondage; what constitutes the promised land as such is that the people promised that land came to it by being "brought . . . out" of Egypt. At the moment of possessing the land, the prescribed response is to tell the story of displacement. As

Daniel and Jonathan Boyarin so neatly put it, "the biblical story is not one of autochthony but one of always already coming from somewhere else."[28] The "somewhere else" is as constitutively significant as the promised land. "Israel was born in exile."

And yet this litany of narrative self-definition seems deliberately to ignore the arché-narrative offered in Genesis of how slavery in Egypt came to be the precondition, the trace, that makes freedom in the promised land what it is. The Deuteronomist's elision of Joseph's story marks, perhaps, a certain ambivalence, an uneasiness about the stories behind the founding story of liberation. For the story of enslavement that must underlie, and by underlying give meaning to, the story of Israel's liberation is full of the troubling Egyptianness of Israel's favorite son. Joseph brought Israel into Egypt. When he asks his brothers, "Am I in the place of God?" he is standing in Egypt and he is still, in a way, Pharaoh's slave. He virtually embodies displacement and exile.

On the other hand, Joseph's story is also the story of how a son of Israel engineered the enslavement of all Egyptians long before Israel itself came to be slaves in Egypt. When they are starving from famine, Joseph requires that all Egyptians, save the priests of On, sell their land, and finally themselves, to Pharaoh in return for food (47:15–22). Joseph, sold as a slave into Egypt, engineers the enslavement of all Egypt to Pharaoh, but he also engineers Israel's residence in the land of Egypt, the earthly Sheol, the Land of the Dead and eventually the House of Bondage. Whether we take Joseph's question genealogically and geographically or in the context of special chosenness and God's inexplicable favor, "Am I in the place of God?" is impossible to answer, because it is a question of place that is impossible to place, always posed from a position of displacement. Even in Egypt, even as an Egyptian, one can be in the place of God. By God's special providence, rather than by physical generation, Joseph becomes a Father of fathers. Having already achieved his boyhood dream of domination over his brothers, he speaks of himself as "father to Pharaoh":

> God sent me before you to preserve for you a remnant on earth, and to keep alive for you many survivors. So it was not you who sent me here, but God; and he has made me a father to Pharaoh, and lord of all his

house and ruler over all the land of Egypt. Make haste and go up to my
father and say to him, "Thus says your son Joseph, God has made me
lord of all Egypt; come down to me, do not tarry." (45:7–9)

Joseph figures himself here as father of Egypt, father of Pharaoh, father of his brothers, and—by virtue of state authority—father of his
own father as he commands Jacob to "come down to me, do not tarry."
The fatherhood celebrated here is insistently not biological or
genealogical; it is metaphorical and metaphysical. Being truly a son of
God makes one a sort of universal Father. Paul's allegory of new birth,
it seems, is not entirely without precedent in the Hebrew scriptures.
What is new is Paul's desire to privilege spirit as absolutely as he can
over body, and to read one as an allegory of the other. But there are
elements of the Christian Gospels that refuse to be so neatly cate-
gorized. Another Pharisee, John's Nicodemus, for example, cannot so
easily allegorize the body, especially "his mother's womb."[29]

Even in Calvin's apparently radically binary version of self and
God, the place of displacement makes itself felt in the metaphor of
birth: "it is not easy to determine which of the two [knowledge of God
or knowledge of self] precedes, and gives birth to the other." This
third thing, the place of displacement, threatens to explode the pure
self/God, father/son binary as not truly binary, but it also stabilizes it,
keeps the elements of the binary from collapsing into each other, into
sameness. Joseph's undecidable place, Paul's unaccountable *me,* and
Calvin's metaphor of the birth of one knowledge from another knowledge, wherein which gives birth to which is undecidable, all tend to
keep the question as a question even when it is disguised as an announcement of the constitutive ground of all "that ought to be
deemed true and solid wisdom."

This third thing, the place of displacement that both threatens and
guarantees the God/self binary, is most evident in the story that interrupts and threatens to displace Joseph's story—the story of Tamar in
Genesis 38. I call it the story of Tamar, but the text introduces it as the
story of Judah, of his energetic activity in pursuit of realizing his place
as a father of a nation. Within the first six verses, we are told, "Judah
went down from his brothers," "saw the daughter of a certain Canaanite," "married her and went in to her" frequently enough to sire
three sons, and "took a wife for Er, his first-born, and her name was

Tamar." At this point, the narrative slows down, Judah's exuberant agency in taking wives and making sons is frustrated, and the rest of the story, except for the very end, is really Tamar's. This narrative structure resembles chapter 37, which introduces the final chapters of Genesis as "the history of the family of Jacob," but rapidly turns into the story of one displaced and enslaved son—the story of Joseph. Joseph's story displaces the family's story. Then, just as Judah's story threatens to displace Joseph's, it is itself displaced by Tamar's.

Tamar's story may be read as the story of how a Canaanite woman makes herself a mother in Israel against great odds. Perhaps it is fitting that this rare story of an energetically agentive mother be a story within a story within a story, and that it not only continue but intensify the themes of displacement already begun in chapter 37. After all, Genesis 2 defined woman as in name and in creation that thing "taken out of Man," a displaced part of man. Because she was created by displacement from man, she also represents the place of man's displacement from father and mother: "Therefore a man leaves his father and mother and cleaves to his wife, and they become one flesh" (2:23–24). Even before the first man is displaced from the garden for listening to the voice of his wife (2:17), he imagines woman, made from displacement, as the site of his own displacement.

In Judah's story, Tamar appears at first as the ultimate threat of displacement, what Mieke Bal calls a "Lethal Woman."[30] Judah took Tamar to be the wife of Er, his eldest son. Before Er sired any sons, he died. So Judah commanded his second son, Onan, to perform the levirate duty of siring sons on his brother's wife and in his brother's name. Onan, apparently as jealous of his place in the genealogy of the promise as Judah, "knew that the offspring would not be his; so when he went in to his brother's wife, he spilled the semen on the ground, lest he should give offspring to his brother" (38:9). Joseph's jealous brothers displaced him by selling him into slavery and reporting him dead, but Onan displaces his brother even after he is dead. In spilling his seed, Onan is an epitome of genealogy interrupted. He is also, paradoxically, an image of resistance to displacement; he refuses to father someone else's child and so be displaced from biological fatherhood.[31] For this, God kills Onan.

The narrator tells us that God slew Er for some unspecified wickedness[32] and Onan for *coitus interruptus,* but to Judah's mind Tamar appears to be the cause of his sons' early deaths. He has but one son left, Shelah, and he is not about to risk his last living bid for fulfilling his promised role as patriarch. He sends Tamar back home, ostensibly to wait until Shelah grows up, but his true concern, the narrator tells us, is that "he feared that he [Shelah] would die, like his brothers" (38:11). Because Judah sees Tamar as the ultimate threat of displacement, the killer of his sons, Tamar suffers a displacement more thorough than Joseph's enslavement. She must live as a childless widow in her father's house, sent back like goods found wanting, a useless vessel.

Shelah grows up and Judah's wife dies, and Tamar is not called back. When Tamar realizes the full effect of her displacement, she shifts from displaced patience to energetic agency, but it is an agency in the service of strategic self-displacement. We are told she "put off her widow's garments, and put on a veil, wrapping herself up, and sat at the entrance to Enaim, which is on the road to Timnah" (38:14). That is, she disguises herself as a whore and places herself in Judah's way as he travels to Timnah to shear his sheep. Judah, having recently buried his wife, propositions her, and Tamar sets her price—a kid from the flock. Since Judah hasn't got the kid with him, she demands a pledge in lieu of payment and specifies the dearest things Judah has on his person—his signet and cord and his staff, the symbols of his status, wealth, and promised role as father of a nation.[33] Judah agrees; he goes "in unto her," and she returns home to her widow's weeds— pregnant with Judah's son? grandson? whoreson? son of incest? She does not wait for the kid; she keeps his pledges and returns to widowhood as a mother.

After three months, people report to Judah that his daughter-in-law is "with child by harlotry." Judah says, "Bring her out and let her be burned" (38:24), but Tamar produces the signet and cord and staff, saying, "By the man to whom these belong, I am with child." Judah calls off the burning, acknowledges his things, and says, "She is more righteous than I, inasmuch as I did not give her my son Shelah" (38:25–26).[34] Tamar gives birth to twin sons, Perez and Zerah, who, like Jacob and Esau, struggle in her womb for primacy of place, that is, to be the first to come out of the place of displacement, Tamar's womb, and assume the title of Son of Judah and Father of Kings.

A growing body of feminist readings of Tamar's story assign her a place among the relatively unsung heroines of an otherwise militantly patriarchal tradition. They call attention to Tamar's apparent transformation from a patient object—taken for Er, then shunted on to Onan, and finally displaced altogether even from the limited role of a vessel for turning fathers' seed into sons—into a very decisive, even transgressive, agent. She takes charge of her fate and turns displacement itself—dressing as a roadside whore—into a scheme for re-taking her place. She demands the signs and tokens of the would-be patriarch who rejected her, and, through seduction and deceit, takes possession of his seed in place of the son she was denied. She even displaces Shelah, the only remaining son of Judah. On this reading we are invited to see a biblical example of a self-made and self-making woman, a woman who re-takes her place even after she has been thoroughly displaced by the patriarch. She takes justice into her own hands and rights the wrong done to her, even by very transgressive means—harlotry, incest, theft, and deceit.

But to what end is Tamar's much-vaunted agency directed? To the end of being restored to the status of a place for Judah's seed, a place for the intrauterine struggle between brothers seeking to displace each other from the promised role as Father of Kings:

> When the time for her delivery came, there were twins in her womb. And when she was in labor, one put out a hand; and the midwife took and bound on his hand a scarlet thread, saying, "This came out first." But as he drew back his hand, behold, his brother came out; and she said, "What a breach you have made for yourself!" Therefore his name was called Perez. (38:29)

Like the perinatal Jacob grasping at Esau's heel, Perez makes a breach for himself in the genealogical rule of primogeniture, even upsetting the rule by which midwives were to have unquestioned powers of witness in such matters, and he becomes the messianic son, the son of the promise.[35] Jacob wrestled and bargained with an angel, or with God, for a blessing, but Tamar wrestles and bargains with Judah for some sperm, some male homunculi who want nothing more than to be the first *brought out* of her and so into the promised name and place of the Father. It is tempting to read Tamar's story as an allegorical epitome of the sons of Israel struggling to be made a place for God. Had Paul written a midrash on Tamar's story, perhaps he would have pursued such a theme: Tamar as an allegory of the old self giving birth to the new. Tamar's role in the effort to realize the promise of a place is to serve as the place of displacement—a whore, an incestuous daughter, a transgressive womb. So, in one sense, is the Egyptian Joseph's role: establishing Israel's originary displacement in Egypt and threatening to demonstrate that chosenness, not genealogy, displacement, not placement, is the covenant's true mode. So, certainly, is that of the Pauline Self, finally and utterly displaced by the Son who is one with the Father.

Tamar's story, embedded as it is in Judah's story of anxious pursuit of the promise through paternity, which is itself embedded in Joseph's story of inexplicable chosenness, which in turn is embedded in the "history of the family of Jacob," that is, the story of Israel's sons, is a deeply displaced narrative—so displaced that it is routinely elided from "Bible-story" and Sunday school versions of the Joseph story.[36] Such deep displacement cannot help but register Tamar's story as somehow central—displaced into the center—perhaps even a paradigmatically central version of the larger narrative's obsession with the place of displacement in all its various manifestations—belatedness, primogeniture, Egypt, names, a pit, slavery, a bloodied coat, bags of grain, brothers, fathers, wives, loss of sons, promises, and disguises.

Tamar's energetic and energetically transgressive effort to recover her place as a mother in Israel succeeds, but she succeeds in bearing twin sons who reestablish—or re-cover—her as the quintessential place of displacement, the deadly-whore-mother in whose womb twin grandsons of Israel struggle to be the first to emerge from the place of displacement as from a bodily Egypt.

At the heart of this part of Genesis, then, is this displaced place of displacement, the oft-forgotten but persistently literal Tamar out of whose womb literally springs the promised line of David.[37] In Genesis, Tamar and her story are displaced, but not metaphorized. She remains literally a mother in Israel, even to the degree of meriting a place—along with Rahab and Ruth—in Matthew's strange (non)genealogy of "Jesus Christ, the son of David, the son of Abraham." Joseph's question, "Am I in the place of God?" like the story that it closes, remains a question, even, by virtue of Judah's and Tamar's displacing interruption, a question still in question as to the possibility of the question. We may think of Tamar as an embodiment, however briefly, of that question and its possibility as her displaced story rehearses the question's own endless displacement, the displacement of maternity by paternity and paternity by God's Fatherhood. Throughout the story, however, the displacement is not re-placement or metaphorization. Tamar remains literally a mother. Only in Pauline and neo-Pauline allegory is literal motherhood displaced across the ontological frontier into pseudo-being. The discourse of new birth, as we shall see, threatens to put an end to the question, and thus an end to interpretation.

Five

"Other Mens Words" and "New Birth": Bunyan's Anti-Hermeneutics of Experience

> Meaning occurs not because things are *per se* meaningful but in spite of their meaninglessness; grace abounds in spite of sin.
>
> Gabriel Vahanian[1]

Bunyan scholars are still upset by Stanley Fish's designation of *The Pilgrim's Progress* as "the ultimate self-consuming artifact, for the insights it yields are inseparable from the demonstration of the inadequacy of its own forms, which are also the forms of the reader's understanding."[2] Since the principal forms of both Bunyan's text and the reader's understanding are the forms of language, many Bunyanists shrink from the suggestion that Bunyan might be seen as some kind of ur-poststructuralist, deeply skeptical, as Fish appears to be, of language's capacity for articulating the truth. They often accuse Fish, explicitly and implicitly, of re-reading and so re-writing Bunyan in his own image as one who believes that true meaning is an "experience" and "that experience is immediately compromised the moment you say anything about it" (Fish, 425). How, they ask, could one of the seventeenth century's most prolific preachers and writers be such a skeptic about the adequacy of language, especially of the Word, to communicate the truth, the Gospel-truth?[3] How could Fish be so unhistorical?

In the first half of this chapter I want simply to point out that, however unhistorical Fish's reading of *The Pilgrim's Progress* may be, far from re-writing Bunyan in his own poststructuralist image, he probably acquired his own skepticism about language and its forms of understanding from seventeenth-century authors like Bunyan rather than from poststructuralist theory. From his earliest writings, Bunyan announces himself as one deeply troubled by what he called the problem of "words in general," by the intractability of language as an instrument for even the simplest kinds of communication, let alone for truth-telling. The radical sects so prominent during Bunyan's youth have left thousands of pages of writing shot through with anxiety about the authority of words—spoken, written, printed, read, uttered, recited. Some experimented with glossolalia, ecstatic utterances; others with arcane hermeneutic methods; still others sought (and sometimes found) the ur-language in which alone truth could be spoken. In what survives of writers and preachers like Thomas Tany, Abiezer Coppe, William Franklin, and a host of other seventeenth-century religious radicals, the problems of language, of representation in language, of word and Word, hearing and *hearing*, saying and meaning, sign and thing signified, origin and echo, "impead" and "inclue" (to use Tany's idiolect), are endlessly debated, redefined, and sometimes twisted beyond recognition. In the waning years of the Age of Faith, the impossible Real of Christian logocentrism obtrudes its presence quite markedly, quite uncomfortably, and quite persistently.[4]

I propose to concentrate in detail on John Bunyan's chronic anxiety over the problem of "words in general," first as it issues from his debate with the Quaker Edward Burrough, the occasion of Bunyan's first sallies into print, and then as it dominates Bunyan's own "Relation of the work of God upon my own Soul," that astonishingly literalized allegory of the self (or allegorized anecdote of the self), *Grace Abounding to the Chief of Sinners*.[5] Bunyan and Burrough, we shall find, formulate the problem in almost the same words, but they finally agree upon no solution, and settle for reproducing the problem in their mutual accusation that each speaks words without "truth" and so cannot hear the words of the other, or for that matter, the Word of God, a human being's primary other. Burrough's solution is his Quaker pledge to a silence he cannot keep; Bunyan's may be what he once termed his "fall" into allegory—always meaning something other than what he says.[6]

Anyone who takes the time to read through Bunyan's first two tracts against the Quakers and Edward Burrough's polemical responses will probably be tempted to conclude that these two ardent opponents allow the debate to degenerate very quickly into semantic quibbles—arguments over words:[7] the "Christ within" versus the

"Christ without," my Christ versus your Christ, a Christ begotten before all worlds versus since the world began, inner light versus special light. In fact, Burrough's most frequent response to Bunyan, aside from accusing him of having wrested his words into senses different from his intentions, is simply to say, "I own the words, and I deny thy voice" (*Memorable Works,* 141). That is to say, Burrough more often than not sees himself in perfect agreement with Bunyan's theology, especially with what Bunyan thinks is their chief difference—Christology—but their agreement, says Burrough, is only word-deep, and so not really agreement at all. Burrough denies Bunyan's central charge against the Quakers, that they preach "a New and false Christ," and says that there is nothing in Bunyan's Christology—the "first sixteen pages" (141) of *Some Gospel Truths*—but what any Quaker would assent to readily. Burrough takes no exception to Bunyan's teaching about Christ, except to say, "what is Truth I own by the Spirit of the Lord, as it is Truth in Christ; but as it comes from thy lying spirit, I do not so well own it; I own the words, and I deny thy voice" (*Memorable Works,* 141).

Burrough's claim that Bunyan speaks true words in a "lying spirit" and therefore preaches a false gospel reveals an assumption common among Puritan radicals of his day: that truth is a matter of intention rather than of words. Two people, even Bunyan and Burrough, can utter precisely the same words, the same gospel, and one may be identified as "lying" and the other as speaking truth. According to Burrough's line of argument, anyone who attacks believers of the "True Faith of the Gospel," however theologically perfect his or her words, cannot be speaking in the "Spirit of Truth," and therefore the words, however true, are voiced as lies: "And the sum of thy doctrine is no less in the profess of thy words, then what we say; then why doest thou condemn us? But it seems thy tongue speakes one thing, and another thing is in thy heart" (*Memorable Works,* 144). "Though the words be true, yet is thy spirit false, and at the best, what thou hast said, is but bearing false witness (as to thy self) of a true thing; I own the words, and I deny the voice" (148). Burrough here carries the Reformation's general suspicions about inauthenticity in language to a logical extreme.[8] Were we to translate this extreme suspicion into literary terms, the result would be virtually the same as George Puttenham's description of allegory as "a duplicitie of meaning or dissimulation vnder

couert and darke intendments."[9] Burrough, in effect, charges Bunyan
with speaking allegorically without knowing it, almost as if he cannot
help it. He even suggests that Bunyan speaks allegorically to and of
himself.

A key to Burrough's distinction between "the words" and "the
voice"—which is analogous to the distinctions between words and
spirit, tongue and heart—is the Quaker insistence that the true Gospel
cannot be learned from "other mens words" and cannot be taught by
anyone but the Spirit. Each believer, thought Burrough, must have
the gospel directly from "the Spirit," from the "Christ within." Moreover, the Spirit must speak directly to the individual. Gospel truth is
source-specific (from the "Christ within") and target-specific (to the
individual). To learn the gospel any other way is to believe "other
mens words" rather than Christ's Word: "He is a false prophet and a
deceiver which hath not the word from the mouth of the Lord but
takes that which the Lord spoke to another, and calls it his" (*Truth
Defended*, 4). Quakers believed they were living in a new age in which
it was no longer necessary, indeed it was perverse, to take the witness
of others, even those in the Scriptures, for the final authority in matters of faith:

> For now the Lord hath rent the vail of the covering which hath been
> spread over all the nations in all professions; and you are all seen by the
> eternal eye which is opened in thousands; even all from the highest to
> the lowest, who have stollen and painted yourselves with other mens
> words. (*Truth Defended*, 1)

This long tradition of taking "other mens words" for the gospel, includes, says Burrough, the Scriptures themselves, insofar as they are
the words of others. Though, says Burrough, Quakers "own" all
Christ's ordinances—preaching, praying, baptism, communion,
singing:

> we witness these things in the eternal substance, having passed through
> the earthly figures, which was but to stand for its time; by the eternal
> have we been led, by the command of it within us and not by tradition
> from the scripture without us. (*Truth Defended*, 10–11)

Christ once bid the Pharisees to "search the scriptures," but that, says
Burrough, was because the Pharisees were among those "who had not

Christs word abiding in them, and who had not heard Gods voice, nor seen his shape" (*Stablishing Against Quaking,* 16). Pharisees, and those like them—Burrough obviously includes Bunyan here—must settle for a represented Christ, a Christ in "other mens words," and by so settling, mark themselves as false prophets.

Quakers often cited Paul's Epistle to the Galatians in support of their claim that the true Gospel cannot be learned from "other mens words." There Paul claims that, unlike the Jerusalem apostles, he preaches a gospel that is "not man's gospel," that is, not received or taught "from man," and he implies that this gospel, which "came through a revelation of Jesus Christ," is to be preferred above the gospel that Peter and James learned from the man Jesus, before he was risen and glorified (Galatians 1:6–17). According to Burrough's understanding of Paul, the true Gospel cannot be learned, for it is not a matter of human words, but of revelation. Even if one were to preach words identical to Paul's, or Jesus', such words do not constitute the Gospel of Truth unless it can be shown they were received by revelation, not by language:

> . . . this gospel we witness to have received not from man, but by the revelation of Jesus Christ, which is contrary to man. . . . And here again I charge the teachers of this generation, that their gospel which they preach is not the Gospel which the saints preached, but another gospel, and they are guilty of that themselves whereof they falsely accuse us; for they have received their gospel from man and by man, *from the Printers and Stationers.* (*Truth Defended,* 9)

The most vexing problem in all of this, of course, is that Burrough recognizes that the words of "another gospel" may sound identical to the words of the true Gospel: "We who are scornfully called Quakers, do live in and declare forth no other thing but the substance of what the Priests have preached upon and the professors have talked upon in their carnal mindes by their imaginations" (*Truth Defended,* 4). Priests and professors, like the Jerusalem apostles of Paul's day, have been preaching words learned from other men rather than a revelation from the risen Christ; therefore their preaching and professing are all lies. Since there is no certain way to know the difference between words with substance and words without substance except by individual conviction, Quakers tried to practice, among themselves at least, "pure Silence":

> And we ceased from teachings of all men and their words, and their Worships, and their temples, and all their Baptisme, and Churches, and, Professions, and Practices in Religion, in times before zealously performed by us, through divers Forms, . . . and we met together often, and waited upon the Lord in pure Silence, *from our own words,* and all mens words, and hearkned to the Voice of the Lord, and *felt* his Word in our hearts, to burn up and beat down all that was contrary to God, and we obeyed the Light of Christ as in us.[10]

Even their own words counted as "other mens words" the moment they were uttered. The Quakers had a theological understanding of the inevitable othering dynamic of language. Once uttered, words are othered, separated irrevocably from a speaker's intention, liable to be wrested and twisted to the intentions of the hearer. Even if spoken with the Spirit, words cannot carry the Spirit with them. Whether words so spoken are heard in the Spirit depends entirely upon the hearer. To be true words, the hearer must hear them as spoken, not by another, nor even by the speaker, but as if spoken by the Spirit. In short, the Quaker version of what Vahanian calls "the verbal condition of man" (Vahanian, 123) is that all words, except those spoken directly by the risen (and so fully other) Christ, are "other mens words."

On the inevitable distance between saying and meaning, Bunyan agrees quite explicitly with his adversary, echoing in his *A Vindication of Some Gospel Truths Opened* Burrough's words almost exactly: "Now friend, this is fairly spoken: but by words in general we may be deceived, because a man may speak one thing with his mouth, and mean another thing in his heart; especially it is so with those that use to utter themselves doubtfully."[11] Bunyan's enemies, the Quakers on one side and the state authorities and established church on the other, may be special cases of those who "utter themselves doubtfully," but "words in general," no matter who speaks them, present a chronic problem. Words without substance, spoken or heard, written or read, are a persistent concern of Bunyan's, not only in his debate with the Quakers but throughout his autobiography. Bunyan reveals that even before he began the process of conversion detailed in *Grace Abounding,* he was ever anxious about the doubtfulness of words and their authority. He confesses that he was an inveterate swearer: "I knew not how to speak unless I put an Oath before, and another behind, to make my words have authority" (*GA*, par. 28). This anxiety over the authority of words—his own, those of others, those of the Bible, those he hears in voices—takes dozens of different shapes throughout Bunyan's spiritual pilgrimage. An almost uncontrollable desire to swear and blaspheme haunts Bunyan throughout, even after, his conversion (*GA*, par. 100–101, 253, 293), a desire he feels most strongly when he is in the grips of that worst and most persistent of his temptations—atheism:

> Of all the Temptations that ever I met with in my life, to question the being of God, and the truth of his Gospel, is the worst, and worst to be born; when this temptation comes, it takes away my girdle from me, and removeth the foundations from under me. (*GA*, "The Conclusion," par. 1)

Both early and late, Bunyan never fully shook off this temptation or replaced it with the certainty of salvation that all his wrestlings with the Scriptures were supposed to have won him.[12] Even well into his preaching career, Bunyan confesses his fear that he "should not be able to speak the Word at all to edification, nay, that I shall not be able to speak sence unto the people" (par. 292). This fear is a local occasion of that more general fear that as true conviction and true conversion cannot ever come by way of "other mens words" unless the Spirit does the work, so his preaching always comes under the condition of being, for others at least, another man's words. At such times, confesses Bunyan, "I have been violently assaulted with thoughts of blasphemy, and strongly tempted to speak them with my mouth before the Congregation" (par. 293).[13]

Blasphemy, it seems, offered a tempting solution to an intractable problem. If one's words are inevitably othered by utterance, floating free from one's own intention and capable of being heard, read, even repeated without the assistance of the Spirit, as Bunyan and Burrough charged each other had done with the Gospels, then preaching, praying, teaching, and writing must be notoriously unreliable vehicles for gospel truth. At such a pass, one may well be tempted to avail oneself of the affective power of cursing and blaspheming, for surely such utterances hold out a strong promise of saying what one means. As utterances, blasphemy and curses can never be mistaken for misappropriations or misstatements of God's meaning; they have an air of sincerity rooted in the Calvinist conviction of human depravity. Perhaps blasphemy is the only reliable way to express what Calvin believed truly to be in a man's heart. Perhaps this is why Ranters often favored cursing and blaspheming over preaching and praying, though of course Bunyan did not. If you are convinced that all religious talk is mere sham, cursing is a refreshing exercise in sincerity.[14] Or perhaps Ranters had a firmer grasp than Bunyan of the logic of alterity by which truth is blasphemy's unspeakable other, and since the truth cannot be spoken directly without automatically raising suspicions of insincerity, blasphemy supplies the sincerity such utterances must always lack.[15]

"Holy Mr. *Gifford*," to whom Bunyan turned for comfort and instruction, taught Bunyan what we might call the sectarian experimentalist's version of skepticism. It is much the same as Burrough's:

> [H]e pressed us to take special heed, that we took not up any truth upon trust, as from this or that or another man or men, but to cry mightily to God, that he would convince us of the reality thereof, and set us down therein, by his own Spirit in the holy Word. (par. 117)

Only God, "by his own Spirit in the holy Word," can say true words in truth (par. 249). "Other mens lines" (par. 285), other men's feelings (par. 129), other men's "Experience" of God's truth cannot be, for Bunyan, "a Word, a Word to lean a weary Soul upon" (par. 250). Such skepticism means Bunyan cannot expect teaching and comfort from the words of others, especially from their books,

> for those who had writ in our days, I thought (but I desire them now to pardon me) that they had Writ only that which *others felt,* or else . . . studied to answer such Objections as they perceived *others* were perplexed with, without going down themselves into the deep. (par. 129, italics added)

As an author now of his own "Relation," as one who has himself gone down "into the deep" of sectarian skepticism and despair, he must now ask their pardon, for now he can see a homology between their experience and his own, but he must have his own before any such homology appears. How does one get his own experience? From the

Bible? But isn't the Bible itself merely a collection of the records of others' experiences, "other mens words"? And what if those experiences, like Paul's, are but "a Fable and cunning Story," an elaborate deception? "How could I tell?" demands Bunyan (par. 96–98).[16]

When Bunyan was hauled before "Justice Keelin" (Sir John Kelynge of Southhill) in November 1660 on charges of "devilishly and perniciously" abstaining from divine service and helping to organize and support "unlawful meetings and conventicles," Kelynge wanted to know why he objected to using the "Common Prayer-book" for prayer and worship.[17] Bunyan responds, "I said that those prayers in the Common Prayerbook, was such as was made by *other men*, and not by the motions of the Holy Ghost, within our Hearts" (114, italics added). When pressed further to define what he means by prayer, Bunyan implies a distinction between mere words and words spoken in the Spirit, a distinction very similar to Burrough's:

> . . . men might have many elegant, or excellent words, and yet not pray at all: But when a man prayeth, he doth through a sense of those things which he wants (which sense is begotten by the spirit) pour out his heart before God through Christ; though his words be not so many, and so excellent as others are. (114)

Genuine prayer, for Bunyan, does not begin with words; to be genuine, it must begin with a sense of lack—which is true desire or "wants"—and this sense must be "begotten by the spirit" in one's heart. A metaphor of conception and birth, so familiar to us already from Paul, Calvin, and Luther,[18] is deployed to account for the relations between God and his proper worshipper or supplicant. The Spirit begets upon the heart a "sense of those things which he wants," a sense of lack under the image of a fetus, which suggests that the supplicant's heart is a kind of uterus in which the Spirit opens up a space felt as desire for the things of God.

The Justices ignore the birth metaphor and simply agree that excellent words alone do not constitute prayer.[19] But Kelynge insists on exploring the matter a bit further. If prayer is not essentially a matter of words, then does that mean that no one can teach another to pray? Kelynge argues that

> Christ taught his disciples to pray, as John also taught his disciples. . . . Faith comes by hearing: And one man may convince another of sin, and

therefore prayers made by men, and read over, are good to teach, and help men to pray. (115)

Kelynge here shows evidence of experience interrogating Quakers on this issue; no doubt he is already all too familiar with this objection to "other mens words."[20] He presses on in this direction because Bunyan has already rejected use of the prayer book on the authority of Scripture—"I did not find it commanded in the word of God" (114)—hoping that he can maneuver Bunyan into rejecting Scripture itself as "other mens words," a fairly common way of convicting Quakers of heresy.

Kelynge knows that Scripture says Jesus taught his disciples to pray what has for centuries been called The Lord's Prayer. He even has a specific passage in mind: Luke 11:1–4, rather than the more familiar Matthew 6, for the Lucan passage is far more explicit than the Matthean passage on the issue of "other mens words." Whereas Matthew records Jesus as saying, "After this manner, therefore, pray ye" and as emphasizing prayer "in secret" rather than in public, the passage in Luke leaves no room for such equivocation: "one of his disciples said unto him, Lord teach us to pray, as John taught his disciples. And he said unto them, When ye pray, say, Our father . . ." Luke records Jesus as teaching his disciples to pray by offering them specific words and sentences as a prayer to be repeated. Is the Lord's Prayer, then, merely another man's words?

Kelynge has Bunyan at a stand. If he holds firm, as so many Quakers have before him, to his denial of "other mens words," even to the point of rejecting Scripture as such, or calls Scripture mere types and shadows of that which he possesses in substance, Kelynge can convict Bunyan of much greater crimes than nonattendance at the parish church and frequenting conventicles: he can charge him with blasphemy, much as Franklin and Gadbury were charged.

But Bunyan, though he often sounds Quakerish, cannot be badgered into "slighting" the Scripture. Indeed, it is Scripture, in the form of a passage from Romans (8:26–27), that comes here to his rescue:

I said, Sir, the Scripture saith, that *it is the spirit as helpeth our infirmities;* for we know not what we should pray for as we ought: But the spirit itself maketh intercession for us, with sighs and groanings which cannot be uttered. Mark, said I, it doth not say the Common Prayer-book teacheth us how to pray, but the spirit. (115)

Far from slighting the Scriptures, as Kelynge evidently hoped he would, Bunyan adduces Scripture as a direct authority for his point about the Spirit, a point the Justices had already conceded. But Bunyan pushes his point even further, having recognized Kelynge's allusion to the Lord's Prayer:

> And as to the Lord's Prayer, although it be an easy thing to say *Our Father, &c.* with the mouth; yet there is very few that can, in the spirit, say the first two words of that Prayer; that is, that can call God their Father, as knowing what it is to be born again, and as having experience, that they are begotten of the spirit of God: Which if they do not, all is but babbling, &c. (115)[21]

Again the metaphor of begetting and birthing, and again the Justice's ready assent while apparently ignoring the metaphor: "Justice *Keelin* said, that that was a truth." Bunyan seems annoyed by Kelynge's assent, as if he believes Kelynge has missed the full force of his point:

> And I say further, as to your saying that one man may convince another of sin, and that faith comes by hearing, and that one man may tell another how he should pray, &c. I say men may tell each other of their sins, but it is the spirit that must convince them. (115)

Bunyan slips easily here into a familiar strain of anaphoric homiletic, preaching to his judges as Paul did to the Philippian jailer:

> And although it be said that *faith comes by hearing:* Yet it is the spirit that worketh faith in the heart through hearing, or else *they are not profited by hearing.*
>
> And that though one Man may tell another how he should pray: Yet, as I said before, he cannot pray, nor make his condition known to God, except the spirit help. It is not the Common Prayer-book that can do this. It is the *spirit that sheweth us our sins,* and the *spirit that sheweth us a Saviour:* And the spirit that stireth up in our hearts desires to come to God, for such things as we stand in need of, even sighing out our souls unto him for them with *groans which cannot be uttered.* (116)

As if "Justice Keelin" were the perfect example of one who has not ears to hear, Bunyan reports his response to this impassioned sermon:

"But says Justice Keelin, what have you against the Common Prayer-book?"

Bunyan has stuck to his contention that prayers "made by other men," other men's words, cannot—in themselves—count as prayer, but he has not been bamboozled into slighting the Scriptures, even though he has insisted that it is not by words, or by the hearing of words, even by hearing the Word, that prayer or reading or preaching are effective as God's means of revelation or salvation.[22] "'Tis the spirit in the word," says Bunyan, "that is God's ordinance." And the mark of the presence of the "spirit in the word" is that it, and it alone, can tell the would-be supplicant what he really desires, "what we should pray for." Without the Spirit, even one who uses Jesus' own words produces nothing but "babbling, &c." Even more significant, when the Spirit does inform the supplicant about his or her true desire—"such things as we stand in need of"—these desires are recognizable as true only insofar as they are utterly unutterable, inarticulable *"groans which cannot be uttered."* Bunyan describes the distance between "babbling, &c." and unutterable "groans" as absolute, a distance that separates real prayer from false prayer. Without the Spirit, one merely babbles words without substance, ignorant of one's true desire, what he or she must pray for. But the identifying mark of the person to whom the Spirit has made true desire known is not clear articulation (presumably the opposite of "babbling"), but *"groans which cannot be uttered."* Whether in speaking or hearing, the sign of true prayer, of praying "with the Spirit," is a kind of non-sign, something unutterable.[23] Without the presence of unutterable groans, prayer is mere words, "other mens words."

What distinguishes true prayer from false prayer, and true preaching from false preaching, then, is something nonlinguistic, even unutterable, a kind of prelinguistic "groan" neither uttered nor heard. This unutterable groan is what fills the gap between words and intention, between what one speaks and what is in one's heart. It is the only guarantee of Spirit-speaking and Spirit-hearing, but it is a guarantee that lies absolutely outside the horizons of normal language: it is either pre- or postsymbolic, or both. This presymbolic (non?)sign guarantees that the Spirit is speaking and the Spirit is hearing. In a sense, then, it might be said to guarantee that the Spirit is speaking to itself, for the Spirit alone can know the true desire that prompts prayer, and the Spirit alone can supply the unutterable groans, and the Spirit alone can hear these groans for what they are. Some such supposition underlies the Quaker devotion to silence.

But Bunyan, unlike Burrough, has no such devotion to silence. Nor does he explicitly reject Scripture as "other mens words," though he comes perilously close. Instead, Bunyan uses allegory to present his experience of Scripture, what would otherwise be "other mens words," as particular instances of the Spirit speaking directly to him. Bunyan presents his knowledge of Scripture in *Grace Abounding* as a knowledge attained not by reading, nor by hearing, but by unuttered and unutterable revelations. And his favorite allegorical model for such experience is physical violence, often imaged as painful physical violence.

Bunyan is painfully convinced of the unutterable quality of revelation, hence he is uncomfortable with ecstatic utterance, but also paradoxically suspicious of Quaker silence. Although Calvinist in so much of his religion and theology, Bunyan spent his youth surrounded by the skepticism of religious radicals, particularly their skepticism about words and language, so he cannot share Calvinism's relatively naive confidence in the spoken and written word. The iconoclastic attitude Calvin reserves for images Bunyan extends to language itself, and so he finds himself thrust into, or as he put it in *The Pilgrim's Progress,* fallen into, the imagistic language of allegory. Bunyan's is a strangely reversed iconoclasm, then, so utterly convinced of the bad faith at the core of all utterance that it partly rehabilitates images under the protection of acknowledging that bad faith. Allegory preserves his conviction that words alone cannot mean what we want them to say, and that intentionality itself, so far as it is human, is a hopelessly muddy slough out of which only the Spirit can stir up a sincere desire. Allegory opens up, or so Bunyan imagines, a space within his own voice for the Other's—the Spirit's—intention. Bunyan imagines that saying something other than what he means is a way to at least chalk out the Other's meaning.[24]

"*No man can say,*" affirms Bunyan, "*that Jesus Christ is Lord, but by the Holy Ghost*" (par. 118). Only the Holy Spirit makes such saying possible, a saying in which there is no gap between words and meaning, intentions and utterance. And the only means by which this gap may be closed, insists Bunyan, is something called "new birth." The old self must be replaced with a reborn self, a Spirit-of-Christ self who alone, because he is God himself, has the power to speak words in truth:

> now I saw clearly there was an exceeding difference betwixt the notions of flesh and blood, and the Revelations of God in Heaven; also a great difference between that faith that is fained, and according to man's wisdom, and that which comes *by a man being born thereto of God, Mat.* 16:15,16, I *John* 5:1. (par. 118, italics added).

The solution to the otherness of "other mens words," even the otherness of the Bible's words, is nothing less than the othering of the self. Until the self is othered from itself by new birth, by being, conversely, de-othered with respect to God, the words of God himself cannot be spoken in truth. Merely reading the Bible, let alone any other book, cannot be sufficient, for it is in the very nature of reading that the distance between one's own words and another's words is maintained.

It is precisely for this reason that Bunyan's experiences of truth are never described in *Grace Abounding* as coming while reading or while hearing sermons. What he has read or heard in the recent or distant past without apparently hearing it spiritually must come to him again from another source, a place other than the book or the preacher, a place no longer that of another, but still not quite that of the self. For it to have authority it must be clearly the Other's words—God's word to him—but for it to carry conviction he must also have some sense of "owning" the words himself. They must be his own words, but not his own, spoken to him from a place that is neither the old self, nor yet the new. Examples of this are everywhere in *Grace Abounding,* and critics have commented upon them frequently, so I cite only one.[25]

For a year or so after taking up with the Bedford congregation, Bunyan reports, he was continually tempted to despair, to believe that he was too great a sinner for God to save. He worried about "Whether the blood of Christ was sufficient to save my Soul" (par. 203). Merely reading the Scripture was clearly insufficient to resolve him about the sufficiency of Christ's blood in the matter of his soul. He reports that after meditating all day on Hebrews 7:25, he "was, as it were, quite worn out with fear lest it should not lay hold on me, those words did sound suddenly within me, *He is able*." What "it" refers to here is significantly ambiguous. Is it the "blood of Christ," or the words of Scripture, or "those words" that "sound suddenly within"? On some level, Bunyan's ambiguity is deliberate, for he shares enough of the Quaker skepticism about "other mens words" to require a sense of the words being spoken specifically to him, even from "within," as did Burrough's "Christ within." On the other hand, the words must not be identifiable as productions of his own imagination; they must be the words of the Other to him rather than to another. In still another sense, the words must be felt as sufficiently intimate to be virtually his own words, words that are not his to begin with, but are made his, and violently so. The words must be felt as laying hold on him, bursting in upon him, violently changing him into a being who can hear the words as his own, both in the sense of spoken to him and spoken by or within him. But he is convinced that to hear them this way requires that he be radically othered from himself.

At least three times in his autobiography, Bunyan uses a strange locution that conveys, though somewhat cryptically, his experience of the word as requiring a radical displacement of the self. Early in his struggle a "sentence fell with weight upon my spirit" (par. 62), a sentence which, though it turned out not to be traceable to the canonical Scriptures (par. 65), "was so fresh, and with such strength and comfort on my spirit, that *I was as if* it talked with me" (par. 63, italics added). Another time, "words did with great power suddainly break in upon me" (par. 206), with the result that his "Understanding was so enlightened, that *I was as though* I had seen the Lord Jesus look down from heaven through the Tiles upon me" (par. 207, italics added). In both places, where we might well expect the locution *it was as if*, we find instead *I was as if,* as if the *I* somehow stands in for the *it,* as if the spiritual experience of Scripture, as opposed to the notional, or reading, experience of Scripture, were a matter of some conflation of *it* and *I,* of experience and self, of Scripture and self, of God's words and one's own words. God's word to Bunyan was made Bunyan's gospel, and like Burrough, Bunyan claimed to "walk in the Life of it."

At points, Bunyan likens the process by which the Other's word to him becomes his own to the dynamic of an echo:

> I cryed, and my Soul cried to him in these words, with strong cries: *O Lord, I beseech thee show me that thou hast loved me with an everlasting love,* Jer. 31:3. I had no sooner said it, but with sweetness it returned upon

me, as an ecco or sounding again, *I have loved thee with an everlasting love.*
(par. 190)

And again,

> Then breaking out in the bitterness of my Soul, I said to my self, with a
> grievous sigh, *How can God comfort such a wretch as I?* I had no sooner
> said it but this returned upon me, as an echo doth answer a voice, *This
> sin is not unto death.* At which I was as if I had been raised out of a grave,
> and cryed out again, *Lord, how couldst thou find out such a word as this?*
> (par. 188)

In these passages, an intensely anxious Bunyan parses his experience of the Word into three, temporarily separate, voices: first is that
of the *I* who cries; second, the soul's cry; and third, the echo. In the
first example, we may be tempted to hear all three voices saying virtually the same thing, but it is Bunyan's point to insist that this is precisely wrong. The self's cry—"I cryed"—is empty of content, at least
of any content that could be called meaningful. No one, Bunyan has
insisted, can speak Gospel truth, or even articulate one's own true desires in prayer, "but by the Holy Ghost." Only a radically other subjectivity knows what one really desires. Meaningful content comes into
play when "my Soul" cries out, or, as in the second example, the primary "Out-cry" of the self is accompanied by or reproduced with "a
grievous sigh." This "grievous sigh," like the "unutterable groans"
prerequisite to true praying, Bunyan figures as an invitation to the
Spirit to begin the process of shifting the site of this utterance's subjectivity, first from self to "Soul," then from "Soul" to "ecco." With each
shift, he imagines, meaningful content gradually replaces the content-
less affect with which the self began. The self's cry is not even a candi-
date for such translation until it is a cry without even the slightest
pretense to understanding, a cry that is virtually all affect and no content, like the oft-repeated outcry of Christian in *The Pilgrim's
Progress*—"What shall I do?" It is not so much a cry as an "Out-Cry," a
crying out from the depths of desperation, a desperation born of the
recognition of the impossibility of saying what he means or meaning
what he says. Only such a cry—"I cryed"—is ripe for being translated
into the soul's cry, filled with the meaning the self has renounced any

competence to mean. The Spirit can help only a truly infirm self to pray, and the self's infirmity is, among other things, the inability to say or do anything meaningful. In the shift from a crying self to a crying soul, the words begin to appear, and they look at first very much like the words of Jeremiah in the Scripture, or more precisely, the words God is said to have spoken to Jeremiah. They are, as yet, God's words to another—another man's words. Bunyan has tried to appropriate these words as words to himself by shifting the personal pronouns to make them appear to address him, but this is merely a hermeneutic, not an experiential, move. It is insufficient. Perhaps this is why Bunyan glosses his soul's version of the passage from Jeremiah with the citation, "Jer. 31:3." It is still mere Scripture, something read rather than heard, interpreted and applied rather than experienced. Nothing Bunyan can consciously do, as reader or hermeneut, can make these words sound as God's Word to him, or as his true words of supplication to God. Only when the words "ecco" from an entirely new site of subjectivity—registered by the shift of pronouns back to "I" and "thou"—do they count as truly spoken and truly heard. And this new site of subjectivity is somehow both Bunyan's—an echo of his self's cry—and radically not Bunyan's—"*I have loved thee.*"

But why figure this experience of true speaking and true hearing as an echo, traditionally an image suggesting a lack of speaking subjectivity and an emptiness of intention? It is as if the self's crying were all signifier and the spirit's meaning were all signified, two conditions which, as we know, are impossible. They are imagined as possible, however, in that place where the self's words, its utterances, go when the self confesses that its utterances cannot mean. This is what it means to "cry out." That place is also imagined as the place where the Spirit sends its unsignifiable meanings. And in this non-place of non-subjectivity (or, paradoxically, absolute subjectivity), saying and meaning are imagined as achieving precisely the fusion Bunyan so chronically feared was impossible. "I had no sooner said it, but with sweetness it returned upon me, as an ecco or sounding again, *I have loved thee with an everlasting love.*" The only voice that can mean what it says and say what it means is, as we already suspected, the voice of God, but God's voice is figured here as a non-voice, an echo of a voice, a voice that has all the appearance of being from nowhere.

Put simply, Bunyan's echo similitude imagines the original voice (his own attempt at supplication) as devoid of the Spirit's meaning, but its "ecco or sounding again" returns "with sweetness," a fullness of meaning his original outcry had lacked. Bunyan's as yet unreborn voice is all "out-cry" ("I cryed, and my Soul cried to him in these words . . ." [par. 190]), lacking what both Bunyan and Burrough call substance. Echo, that most traditional emblem of voice without substance, sound without meaning, without any grounding in personal intention, proverbially mistaken for a grounded voice, mistaken for an original, is, in this case, taken for the absolutely original voice—that of God.

But putting it simply will not, of course, suffice, for Bunyan insists here that taking the echo for the original is no mistake: "when I awaked the next morning, it was fresh upon my Soul and I believed it" (par. 190). "It," the "ecco" full of the Spirit's meaning, God's voice under the figure of a non-voice, spoke directly to Bunyan's soul with authority. In one sense, this authority is none other than the authority of Scripture, since the "sounding again" has transformed Bunyan's appropriation of Jeremiah's words back into the words as they appear in the book. But Bunyan wants to suggest that this process has produced something radically different, and more truly meaningful, than simply Scripture words, words "a man might say" but not "own." When the voice returns as an "ecco," Bunyan hears the words, not as written, printed, read, or recited, but as if originally said. In a sense, it is mere coincidence—though for Bunyan, a necessary coincidence—that the echo-voice speaks words one might read in Jeremiah. What Bunyan wants, and needs, every bit as much as Burrough did, is to believe that he has heard the voice of God—that most original and originating voice—speaking to him, without mediation: without book, without the self's words or "other mens words," but simply God's Word to Bunyan.[26]

What, then, becomes of Bunyan's own voice, once thought to be original but now redefined as what Derrida would call the "imperfect of that echo"[27] that Bunyan takes to be the original? What becomes of the "I" in Bunyan's "I went," "I prayed," "I cryed," "I . . . said it"? Bunyan the crier is now thoroughly abjected, the sayer who cannot mean, the "I" that is really "Not I." Since what seemed to him an echo is revealed as the only original voice, the "I," once thought to be the point of origin, is transformed into a mere similitude: "At which *I was as if I* had been raised out of a grave, and cryed out again." *I* becomes an *as if I*, a ghostly I, an I from the grave. Once the echo is redefined as the original voice, Bunyan's voice is rendered an echo, his being an "as if." The only way both to say and to mean one's own words is to lose the self, to be reborn as "Not I, but Christ" (Galatians 2:20).

When we return to our example of Bunyan's experience of the Word, it is as clear as it can be that reading is exactly the wrong way to understand the Word:

> One morning when I was again at prayer and trembling under the fear of this, that no word of God could help me, that piece of a sentence darted in upon me, *My Grace is sufficient*. At this me thought I felt some stay, as if there might be hopes. But O how good a thing is it for God to send his Word! for about a fortnight before, I was looking on this very place, and then I thought it could not come near my Soul with comfort, and threw down my Book in a pet; then I thought it was not large enough for me; no not large enough. (par. 204)

"Looking on this very place," the "place" in the "Book," is precisely the problem with reading. For the place of the word as the Word cannot be in a book; it cannot even be in a place. Words, even Scripture words, are the Word only when sounded from the (non)place located somewhere between, or in the overlap of, his subjectivity and God's.

> Wherefore, one day as I was in a Meeting of Gods People, full of sadness and terrour, for my fears were strong upon me, and as I was now thinking, my soul was never the better, but my case most sad and fearful, these words did with great power suddainly break in upon me, *My grace is sufficient for thee, my grace is sufficient for thee, my grace is sufficient for thee;* three times together; and, O me-thought that every word was a mighty word unto me. (par. 206)

The echo of the words Paul claims "the Lord . . . said unto me" (2 Corinthians 12:8–9) Bunyan hears as God's Word breaking in upon him, assaulting him, with all the power and force of an original. Its threefold repetition, as if echoing itself into the status of originality, is both a reminder of Paul's threefold beseeching of God for relief from his peculiar infirmity (2 Corinthians 12:8), and, paradoxically, a reminder that it is precisely such utter infirmity—for Bunyan the infirmity of unbelief and its resultant incapacity for speaking meaningfully

—that enables his utterly meaningless cries to be conjoined with unutterable meanings to produce the effect of a non-echo—a voice. Bunyan's threefold echo of Paul is not, for Bunyan, an echo at all, but "a mighty word unto me." Bunyan's greatest torment, his conviction that words are irrevocably alienated from intention, from meaning, he transforms into a prerequisite for receiving God's saving Word. Without such a conviction, his own words would always remain—to himself, to others, and to God—another's words in which one thing was said while another thing was in his heart. Since he cannot ever "own" words of truth, always and only God's Word, he must undergo instead an utter loss of self, an abjection so complete as to render him a transparent vessel for the Other who alone can truly own both words and voice. The self that truly hears and speaks the Word must be a kind of non-self. Allegory is a perfect rhetorical vehicle for expressing the newly born non-self under the figure of a self.

As I have suggested along the way, this utter loss of self is most frequently figured under the similitudes of birthing and motherhood. As similitudes, these figures serve as a kind of echo in reverse of the primary loss that is both the precondition and the result of access to the symbolic order. Exercising the symbolic order's powers of representation always carries with it an unutterable sense of that loss, the loss of unrepresented meaning. More precisely, this sense of loss is an effect of the very activity of representation, an effect that the representing activity then regards as a constitutive loss. In short, the activity of representing always produces an echo-effect of itself, which Bunyan senses as echoing not just representation, but the loss of a meaning that did not require representation, unmediated meaning, a sort of meaning for which the distinction between sense and meaning, words and intentions, is nonsense. And this echo Bunyan takes for that lost original.

Thus, when Bunyan figures the recovery of that loss as new birth, he also reenacts the replacement of voice by echo in the replacement of literal birth by figurative birth. Just as the echo must be taken for the original, so the figurative new birth must be taken for the original birth, of which literal birth is now merely an echo. Speaking, hearing, being born—all experience on this side of the next world—is but an echo of true experience, but from this side of the next world, the truth itself still sounds like an echo. Bunyan deploys this figure most poignantly in an allegory set in the midst of his autobiography, an allegory complete with its own allegoresis.

The story begins in the familiar register of an anecdotal digression:

> But upon a day, the good providence of God did cast me to *Bedford*, to work on my calling; and in one of the streets of that town, I came where there was three or four poor women sitting at a door in the Sun, and talking about the things of God; and being now willing to hear them discourse, I drew near to hear what they said; for I was now a brisk talker also my self in the matters of Religion: but now I may say, *I heard, but I understood not;* for they were far above out of my reach, for their talk was about a new birth, the work of God on their hearts, also how they were convinced of their miserable state by nature. (par. 37)

Bunyan describes this event as a threshold in his soteriological progress. The "poor women" he admires so much sit "at a door in the Sun." It marks his passage from being a "doer" and "talker" of religion into the desperate condition of one who "could not tell what to do" and who "was driven to [his] wits end, not knowing what to say" (par. 59–61). This is the abjection that is prerequisite to new birth, just as it is prerequisite to saying, meaning, and hearing. Just before this event, he says he was confident—"I thought no man in *England* could please God better than I" (par. 35); in the paragraphs that follow, versions of the desperate outcry, "What shall I do," forge a new refrain.[28]

The story's opening—"But upon a day"—marks its genre ambiguously, for it is a beginning equally indicative of a personal anecdote or a fable.[29] Thus it brilliantly captures the affect of radical ambivalence Bunyan goes on to describe as driving him to his "wits end" for a period of years. As an anecdote, it functions in much the way Joel Fineman says anecdotes function, as both an interruptive opening of the otherwise seamless teleological narrativity of history and also as the constitutive event of what becomes a new narrative whole with a new telos. One apparently meaningless incident triggers Bunyan to rewrite his life story as an entirely new story with a new point of origin and a new destination. What he took to be significant turns out to be "naught" and what first appeared as incidental is now crucial. To use Fineman's suggestive terms, the anecdote opens a "hole," an apparently disjunctive gap, in the existing narrative, which by its utter contingency—a happening without apparent significance—threatens to obliterate what seemed to be the integrity of the "whole" narrative up to this point—Bunyan's hitherto apparently steady progress in "righteousness."[30] Confidence gives way to utter despair. The happening leaves him radically uncertain about what to do, what to say, even "where I was" (par. 56). Even more upsetting, it leaves him completely at a loss about the happening itself: he has heard the poor women talk of numerous things about which he hasn't a clue. His actions, his words, his entire world up to this point appear to be rendered "naught" by this happening:

> And me thought they spake as if joy did make them speak: they spake with such pleasantness of Scripture language, and with such appearance of grace in all they said, that they were to me as if they had found a new world, as if they were people that dwelt alone, and were not to be reckoned among their Neighbors, Num. 23:9.
>
> 39. At this I felt my own heart began to shake, as mistrusting my condition to be naught; for I saw that in all my thoughts about Religion and Salvation, the New birth did never enter into my mind, neither knew I the comfort of the Word and Promise, nor the deceitfulness and treachery of my own wicked heart. (par. 38–39)

This is a story about Bunyan's encounter with what appears to be an utterly new symbolic order—words about things Bunyan never even guessed existed—and he feels "at a great loss" (par. 52). Almost immediately he suspects that his world, his story so far, is "naught" and that the poor women's "new world," which appears to him at this point as little more than a hole (a threshold, a disjunctive opening or gap) in his own world, is more real than his own. The rest of Bunyan's autobiography can easily be seen as a desperately elaborate series of attempts to plug up this hole in the whole, to forge a new teleological narration in which this disjunctive hole is re-read as the constitutive origin of a new story about "New birth" into a "new world." A mere glance at Bunyan's *Map Shewing the Order and Causes of Salvation and Damnation* reveals that of course there is nothing at all disjunctive or out of place about this happening; it turns out not to be a mere happenstance at all, but rather *the* constitutive event in the story of Bunyan's new being.[31] And, of course, we know this almost from the beginning of the anecdote itself, since Bunyan tells us that "the good providence of God did cast" him into this apparent hole to begin with. At the time Bunyan thought he went to Bedford "to work on my calling," but the newly born Bunyan who narrates this story knows God "cast" him to Bedford to hear another sort of calling.[32]

Fineman's thesis on anecdote and history offers a guide to understanding how this story of the Bedford women's "talking" works in Bunyan's "Relation of the work of God upon my own Soul" ("Preface" to *GA*, 1–2):

> the anecdote is the literary form that uniquely *lets history happen* by virtue of the way it introduces an opening into the teleological, and therefore timeless, narration of beginning, middle, and end. The anecdote produces the effect of the real, the occurrence of contingency, by establishing an event as an event within and yet without the framing context of historical successivity, i.e., it does so only in so far as its narration both comprises and refracts the narration it reports. . . . I want further to maintain, . . . that the opening of history that is effected by the anecdote, the hole and rim—using psychoanalytic language, the orifice—traced out by the anecdote within the totalizing whole of history, is something that is characteristically and ahistorically plugged up by a teleological narration that, though larger than the anecdote itself, is still constitutively inspired by the seductive opening of anecdotal form—thereby opening up the possibility, but, again, *only* the possibility, that this new narration, now complete within itself, and therefore rendered formally small—capable, therefore, of being anecdotalized—will itself be opened up by a further anecdotal operation, therefore calling forth some yet larger circumcising circumscription, and so, so on and so forth. (Fineman, 61)

Fineman's thesis can offer us some insight into the "so on and so forth" character, not only of Bunyan's autobiography, but of *The Pilgrim's Progress* as well, indeed, of Bunyan's entire *oeuvre*. It offers to explain why the stories of progress have about them such an insistent theme of the lack of progress, why *"hope* and *fear"* must be the perpetual *"Goad"* in the pilgrim's sides to "prick" him forward "in the way" that seems so often to reveal itself as a way precisely when the pilgrim is "at a stand."[33] I shall reserve such observations, however, for the next chapter, and concentrate here on how Bunyan's meditations

upon his encounter with the "poor women" of Bedford drama-
tize Fineman's thesis about "the formal play of anecdotal hole and
whole."

Among all the "things of God" the Bedford women talked about,
the one thing most fascinating and mystifying to Bunyan was "their
talk . . . about a New birth." This is so, I suspect, because the "New
birth" offers itself almost immediately to Bunyan under the similitude
of the incident itself as a "narrow gap," a "passage . . . very straight,
and narrow," "like a little door-way," (par. 54, quoted in full below) or
what Fineman calls a hole in the narrative integrity of Bunyan's life so
far. We have already seen that Bunyan confesses he felt this happening
as a threatening hole in the story of his progress in righteousness: it
made him fear that his "condition" was "naught"—an utter zero, a
nothing—instigating in him the fear that his world might be nothing
more than a deceitful fable compared with the "new world" he now
only dimly glimpses in the women's discourses. This fear is homologous to Bunyan's chronic temptation to atheism, to conclude that
"Faith, and Christ, and Scriptures" are but a "think-so," a "Fable and
cunning Story," but here the fear works in reverse—it is his own
fleshly life Bunyan suspects to be a mere "Fable and cunning story" he
has been telling himself right up to the moment he sees the women
"sitting at a door in the Sun." The figure of birthing, of passing
through a "narrow gap, like a little door-way in the wall" of his experience, quite unsurprisingly dominates his sense of his encounter with
the Bedford women as revealing a hole in his life-narrative, an orifice
that desperately needs either plugging up or passing through—or
more likely, a plugging up imagined as a passing through.

The disturbing experience of hearing but not understanding the
Bedford women's discourse on new birth begins its progress toward
becoming the originary event of Bunyan's new life by being translated
into a "Vision," a vision that replays the apparently meaningless incident as a significant event by allegorizing it. The progress of the experience from incident to "Vision," then from "Vision" to allegoresis, is
much like the process by which Bunyan's "out-cry" was transformed
to his soul's cry and finally to an echo. And as with the echo, Bunyan
designates the allegoresis of the vision as the originary event. The incident, it turns out, was an allegory of a real experience:

53. About this time, the state and happiness of these poor people at *Bedford* was thus, in a kind of Vision, presented to me: I saw as if they were set on the Sunny side of some high Mountain, there refreshing themselves with the pleasant beams of the Sun, while I was shivering and shrinking in the cold, afflicted with frost, snow, and dark clouds; methought also betwixt me and them I saw a wall that did compass about this Mountain; now thorow this wall my Soul did greatly desire to pass, concluding that if I could, I would goe even into the midst of them, and there also comfort myself with the heat of their Sun.

54. About this wall I thought myself to goe again and again, still prying as I went, to see if I could find some way or passage, by which I might enter therein, but none could I find for some time: at the last I saw as it were, a narrow gap, like a little door-way in the wall, thorow which I attempted to pass: but the passage being very straight, and narrow, I made many offers to get in, but all in vain, even until I was well nigh quite beat out by my striving to get in: at last, with great striving, me thought I at first did get in my head, and after that, by a side-ling striving, my shoulders, and my whole body; then I was exceeding glad, and went and sat down in the midst of them, and so was comforted with the light and heat of their Sun.

An allegorical version of Bunyan's encounter with the Bedford women's talk about new birth, says Bunyan, "was thus, in a kind of Vision, presented to me," that is, it comes to him, not as his own figural version of the encounter, but as someone else's—presumably God's—presented to him for meditation and interpretation. On the other hand, though the chief allegorical elements of the vision—the mountain, the "Sun," the cold, and the wall—are among those presented to him, the allegorical status of "my Soul" and its "desire to pass" through the wall and sit in the "Sun" is ambiguous. Is his soul's desire part of the vision presented to Bunyan—that is to say, is "Soul" here an allegorical figure? Or are we to understand here that Bunyan is describing his own soul's affective interaction with the allegorical vision? Another way of asking much the same question is: are we to understand this as a dream-vision in which "my Soul" is a dream projection that Bunyan watches, or are we to take Bunyan's talk about his soul's desire as the dreamer's affective responses to the dream? Bunyan does not allow us to choose between the two. The problem of whether or not we are to read Bunyan as inside or outside of the dreamlike vision is homologous to the problem the vision thematizes—being outside in the cold, or inside with "the light and heat of their Sun." If Bunyan succeeds in getting inside, becoming reborn into the new world the Bedford women talk of and live in, then his entire life up to that point will turn out to have been the dream, the "naught," and the new world inside the allegorical wall will turn out to be reality. If he succeeds, as he dreams his soul succeeds, in getting inside the vision, then vision and reality, dream and waking, allegorical and literal, will have exchanged places; in fact, they will be revealed to have been each other's opposite all along. This means that the allegorical version of the incident will turn out to be reality, and the incident itself will turn out to have been a mystifying allegory of that reality.[34] In this exchange, what appeared at first as a disruptive hole in Bunyan's narrative world will turn out to be the most significant event of his new life, his new whole.

The same radical ambiguity, then, must apply to the startling image of birthing at the vision's climax—is this image Bunyan's similitude, his articulation of his soul's desire in the terms offered by the vision, or is this similitude presented to him as part of the vision? In short, is this similitude of birthing—more precisely, reverse birthing—Bunyan's similitude or God's, presented to him for interpretation? Once again, Bunyan makes any such choice impossible. The difference between being presented with a vision in which his allegorical "Soul" passes through to the inside and Bunyan thinking himself—"I thought myself"—"prying" and "striving" to get inside is precisely the difference that will be erased by his experience of new birth when it finally comes. Once he has experienced the new birth, Bunyan and his soul will be one, for he will have been literally reborn as his soul's desire. The difference and distance between the self and the self's desire, between the self and the soul, and between the soul and Christ will, Bunyan imagines, finally be lost. This difference, experienced by Bunyan as "a great loss," will itself be lost, and the loss of this loss is, quite appropriately, figured as a birth in reverse, as "a sideling striving" to return to substantial unity with the (m)Other.

In Bunyan's vision Christ is certainly the Other Bunyan desires to see himself returned to unity with, but Christ is not explicitly figured as a mother. However much Bunyan imagines his return to union with

Christ as a reverse birth, a "side-ling striving" to pass through the narrow "passage" or "gap" in the wall that separates one world from the other, the "naught" from the true, the "inside" of the wall is not so much a person as a place, the place upon which "the Sun" shines with his "mercifull face." But Christ is also, thinks Bunyan, represented as "the gap" in the wall of "the Word" that separates this world from the next, where the next world is realized to have always already been the truly real, truly originary world, the world out of which we were thrust by carnal birth:

> Now, this Mountain and Wall, &c., was thus made out to me; the Mountain signified the Church of the Living God; the Sun that shone thereon, the comfortable shining of his mercifull face on them that were therein: the wall I thought was the Word that did make separation between Christians and the world: and the gap which was in this wall, I thought was Jesus Christ, who is the way to God the Father, *Joh.* 14:6 *Mat.* 7:14. (par. 55)

Spiritual birth, imagines Bunyan, undoes carnal birth. The way back to God the Father is through Christ, "the gap" in the wall of words, which is how the Scriptures appear to those not yet reborn. By figuring "the Church of the Living God" as a womblike enclosure, where what appeared to be darkness is really light and what appeared to be a barrier is really a wall that shuts out the cold of the carnal world, Bunyan effectively produces a new imagery of anti-motherhood. The truly motherly womb is the place of "God the Father." The true way back to this originary place is through "the gap," or new-birth canal, of Christ. Once inside, mere words disappear and are replaced by meaning.

As yet, Bunyan has only a fantasy of new birth, a kind of allegorical vision of what new birth might be like. This vision of new birth Bunyan describes as part revelation—"presented to me"; "made out to me"—and part his own fantasy—"I thought"; "I attempted"; "I made many offers to get in." We might say that his fantasy is to install himself, to get into the revelation itself and live in it, so that new birth is no longer an image, an idea, a vision, a story, but simply his own experience. And new birth is also the process of getting into, and living in, the revelation. Bunyan wants not to go through the fantasy, but to live in the fantasy, to be reborn (or un-born) into that other world compared with which his old world is naught. And, of course, once inside the fantasy, it is no longer for him a fantasy, not even a revelation, but simply his reality:

> The Lord did also lead me into the mystery of Union with this Son of God, that I was joyned to him, that I was flesh of his flesh, and bone of his bone. . . . Now could I see myself in Heaven and Earth at once. (par. 233)

Bunyan's fantasy of getting through the wall and into the sunshine is also a fantasy of getting into what is as yet merely a vision. Once inside the vision, reality and revelation will exchange places, and he will live inside what is as yet merely an allegory of inside and outside. And this getting in, both in the vision and in the allegoresis of the vision, is figured as the very new birth he expects to understand once inside. Experience of new birth and understanding of new birth will be identical. He will understand the new birth the Bedford women spoke of, not by talking, as he at first supposed, but by experiencing it. Even the revealed interpretation itself suggests this, since Bunyan takes the wall that separates the newly born from the world to be the Word itself—"the wall I thought was the Word that did make separation between the Christians and the world." Talking and words, even talking about or repeating the Word, is not the way to experience, it is precisely the barrier to experience. Christ, according to the allegory, is the "gap" in that barrier. Christ, in this similitude, is not the Word, but the gap in the Word, the aperture or "narrow passage" through the wall of the Word. Christ is the opening in Scripture words that permits one to pass through "other mens words" to being in the Word itself, a Word that is experience unmediated by words. Words always other experience, they are about experiences or representations of experience; Bunyan wants a Word that simply is experience, and so he imagines it here as the experience of passing through "the gap" in Scripture words, the "little door-way" circumscribed by the rim of representation. As "the Way" from one world to the next, Christ is the gap or hole that is desire's true object, the impossible nothingness covered with an equally impossible double mask of manhood and Godhood. Getting into that space, passing through gap in representation, in language, Bunyan occupies, for a moment, the place of nothingness, fills it in much the same way a baby/fetus fills the birth canal, but headed in the opposite direction, on the threshold between being a self and being part of the Other's body. New birth reverses literal birth and then recasts it as a faulty allegory of the true experience it only dimly shadows—being made one with Christ. Only by filling that gap, taking the place, with his body, of the Name of Christ, the name of that gap in the Word, can Bunyan be re-born (reverse born) into the fantasy of living in Christ.

Six

Faring Otherwise: Allegory and Experience in *The Pilgrim's Progress*

At least since Coleridge's famous diagnosis of Bunyan's writerly schizophrenia—a "Bunyan of the conventicle" at odds with a "Bunyan of Parnassus"—critics have tried, some rather desperately, either to reconcile the two or to assert that one or the other is the real Bunyan.[1] Few have been willing to acknowledge that reality is a particularly problematic category in Christian discourses, especially those of the Puritan sects of the English seventeenth century. The real Bunyan is no easier for Bunyan's readers to pin down than it was for Bunyan in reading himself, and we have seen already in *Grace Abounding* how complicated and conflicted that process was.

I have speculated that Bunyan "fell" into allegory while reading himself because allegory is a mode peculiarly suited to finessing the issue of the real, allowing Bunyan to substitute spiritual "experience" for reality. This means that what is real will be different for each of the two classes of people Bunyan is interested in: those "blest" and those "not" ("The Author's Apology," *PP,* 7). Those not blessed with the experience of new birth are doomed forever to mistake types and shadows, figures and similitudes, all the things of "this World," including themselves, for what is real. These are the wretchedly "carnal," the people who, for lack of the "vision" afforded by new birth, will "perish."[2] Whether named "Atheist," "Worldly-Wiseman," "By-ends," or "Hold-the-World," all such people are simply different versions of that larger and older class of people known as the Jews—those who don't realize that their experience of "this world" is but an allegory of the real "world which is to come."[3] Those born again, who have experienced the true birth of which birth into this world is a mere shadowy figure, walk through this world as if walking through an allegory, just as Christian, Faithful, and Hopeful walk through the landscape of *The Pilgrim's Progress*. Gaining entrance at the gate of the Celestial City, in fact, depends upon how successfully one has passed through this world as if it were a dream or an allegory. As John Knott observes,

> In the terms of Bunyan's narrative one can gain entrance to heaven only by learning to understand the visible world of ordinary experience in the metaphoric terms established by the Word: as an alien, and ultimately insubstantial country through which God's people must journey until they attain the ultimate satisfaction of communion with God.[4]

The things they see there and the things that happen to them there are shadowy figures of true reality, as far removed from it as printed words are from meaning.

Virtually the entire plot of Bunyan's allegory is generated by a string of occasions in which the pilgrim characters temporarily forget the allegorical status of their experiences in this world. Mistaking this-worldly experience for reality, they fall, as it were, back into the allegory and take it for the real thing. At such moments, their spiritual empiricism—"the evidence of things not seen"—is exchanged for a more mundane empiricism of things seen. At such points they risk, however briefly, falling back into the status of the Jew, mistaking the temporal world and its experiences for reality. Rescue usually takes the shape of an act of sudden grace that redefines worldly experience as allegorical, then submits it to interpretation that yields not knowledge, but the conviction that true knowledge is had only by way of such sudden acts of grace that repeatedly disqualify worldly experience as real or meaningful. This state of abjection, in which the pilgrim fully acknowledges the meaninglessness of this-worldly experience and the utter infirmity of his or her capacity to articulate true meaning from such experience, qualifies one for new birth, which instantly re-creates one as the meaning that always lay hidden behind the old self. This chapter will examine in detail several narrative versions of this dynamic in *The Pilgrim's Progress*, but I would like to find my way into such readings by way of Stanley Fish and his theory of "literature in the reader."

Stanley Fish is one of a very few critics to direct concentrated analytical attention to the all-too-apparent paradoxes of *The Pilgrim's Progress*. Fish, unlike most Bunyanists, is not content simply to point to the paradoxes and then admire their depth and richness. His detailed analysis of the reader's experience of Bunyan's allegory leads him to startling conclusions: that there is "no progress in *The Pilgrim's Progress*," and that "*The Pilgrim's Progress* is the ultimate self-consuming artifact, for the insights it yields are inseparable from the demonstration of the inadequacy of its own forms, which are also the forms of the reader's understanding"[5] Most attempts to challenge Fish's landmark reading (including my own past attempt) focus on his first conclusion.[6] Fish's second conclusion, however, deserves closer attention, for this conclusion makes much more far-reaching claims about what counts as "meaning" in Bunyan's allegory and how we as readers are expected to learn this. In fact, Fish's conclusion is even more far-reaching than his own readings of Bunyan seem to acknowledge, for his conclusion designates *The Pilgrim's Progress* as a text that repeatedly disqualifies its own capacity for meaning, while his readings continue to assume that there is such a thing as interpreting Bunyan's allegory "correctly" (Fish, 264).

Like any interpreter, Fish assumes that the text under consideration yields "insights" roughly equivalent to the "insights" its author intended it to yield, if only a reader interprets "correctly." This is a fairly standard hermeneutic assumption, but Fish goes on to conclude that the reader's experience of *The Pilgrim's Progress*, if the reader proceeds correctly, is precisely the experience of having this assumption repeatedly challenged, even finally invalidated. Thus Fish, although he identifies with some precision the conflictedness about meaning and intention at the heart of *The Pilgrim's Progress*, manages to reproduce almost precisely the same conflictedness in his interpretation, an interpretation that he later deploys as a crucial example of his "method" of reading. One of the "advantages" of his "method," Fish remarks, "is its ability to deal with sentences (and works) that don't mean anything, in the sense of not making sense" (397). "Literature," we are reminded, "is largely made up of such utterances." When one employs

Fish's "experiential analysis," however, it really doesn't matter at all whether the text under consideration makes sense or not as "a logical utterance" (397, 398). The only thing that matters is the experience a reader can be said to have in the inevitably vain attempt to "make sense" out of it. Literature that refuses "to mean in that discursive way," that is, as "a logical utterance,"—and this accounts for most if not all literature—"creates the experience that is its meaning; and an analysis of that experience rather than of logical content is able to make sense of one kind—experiential sense—out of nonsense" (398).

Fish follows Bunyan in redefining meaning as experience rather than as "analysis . . . of logical content," but here he appears to suggest that the special "kind of sense" he is after—experiential sense—is the result of an analysis of the experience of reading that is a text's meaning. At this point, at least, Fish parts theoretical company with Bunyan by implying that what he is after is an analysis of experience, rather than the experience itself. In other words, Fish is not, at least here, primarily interested in meaning at all, but in an analysis of meaning-experiences. Bunyan is more forthrightly anti-hermeneutic in that for him the experience is the only goal—having the experience of one's absolute inability to "make sense" is the meaning. Once the pilgrim reader is cajoled into stopping the effort to "make sense," the Spirit, believes Bunyan, is free to do its work.

Having said as much about Fish in his guise as critic, it is also worth noting that Fish occasionally drops this guise and appears more evangelical, more Bunyanlike. At many points in his account of his "method," Fish appears to embrace Bunyan's anti-hermeneutic position more openly. In his conclusion, for example, Fish acknowledges, somewhat coyly, that his "method" is not really "a method at all."

> Its results are not transferable because there is no fixed relationship between formal features and response (reading has to be done every time); and its skills are not transferable because you can't hand it over to someone and expect him at once to be able to use it. (It is not portable.) . . . Moreover, its operations are interior. It has no mechanism. . . . Becoming good at the method means asking the question "what does that . . . . do?" with more and more awareness of the probable (and hidden) complexity of the answer; . . . it is a method which processes

its own user, who is also its only instrument. . . . In short, it does not organize materials, but transforms minds. (425)

In a brilliant act of anti-hermeneutic bravado, Fish drops virtually all pretensions to literary criticism and analysis and throws in his lot with the sectarian experimentalist. Each reader's experience of the text is idiosyncratic; that's what it means to be experience. As with Bunyan's Gospel-sense of Scripture, neither the experience nor the "skill" in having such experiences is transferable without the risk of experience degenerating into "other mens words." Experience of the meaning, like experience of the truth, is "not portable."

Fish tries to avoid religious language, but some of the sectarians' favorite concepts do appear, almost euphemistically. When he says that the method's "operations are interior," it is very easy to supply "the Spirit" for "the method," especially if we remember that the method "is not a method at all." Earlier in his essay, Fish had spoken of a "regulating and organizing mechanism, preexisting the actual verbal experience, . . . In short, something other than itself, something existing outside its frame of reference, must be modulating the reader's experience" (404). It is hard not to recognize here a religious metaphysics at work. This preexistent "something" that governs a reader's experience (which is meaning) Fish further defines, rather secularly, as "everything the reader brings with him, by his competences" (404), but if the meaning produced by these "competences" is "the demonstration of the inadequacy of its own forms, which are also the forms of the reader's understanding," that is, utter incompetence, then clearly Fish's "something" is something other than a reader's "competences." His "something" is much more like the "everything" of a preexisting alpha and omega (424). Fish claims that, like Bunyan's "Spirit," his "method" "processes its own user" and "transforms minds" (425). With a patina of secularism, Fish is also preaching new birth—"it does not organize materials, but transforms minds."

Fish's injunction to repeatedly ask, "what does this _____ do?" (398) is a version of Christian's endlessly repeated question, "What must I do?" It is also, therefore, a version of both the Philippian jailer's and Nicodemus's famous questions (Acts 16:29, John 3). Fish's version shifts the assumption of agency from pilgrim reader to text, but the implied answer to both questions is much the same: nothing. Neither the text, nor the reader, nor the would-be pilgrim can do anything; that is the message. Meaning, if it is true meaning, is always produced by "something other than itself [other than the text, other than the reader, something radically other]; something existing outside its frame of reference [outside the text's, outside the reader's, something radically outside] must be modulating the reader's experience"— something so radically outside as to be radically inside. Since experience is the transformation of minds—"And be not conformed to this world: but be ye transformed by the renewing of your mind, that ye may prove what is that good, and acceptable, and perfect, will of God" (Romans 12:2)—the new-born reader has this non-portable method, what Bunyan calls "the Spirit," on the inside. The reader as experiencer is him- or herself radically other and radically outside of "this world."[7]

It is not surprising, then, that Fish's first example of how his method—what he calls a "saving" operation—works when "applied" to "units larger than a sentence" is his proclamation of "the basic experience . . . (do *not* read basic meaning)" that "occurs at every level" of *The Pilgrim's Progress* (398). What happens to the reader in "the basic experience of *The Pilgrim's Progress*," says Fish, is this: "Again and again he settles into temporal-spatial forms of thought only to be brought up short when they prove unable to contain the insights of Christian faith" (399).[8] If temporal-spatial forms of thought cannot contain the insights of Christian faith, then the only point of reading is to be reminded to stop reading; the only point of interpretation is to be reminded "again and again" to stop interpreting; the only point to living in this world of temporal-spatial forms is eventually to stop living in it, to "*go out of the world*" altogether, which is, of course, Bunyan's hope for every reader who truly becomes a "traveller" (*PP*, 89).

The Meaning of Meaninglessness

WHEN FISH SAYS OF *The Pilgrim's Progress* that "the insights it yields are inseparable from the demonstration of the inadequacy of its own forms, which are also the forms of the reader's understanding," Bunyan critics generally resent what they take to be a rather cavalierly deconstructionist treatment of a great Christian allegory. They fear that

Fish, by calling it "the ultimate self-consuming artifact," has recast Bunyan's masterpiece as some dreadfully postmodernist exposure of the abyss of meaninglessness that lies just beyond the meaning-effect of language itself. This finally proves to be a baseless fear, but I want to follow it up in the interest of showing how central to both Fish's and Bunyan's soteriology is the experience of utter meaninglessness.

It is possible to read Fish's "insights" here as a euphemism for "meaning," but that would be too easy. Fish has deliberately avoided the expected, somewhat more technical term (at least in traditional hermeneutics) in favor of the annoyingly vague, and always suspicious, term "insights." We might want to paraphrase Fish as proposing that Bunyan's allegory yields not meaning, but insights, where insights is something significantly different from meaning. Fish offers support for such a paraphrase in his theoretical chapter, "Literature in the Reader," when he suggests "that there is no direct relationship between the meaning of a sentence (paragraph, novel, poem) and what its words mean" (393). This provocative suggestion nicely reproduces Bunyan's own tantalizing conundrums about meaning—the puzzle over "the way" and "the way" (*PP*, 39–40; Fish, 227–28), the apparent but hard to grasp difference between Talkative's "talking" and Christian and Faithful's "talking" (*PP*, 85), and Faithful's assertion that "There is therefore knowledge and knowledge" (*PP*, 82). Fish seems to echo Bunyan and his pilgrims by saying there is meaning and meaning and that grasping this distinction is crucial to interpreting "correctly."

Like Bunyan's Faithful, Fish offers some explanation of his distinction:

> the information an utterance gives, its message, is a constituent of, but certainly not to be identified with, its meaning. It is the experience of an utterance—*all* of it and not anything that could be said about it, including anything I could say—that *is* its meaning. (393)

As is usually the case with binary distinctions, especially binary distinctions between two apparent identities like meaning and meaning, there is a third thing hiding somewhere in the formula. Fish here glosses one of the two meanings in his distinction as "message," or "information," and he implies that it should be obvious that "message" and "meaning" are two different things. Message is a constituent part of meaning, but meaning itself is a much larger affair. The meaning Fish is after is "the experience of an utterance—*all* of it." This "*all* of it" is further specified as "not anything that could be said about it, including anything I [Fish, or anyone else for that matter] could say."

To sum up, then: when Fish says that "there is no direct relationship between the meaning of a sentence . . . and what its words mean," we are invited to understand "what its words mean" as "information" or "message," and "meaning" as "the experience of an utterance—*all* of it." Presumably an utterance offers information in the form of a "message," but it is the experience of receiving that message that is truly meaning. But this meaning is itself unutterable—it is "not anything that could be said about it," where "it," presumably, is the experience itself. This must be even more the case if the meaning is somehow the experience of being convinced of the "inadequacy" of "the forms of the reader's understanding" as well as of the text's attempts at articulation. Logically, the text proves itself to be no better, or worse, than "nonsense," and the meaning is the experience of that nonsense that a reader undergoes. Fish does not say that nothing can be said about this experience; he simply warns us that nothing that can be said about it should be mistaken for the meaning, which is the experience itself. The three things, then, are first, meaning$_1$, or "what [an utterance's] words mean" (their "logical content"), second, meaning$_2$, or experiential meaning, and third, whatever can be said about that experience, which should not be mistaken for either of the other meanings. Fish allows that meaning$_1$ is a constituent of meaning$_2$, but whatever can be said about meaning$_2$ is an altogether new utterance that is itself subject to division into "message" and "meaning." Like any other utterance (Fish heaps scorn on the notion of any significant distinction between ordinary and literary utterances), the meaning of what we can say about meaning must also have an unutterable experiential surplus beyond the message, which qualifies it as having true or full meaning. The sign (or non-sign) of meaning's presence is always this unutterable surplus beyond the message.

Bunyan's term for this experiential meaning is, of course, "the truth," or "the Gospel-sense," and Fish does not consistently shy away from using "the truth" in much the same way Bunyan does. Fish closes his essay on *The Pilgrim's Progress* by quoting from Bunyan's concluding address to the reader:

> Now Reader, I have told my Dream to thee;
> See if thou canst Interpret it to me;
> Or to thy self, or Neighbor: but take heed
> Of mis-interpreting: for that, instead
> Of doing good, will but thy self abuse:
> By mis-interpreting evil insues.
>
>   Take heed also, that thou be not extream,
> In playing with the *out-side* of my Dream.
>
>   (*PP*, 164; Fish, 263)

Fish explains: "To play 'extremely' with the outside of the dream is to take its linear form seriously by failing to pierce through to the truth it cannot itself image or contain; it is then that misinterpreting and evil ensue" (Fish, 263–64). The meaning or the truth of *The Pilgrim's Progress,* then, is something that the message of the text, "what the words mean," "cannot itself image or contain." It is not something in the words as "logical content," nor is it projected imagistically by the words, but must be thought of as something on the other side of the words from the reader. Like Bunyan's wall of the Word, both the text and the reader's "forms of understanding" texts stand between the reader and meaning or experience. Both are obstructions that must be pierced through. A reader who would avoid misinterpreting Bunyan (or Fish) must "pierce through" both the text's forms and the forms of his or her own understanding to experience something that the words are inadequate to contain or project, something on the other side of what is utterable by text or by reader. Nevertheless, Fish asserts that the text's repeated "demonstration of the inadequacy of its own forms" somehow yields the very "insights" it is at pains to disqualify itself from yielding and the reader's understanding from comprehending. This contradiction can only be unraveled by glossing Fish's "insights" as "the insights of Christian faith" (Fish, 399), which, of course, are things completely other from this world's forms of articulation and understanding—"the substance of things hoped for, the evidence of things not seen" (Hebrews 11:1).

    By now it should be abundantly clear that the only thing that can save *The Pilgrim's Progress* and Fish's reading of it from being hopelessly nonsensical is a theology very much like Bunyan's own, a theology of grace that endows the experience of meaningless utterances with meaning, that "yields insights" in spite of, rather than as a result of, the various acts of interpretation one performs in reading. This theology is finally an anti-hermeneutic theology.

Fish acknowledges that his method (which he frequently calls "*the* method," but which he also says "is not a method at all") commits him to "a monistic theory of meaning" (424). He also claims that, unlike most monistic theories, his "permits analysis, because it is a monism of effects, in which meaning is a (partial) product of the utterance-object, but not to be identified with it" (424). Meaning, then, if it is not to be discarded as a hopelessly misleading term (425), should be redefined as meaning-effect, a small part of what counts as true meaning, which is, Fish repeats, one's unutterable "experience" of an utterance—"*all* of it." There is no such thing, therefore, as "*the* meaning," because *the* meaning, to qualify as such, would have to take full account of everything that happens in any full experience of an utterance, all the "something[s]" that "happen" to a reader experiencing a text, especially a text's demonstration of its own inadequacy. This would be Fish's idea of what Whitaker and Perkins called the "full literal sense," but Fish knows enough to acknowledge that such a sense is beyond articulation.

"The key word is, of course, experience." Actually there are several key words here besides "experience," words which at different moments in Fish's argument stand in euphemistically for experience. These words are "something," "everything," and "nothing." Each euphemism renders a slightly different aspect of the monist meaning Fish believes in. Because the true meaning "is immediately compromised the moment you say anything about it" (425), strictly speaking, Fish is perfectly correct to respond to the question, "What is the meaning?" by saying simply, "Nothing is." We could call this the Quaker moment in Fish's monism. Quakers, had they really kept silence in the face of such a question, would have gone Fish one better by saying nothing, rather than "Nothing is," since any attempt at articulation of the "everything" that comprises "the meaning" is bound to fall short of adequate fullness. It is only "human," however, to be unable "to resist the impulse to investigate" the processes of meaning production (425). Presumably this is why even Quakers devoted to silence preached and wrote so prolifically. They, like Fish, were only human. Since such investigation inevitably results in statements that compromise "the meaning" by other men's words, the prudent analyst must "proceed in such a way as to permit as little distortion as possible" (Fish, 425). A prudent analysis should simply conclude that "something (analyzable and significant) is always happening" to readers and that the best we can hope for is to participate in the never-ending process of asymptotically approaching an adequate description of these "something[s]" that happen, careful to remember that the discursive forms of such attempts will inevitably always be inadequate, distortions of the "everything" that is truly the meaning.

Because Fish's (non)method is a barely secularized version of Bunyan's own anti-hermeneutics of experience, it can serve quite nicely as a guide to some of the more perplexing passages of *The Pilgrim's Progress* and the ways in which the allegory makes perpetual "travailers" and "travellers" of its readers.

"Discoursing of Things": Something, Everything, Nothing

WHEN CHRISTIAN AND FAITHFUL MEET UP on "the way" to the Celestial City, they settle in for several peripatetic pages of what the narrator calls "sweet discourse of all things that had happened to them in their Pilgrimage" (*PP,* 66). This business of discoursing about "things" is, as it turns out, very dangerous. For it is the prime task of pilgrims to keep themselves as clear as possible from the things of this world and to concentrate on the true things, which are both invisible and, largely, unspeakable. Insofar as "the way" is allegorized in *The Pilgrim's Progress* by the various things that happen to true pilgrims on "the way," it would seem that Christian and Faithful here are meant to represent Bunyan's own attempt to construct a discourse in writing of "the Way / And Race of Saints" ("The Author's Apology," *PP,* 1). Their discourse of "things that happened to them" is a model for Bunyan's discourse as a whole. But, as Fish points out so cogently, Christian's pilgrimage and Faithful's pilgrimage up to this point look like two rather different things. "The Way / And Race of Saints" appears here as two different ways for two different saints, precisely because each reports to the other different "things that happened to them in their Pilgrimage." We are tempted, much as Christian is tempted, to re-write "Pilgrimage" as plural, just as "Saints" is plural. Christian responds to Faithful's account of the things of his pilgrimage: "I am sure it fared otherwise with me." Fish's conclusion—"It fares otherwise with everyone"—simply makes explicit the threat to any certainty about the way implicit in Bunyan's discourse about it: "When Faithful and Christian compare notes, we discover that there is not one, but an infinity of ways, each of which shapes itself to the inclinations of its single traveller" (Fish, 230).

If there is indeed an "infinity of ways," then any attempt to write about "the Way / And Race of Saints" is doomed to failure. But Bunyan is not the pluralist Fish pretends to be at this moment in his interpretation. True, when he tries at first to write about "the way to Glory," Bunyan quickly discovers how inadequate any discourse about the things of the way must be:

> In more than twenty things, which I set down;
> This done, I twenty more had in my Crown,
> And they again began to multiply,
> Like sparks that from the coals of Fire do flie.
> ("The Author's Apology," 1)

Such "sparks" present a threatening image of infinite numbers of different things that happen to pilgrims on "the way to Glory," which by their very infinity threaten to expose any discourse about "the way" as hopelessly inadequate:

> Nay then, thought I, if that you breed so fast
> I'll put you by your selves, lest you at last
> Should prove *ad infinitum*, and eat out
> The Book that I already am about.
> ("The Author's Apology," 1)

Bunyan acknowledges right up front that he feels himself caught in something like Fish's all-or-nothing dilemma. Either he tries to account for the *"all* of it," the "everything" of the pilgrim experience, and inevitably fails, or he settles for "something" of the whole and so compromises the truth.

Where Fish's solution is to fall into a kind of critical doublespeak (the method that is "not a method," approaching meaning by refusing to ask "what this work is about," describing structures of "response" that contrast with "the structure of the work" [Fish, 399]), Bunyan's solution is to fall into allegorical discourse, that most popular method

for speaking otherwise. Bunyan presents his fall as quite uninten-
tional, not so much a solution to his dilemma as an experience of it:

> And thus it was: I writing of the Way
> And Race of Saints in this our Gospel-Day,
> Fell suddenly into an Allegory
> About their Journey
> ("The Author's Apology," I)

Neither Christian's nor Faithful's account of the experience of the way
is the "*all* of it" required. Bunyan's intended discourse of "the Way /
And Race of Saints" is set aside and left unspoken, for it is unspeakable. In its stead appears "suddenly" an "Allegory / About" the way, a
breeder-reactor of "things" that both enables Bunyan's own attempts
at discourse and threatens to misrepresent the one-truth, one-way
message of his "Book." Central to the result is Bunyan's implicit denial, facilitated by allegory, that the things he has finally "set down" on
paper actually represent "the way." The way is always the something
other behind the text, the unutterable "*all* of it," what Bunyan in his
"Conclusion" calls the "substance of my matter" which is not "the *outside* of my Dream" (*PP*, 164). Bunyan does not allow, as Fish pretends
to, that there is "an infinity" of ways. Bunyan is certainly not a pluralist. There is for Bunyan only one way. If that way looks or sounds different in different pilgrims' perceptions or discursive accounts of it,
this is an unfortunate effect of the pilgrims' stubborn attachment to
the things of this world. True pilgrims are on the way to another
world, one allegedly free of the distortions presented by things and by
talk of things. They set their sights, with intermittent success, on a
land free of worldly things, that is to say, on what Augustine called
"things, strictly speaking"—things not seen.

Fish observes that in *The Pilgrim's Progress* "the perils of the way
are generated by a pilgrim's weakness" (230), and this appears to be
equally the case with the many false pilgrims Christian and Faithful
(and later, Hopeful) meet on their way. The false pilgrims are reified
personifications of the true pilgrims' stubborn attachment to worldly
things and worldly thinking. Talkative appears on the landscape just
after Christian has finished explaining how "otherwise" his experience
of the way has been. All this talking, however "sweet," of "all things
that had happened to them" presents a serious risk of distortion. Talk-

ing about the experience, the way, always reduces the truth to "other mens words." Just when the way seems to have multiplied into two ways, allegory saves the appearances of contradiction: Talkative appears as the personification of this threat. He must now be carefully and deliberately exposed and destroyed.

"Faithful *and* Talkative," says the marginal note, *"enter discourse,"* as if *"discourse"* about things were another threatening feature of the landscape like the Slew of Despond or Mount Sinai. The pilgrims here enter a patch of rough ground, and this rough ground is none other than worldly talking itself, the "sweet discourse of all things." Because discourse inevitably transforms experience into things, installing a distorting distance between the self and its experience, to discourse about the way is to dis-course one's self from the way. So the rough ground Christian and Faithful find themselves traveling over here is precisely the same rough ground occupied by Bunyan, who is compelled by his unfortunate humanness, his fallenness, to speak of the way as if it were a matter of things, rather than the unutterable substance of experience. Christian and Faithful, the landscape, and the narrator himself are all distortion-effects of this discursive ground, and this episode, like many others, threatens to expose them as such.

In this fallen condition, the way appears a bit broader than the "strait and narrow" path Evangelist directed Christian to follow. Talkative appears, not behind or in front of the pilgrims, but "walking at a distance besides them, (for in this place there was room enough for them all to walk)" (75). "This place," because it is so suddenly broad, immediately raises the suspicion that the pilgrims are significantly out of the way. Fish would have us understand "this place" as the pluralism of the way, but Bunyan would not. Talking, even before Talkative appears, threatens to broaden the way into no way, just as the "sparks" in Bunyan's "Crown" threatened to "eat out" the "Book" he never could write.

At first, Faithful finds Talkative attractive and is eager to have him as a companion "in discoursing of things that are profitable" (75). Faithful, being as his name implies full of "the substance of things hoped for, the evidence of things not seen," exclaims "what things so worthy the use of the tongue and mouth of men on Earth, as are the things of the God of Heaven?" (75). Just what are such things? How do men on earth talk of what they have not seen and cannot see? What kind of talk might this be? Are the tongues and mouths of men "worthy" enough, in the sense of adequate, to articulate such "things"? Is talk about "all things that had happened to them in their Pilgrimage," the very talk that broadened the way to make room for a false pilgrim, the same as talk about the "things of the God of Heaven"?

What the margin sarcastically calls "Talkative's fine discourse" is, in fact, chock-full of what Bunyan elsewhere subscribes to as sound doctrine: "the vanity of earthly things, and the benefit of things above, . . . the necessity of the New-birth, the insufficiency of our works, the need of Christs righteousness, . . . the necessity of a work of Grace in [the] Soul" (76). "All this is true," says Faithful, "and I am glad to hear these things from you," but something about the way Talkative has so briskly rattled off these things, these "truths," gives Faithful some pause. We might recall Bunyan's own suspicions about the "brisk" way Quakers like Edward Burrough allegedly talked about such things. Faithful objects specifically to Talkative's suggestion that "a man may learn" these things "by talk." "But by your leave, Heavenly knowledge of these," says Faithful, avoiding the word *things,* "is the gift of God; no man attaineth to them by humane industry, or only by the talk of them" (76). But Talkative has no trouble agreeing with this. He doesn't even see it as an objection relevant to what he has been saying:

All this I know very well. For a man can receive nothing except it be given him from Heaven; all is of Grace, not of works: I could give you an hundred Scriptures for the confirmation of this. (77)

Neither Talkative nor Faithful, for the moment, appears aware of the contradiction between "a man can receive nothing except it be given him from Heaven" and "I could give you an hundred Scriptures."

This is, after all, precisely the contradiction that Bunyan's own discourse inhabits. Every page bristles with the promise of giving its reader knowledge of the way, and the margins are littered with hundreds of Scripture references, apparently for confirmation. Talkative, the false pilgrim, is a personification of the inevitable inadequacy, even self-contradiction, of Bunyan's own project. But this conclusion fails to take account of Bunyan's project as allegorical. Unlike Talkative, Bunyan's allegory never really claims to affirm, let alone confirm, anything.[9] It only promises to make perpetual "travellers" and "travailers" of its readers, ever taking, then rejecting as inadequate, one false step after another until there are no more steps because all the steps one can take are found to be false.

Faithful, says the margin, is "beguiled by Talkative" (77), but how exactly is he beguiled? Faithful is careful to object to Talkative's suggestion that "a man may learn by talk," but he mistakes Talkative's talk of doctrine for the real thing—an experience of grace. Readers, of course, are in much the same position vis-a-vis Bunyan's text. Without a "work of Grace" (83) "given from Heaven," Bunyan's text is no better (or worse) than a Talkative, an impersonation of a true pilgrim. Indeed, in his prefatory verses to *The Second Part,* Bunyan represents his own text as a personification of a "Pilgrim."[10] What is the difference between a personification and an impersonation? This is precisely the question that was at stake in the case of William Franklin, and in the case of James Nayler, and of other Quakers who went naked "for a sign" of Christ's presence within them. Were they impersonating Christ or personifying Christ? Again, the same question is at stake in Bunyan's claim that the Quakers' "Christ within" is a "false Christ," while he claimed to have within himself the "true Christ," who was also a "Christ without."[11] How do we know?

Bunyan's Faithful articulates the answer as, "There is therefore knowledge and knowledge":

> Knowledge that resteth in the bare speculation of things, and knowledge that is accompanied with the grace of faith and love, which puts a man upon doing even the will of God from the heart: the first of these will serve the Talker, but without the other the true Christian is not content. (82)

Faithful tags his explanation of the distinction between "knowledge and knowledge" with a quotation from Psalm 119. Faithful's distinction resembles that articulated by Luther more than a century and a half earlier when he distinguished between approaching Scripture as "testimonies" and approaching it as a source of "sure knowledge." Luther scholar Warren Quanbeck has argued that in the course of preparing his *Lectures on the Psalms,* especially those on Psalm 119, Luther "discovered the Gospel," that is, he forged a hermeneutic method that was to become a lasting hallmark of Protestant, and especially Puritan, approaches to Bible reading.[12] Understanding Scripture in what Bunyan would later call its "Gospel-sense," argues Luther, requires that a reader take it as "testimonies," rather than as a source of knowledge:

> these are testimonies one must first believe, not testimonies one may rightly expect to understand directly. He who wants to understand before he believes has not testimonies, but sure knowledge, as it seems to him. And they are the testimonies not of Scripture but of knowledge.[13]

This is not hermeneutics, but a kind of anti-hermeneutics, for it insists that understanding comes, not by acts of interpretation, but by believing without knowledge or understanding. The person who tries to interpret ("to understand directly") before believing will, according to Luther, miss the chance for true understanding altogether and wind up with testimonies of "knowledge" rather than "of Scripture." Interpretation yields knowledge of things; believing yields experience of the promises, the "testimonies" of things beyond human understanding. Even when belief comes first, what one obtains is not "sure knowledge" in the sense of seeing is believing, but faithful knowledge, for the Gospel-sense of Scripture has to do with things that are not seen. When Richard Baxter, Bunyan's close contemporary, speaks of "knowledge of another kind," or Bunyan's Faithful distinguishes between "knowledge and knowledge," they both draw on this Lutheran distinction between "sure knowledge" and "testimonies."[14]

To know something as a testimony, then, is to make a deep acknowledgment of the fact that you cannot really know it at all. The true Christian can never rest, is not content, because he or she admits that in fact, there is no knowledge at all, only faith in promises of knowledge. Luther reworks the medieval letter-spirit formula by identifying the "letter" as the "lack of knowledge" a Christian must continually confess. Only by such confession does "lack of knowledge" qualify as the "letter," the sign, of "the following knowledge," the knowledge that is promised as a gift, but can never be an achievement: "This is what being 'testimonies' means" (*Luther's Works,* 11:433–34). Once one claims, as Talkative does, "Great knowledge of *Gospel Mysteries,*" one stops experiencing Scripture as testimonies and allows it to harden into "sure knowledge," a thing rather than an experience, and so useless, worse than nothing. Such knowers rest "in the bare speculation of things," stop experiencing the promise, and "act in their own way, as the heretics and hypocrites and those zealous of peculiarities do [they are the ones who do not understand the Scriptures to be testimonies], they do not accept them all as testimonies, but as the truth already finished and resolved" (11:434; brackets in original). When experienced as testimonies, Scripture puts a reader "altogether in another world, far from reason" (27:229).

In the Talkative episode Bunyan not only assigns himself the task of exposing notional knowledge as no knowledge at all and exposing talk of the way as a threat to the experience of the way, he also must accomplish this without indicting his own textual practice. Christian and Faithful have no other choice but to use talking to expose Talkative. But exposing Talkative as a hypocrite notionist who "*talketh* of Prayer, of Repentance, of Faith, and of the New-birth: but he knows only to *talk* of them" (78) always involves Bunyan in self-indictment. Talkative came into being, after all, as a personification of Christian and Faithful's own talking, talking that threatened the unity of the way. Exposing and condemning Talkative is more like a self-exorcism than a catechetical examination of another would-be pilgrim. When the pilgrims condemn Talkative as one "who may yet be nothing, . . . no child of God" (82), one of those "Things without life, that is, without the true Faith and Grace of the Gospel; and consequently, things that shall never be placed in the Kingdom of Heaven" (80), they also condemn their own wayward tendency to trust discourse over experience. In this very talky episode, Christian and Faithful first bring Talkative into being as a personified projection of their own error, then they proceed to exteriorize and condemn him as a false pilgrim, an other.

How can Christian know Talkative so well, "better than he knows himself" (77)? Some of what Christian says of Talkative he says he has by the reports of others, from "the common People," "His poor Family," and "Men that have any dealings with him" (78). But none of this counts as experiential knowledge of Talkative, which by the pilgrims' own strict definition would be insufficient. Christian says to Faithful, "Had I known him no more than you, I might perhaps have thought of him as at the first you did," but Christian claims he knows these things about Talkative "of my own knowledge" (79). He claims "th[o]rough acquaintance with him" (77): "I have been in his Family" (78). In short, he has been intimate with Talkative, for he has been

Talkative, or Talkative has been in him. That is how Talkative came to be next to Christian on the suspiciously broadened way. He has, until just this moment, been in Faithful as well. Faithful's ignorance of who Talkative really is, is simply ignorance of himself, or his own waywardness.

Together Christian and Faithful expose Talkative as one who is impatient of "Experience" and "Conscience" (84), oblivious to the distinction between "the power of Religion" and "the power of things" (81), one who cannot hear the difference between "crying out against, and abhoring of sin," which Christian and Faithful now agree is crucial to the difference between talk of the way and experience of the way (81). In doing so, they expose themselves, and then exteriorize their own inward carnality as that of another. As if by magic, the threatening quandary with which the episode began—"I am sure it fared otherwise with me"—disappears. Christian and Faithful, the narrator tells us blithely, "went on their way talking of what they had seen by the way" (85), and there seems to be no more problem about how different their respective ways once appeared.

It is not, of course, magic, but sleight-of-hand, even a violent sleight-of-hand. Christian dismisses their little encounter with Talkative, an encounter with their own tendency to substitute discursive matter for the unutterable substance of experience, with these words: "I have dealt plainly with him; and so am clear of his blood, if he perisheth" (85). He speaks of Talkative no longer as a personification of his own error, but as an impersonator, a false pilgrim who, if he doesn't "think of it again" (85) and repent, will perish. He feels comfortable contemplating Talkative's eternal damnation; he is "clear of his blood." How did Talkative get transformed into a being capable of either salvation or damnation? How did he come to have "blood"? Much the same question arises when we consider Ignorance, whose fate it is to be cast into the pit as the very last event of the first part of *The Pilgrim's Progress.* At this point it is enough simply to say that salvation of the self in Puritan thought is always coincident with damnation of the other, and the other who is damned always begins its life as the old self. The old self must be "outed," exteriorized, before it can be damned, and its damnation most often takes the form of being attached to another, who becomes the personification of the old self. It is as if Christian were to say, "I used to be talkative, but now I see what it means to be Talkative, and that man over there is really Talkative, and he is damned." Self-accusation and its purifying effects virtually require that another take the place of the saint's exteriorized sin, and that that person perish. More people perish in *The Pilgrim's Progress* than reach the "world which is to come." The new birth of the self as Christ first requires self-erasure, an othering of the "carnal" self, and the process of that othering inevitably attaches what is othered to another of flesh and blood, capable of perishing.

Now, what of the experience of Bunyan's readers? Do they experience this episode as so much talkative discourse or as "Gospelstrains"? Does Bunyan's own printed discourse run the risk of being, like Talkative, a thing "without life," "other mens words"? The only consistent answer is "Yes," and Bunyan acknowledges as much when he cautions readers against "playing with the *out-side* of my Dream." We must agree with Fish that there is no progress in *The Pilgrim's Progress* because the progress Bunyan encourages his readers to experience, the "work of Grace" in the heart, is not something "a man may learn by *talk,*" even by Bunyan's talk. Even when one feels one has experienced this "work of Grace," says Faithful, "it is but seldom that he is able to conclude that this is a work of Grace, because his corruptions now, and his abused reason, makes his mind to mis-judge in this matter" (83). What Luther called "sure knowledge" transforms testimonies of the Spirit, taken on faith, into testimonies of knowledge. As Fish puts it, "that experience is compromised the moment you say anything about it" (Fish, 425). We recall that in *Grace Abounding,* Bunyan represents his "Gospel" experiences as things that come to him not while reading or interpreting, but suddenly and often violently. All Bunyan promises his readers in his allegory's title is a "similitude" or a "figure" of such experience, a kind of chalking out of such experience, not the experience itself.[15] The "out-side" of Bunyan's "Dream" is a nothing, or worse.

The insights Bunyan's allegory yields, then, are more than "inseparable from the demonstration of the inadequacy of its forms"; those repeated demonstrations are the only insights it can yield. This is a more radical version of Fish's conclusion, one he shrinks from making, but one to which both his and Bunyan's methods inevitably lead. If the meaning or experience Fish and Bunyan are interested in requires readers "to pierce through it [the dream matter] to the truth it cannot itself image or contain," then such experience must be something other than the text or the reading of the text. The substance Bunyan points to, like the "shining light" Evangelist points to and the Celestial City the Shepherds point to, but which the pilgrims never quite see, always lies on the other side of the matter:

> Put by the Curtains, look within my Vail;
> Turn up my Metaphors and do not fail;
> There, if thou seekest them, such things to find,
> As will be helpful to an honest mind.
>
> (*PP*, 164)

If "Curtains," "Vail," and "Metaphors" are all equivalent to "the Similitude of a Dream," then the "There" where meaning is experienced is radically "out-side" the world occupied by both the text and the reader, the world of "the forms of the reader's understanding." Both the destination and the way to it are simply unrepresentable.

Like Fish, however, Bunyan equivocates. Without equivocation there would be no *Pilgrim's Progress* at all. He still refers to the meaning of his Dream as a "thing," even though the episode with Talkative so thoroughly disqualifies worldly things as nothings. He persists in speaking of his allegory as a container of truth—

> It seems a Novelty, and yet contains
> Nothing but sound and honest Gospel-strains
>
> ("The Author's Apology," 7)

—even though his characters have so convincingly demonstrated that, from the perspective of the "world which is to come," the perspective the text everywhere encourages its readers to adopt, the things one encounters on the way should appear as they do to Mr. Valiant-for-Truth: "as so many Nothings" (*PP*, 295). Bunyan claims his "fancies . . . will stick like Burs" (7), but he also recommends that readers treat such "fancies" as "dross" to be discarded once the "Gold" of truth is experienced.

Nowhere is Bunyan's ambivalence about the status of his matter more apparent than in the concluding lines of "The Conclusion" to *The Pilgrim's Progress:*

What of my *dross* thou findest there, be bold
To throw away, but yet preserve the Gold.
What if my Gold be wrapped up in Ore?
None throws away the Apple for the Core:
But if thou shalt cast all away as vain,
I know not but 'twill make me Dream again.

(*PP*, 164)

Bunyan leaves unresolved the conflicted twinning of these two figures—the gold and the apple core. The gold wrapped up in drossy, and therefore disposable, ore is swiftly supplanted by the figure of the altogether disposable core surrounded by nourishing fruit. The relative values of outsides and insides are suddenly reversed in what looks like a desperate attempt in the very last lines to save figures, similitudes, dream-matter, discourse itself as something not only valuable, but necessary. One must consume the outside, but there is no guarantee that once the outside is consumed, you won't be left with only an inedible core and no gold. What better figure for what Bunyan takes to be the stubborn fallenness of the human mind, forever attached to things and outsides, than this image of his own discourse as an apple, the tempting fruit of knowledge. Quoting 2 Corinthians 4:18, Bunyan's Interpreter warns Christian that

> the things that are seen, are Temporal; but the things that are not seen, are Eternal: But though this be so, yet things present, and our fleshly appetite, *are such near Neighbors one to another;* and again, because things to come, and carnal sense, are such strangers one to another: therefore it is, that the first of these so suddenly fall into *amity,* and that *distance* is so continued between the second. (*PP,* 32)

The Pilgrim's Progress everywhere claims to be directing readers to "that shining light" that neither it nor the Scriptures it recommends in its margins is capable of representing without the distortion of "other mens words," but it finally admits its own complicity in continuing the "distance" between "things" and "things to come." Unlike William Franklin, or Fifth Monarchists, or even (in their own way) the Quakers, Bunyan is unwilling to announce the arrival of "things to come" in the flesh and in the present. Allegory preserves him from the chiliastic moment he so devoutly hopes for and so resolutely resists.

Christ remains "without" even as Bunyan claims he must be experienced "within." With Bunyan, radical nonconformity falls from chiliasm back into allegory, which continues the distance between "two worlds" and so renders it mainstream enough politically and culturally to become what N. H. Keeble argues was a lasting, if not dominant, cultural and "literary movement."[16] Bunyan's fall helps to shift radical antinomianism into mere dissent.

Bunyan's ambivalence resolutely avoids any resolution, boiling away just below the surface of his text and erupting more and more frequently as the narrative proceeds in startling images of violence. We have already seen how Talkative is subtly shifted from being an outward personification of Christian's own inner waywardness (an allegory) to being a flesh-and-blood false professor, an impersonator who must be shunned and damned in order that Christian and Faithful may return to the way freed from the very doubts that first gave rise to Talkative. For Christian and Faithful to achieve identity with Christ, others must be thrust into identity with all that is not Christ. Christian and Faithful violently "out" their own carnal nature and attach it to others, who then must be destroyed.

The Pilgrim's Progress and its sequel are littered with the corpses of false professors, flesh-and-blood beings whom the pilgrims expose as "nothing[s]" (82) or "Things without life" (80), but who are not permitted simply to vanish from the landscape like phantoms, but must perish. The laborious process of ridding themselves of their own worldly ways, it seems, is inextricable from the process whereby worldly others meet destruction. Once Talkative has been exorcised and doomed to perish, Evangelist reminds the pilgrims to

> believe steadfastly concerning things that are invisible. Let nothing that is on this side the other world get within you: and above all, look well to your own hearts, and to the lusts thereof; for they are deceitful above all things and desperately wicked. (87)

Talkative belongs to that order of things "that is on this side the other world," but he is also an effect of the pilgrims' own deceitful lusts. What the un-blessed like Talkative, Pliable, Worldly-Wiseman, Ignorance, Hypocrisy, Formalist, Hold-the-World, Wanton, By-Ends, Mony-love, and (especially) Save-all take to be the world must be redefined by the pilgrims as nothing more than the reality-effect of the pilgrims' own deceitful lusts. They and their world must be seen as nothing more than allegorical personifications of the many weaknesses of those who are truly "blest." The false professors live in an allegory and are themselves allegories of the pilgrims' progress in purification as they pass through this allegorical (non)existence to a new reality. Yet they are real enough, or threaten to appear real enough, that they must be violently destroyed in order to be made truly unreal. They do not evaporate; they suffer eternal torment in Hell, and their very real suffering somehow guarantees their status as having always been unreal.

There Is, Therefore, Ignorance and Ignorance

BUNYAN SAVES HIS ACCOUNT of Ignorance's perdition as the final episode of *The Pilgrim's Progress,* a kind of coda to the story of "the Way / And Race of Saints" that jarringly refocuses a reader's attention on the fear of being left among the false professors, one of the allegorical others constitutive of Christian's new reality. The last thing the narrator sees in his dream is Ignorance being bound hand and foot and thrust into the pit of Hell (163). He is damned precisely because he never believed sufficiently in the invisible things. He never even knew there were such things. Like the Jew of Protestant typology, he lived and breathed in the unreal world of temporal things, always mistaking them for the invisible reality of the promises. He is the personification of the true pilgrims' fleshly existence. He is the allegorical distortion of their experience of salvation. He is the flesh and blood of types and shadows.

Yet, like Talkative before him, Ignorance comes into being as a projection of Christian's and Hopeful's sinful carnality, specifically, their tendency to doubt the reality of "things not seen." He appears on the landscape at just those moments when Christian and Hopeful are most prone to the error he both is and represents. Having just come from their sojourn with the Shepherds in Immanuel's Land, Christian and Hopeful are still shaken by what the Shepherds had shown them, and by what they had failed to see, and by their failure to acknowledge that they had failed to see.

It gradually dawns on the pilgrims that many other pilgrims have come as far as they have only to wind up in Hell. "I perceive," says

Hopeful, "that these had on them, even every one, a shew of Pilgrimage as we have now" (122), yet they, and even some who progressed farther still, "were thus miserably cast away." Are the pilgrims truly pilgrims, or do their deceitful hearts merely make them think they are pilgrims? Might they really turn out to be, like Talkative and the rest, false professors? The Shepherds refuse to confirm the pilgrims, either to themselves or to us, as true wayfarers:

> *Chr. Is this the way to the Celestial City?*
> *Shep.* You are just in your way.
> *Chr. How far is it thither?*
> *Shep.* Too far for any, but those that *shall* get thither indeed.
> *Chr. Is the way safe, or dangerous?*
> *Shep.* Safe for those for whom it is to be safe, *but transgressors shall fall therein.* (119)

By his questions, Christian gives every indication that he has not yet relinquished his carnal notions of the outward thingness of the way. He still mistakes the figures or the similitudes, the appearances of the landscape, for the way itself, and so elicits from the Shepherds precisely the equivocal responses he had hoped his questions would settle. That he asks such questions at all indicates that he does not yet see the way for what it is, so the doubts that prompt such questions must also produce doubtful answers. Christian still seeks knowledge of the way because he has yet fully to achieve belief in the way as "testimonies." In the episodes that follow, Christian and Hopeful encounter many dangers that simply increase their—and our—doubts about their legitimacy as pilgrims.

The pilgrims' doubts and fears are further aggravated by their lack of skill with the Perspective Glass, but Christian and Hopeful choose to deny these doubts. Though they stand atop the "Hill called *Clear*" and look through this special glass, "slavish fear" (123, marginal note) causes their hands to shake; thus they only "thought they saw something like the Gate, and also some of the Glory of the place" (123). Despite what the text and margin identify as their failure of vision, they think they saw what they should have seen, or what they wanted to see, and they rejoice in song, quite pleased with the "skill" (123) they have just demonstrated they lack. What if it was all but a "think-so"?

It should be no surprise, then, that Ignorance appears from the "left hand" (perhaps the shaky hand that rendered the Perspective Glass virtually useless?) as soon as they take leave of the Shepherds. Ignorance appears again later just as Hopeful is confessing that his visionary experience, one particularly reminiscent of Bunyan's own,[17] failed to comfort him as much as it should and instead "confounded me with the sense of my own Ignorance" (144). Hopeful no sooner finishes speaking than he looks back and sees Ignorance "coming after" him.

Ignorance, we discover from the ensuing dialogue, scorns revelations and visions as "but the fruit of distracted braines" (148). Roger Sharrock and Christopher Hill read Ignorance as a personification of latitudinarians like Edward Fowler, later Bishop of Gloucester,[18] but in the immediate context of the narrative, he personifies Christian's and Hopeful's (and Bunyan's) inability to keep hold of their experiences of ecstatic revelation as experiences. He is an exteriorized version of their own inward fears that their experiences of revelation and of new birth may turn out to be all "a shew" (122), or something they only "thought they saw"—in a word, "so many whimzies" (149). Ignorance personifies the inner latitudinarian, the this-worldly tendency of revelatory experience to dwindle into a doubtful thing by being reflected upon, discoursed about, made an object of carnal forms of understanding, and so claimed as one's own.[19] As with Talkative, Christian manages to exorcise his own ignorance by "boldly" affirming "that no man can know Jesus Christ but by the Revelation of the Father," by a work of grace "wrought by the exceeding greatness of his mighty power" (149). There is, it seems, ignorance and ignorance. Ignorance's brand of ignorance consists in not knowing that he does not, and cannot, know Jesus Christ; Christian's ignorance is "blest" because it knows precisely that and nothing else. Perhaps this is why Ignorance has been permitted to come so far on his apparent pilgrimage before being exposed at the very end of the narrative and pitched headlong into the pit—his ignorance, unless we look very closely, looks a lot like pious ignorance.

Once again, the role Scripture reading and interpretation are allowed to play in such "Revelation" is a crucial issue. Ignorance claims that he enjoys "good thoughts" of himself, thoughts that "agree with the Word of God" (146). But Christian counters that the only thoughts of "our selves" that agree with the "Word of God" are those that convince us of the utter vileness of all our thoughts, what Fish calls the complete "inadequacy . . . of the forms of the reader's understanding" (Fish, 264).

> *The Word of God saith of persons in a natural condition,* There is none Righteous, there is none that doth good. [Rom. 3] *It saith also,* That every imagination of the heart of man is only evil, and that continually. [Gen. 6:5] *And again,* The imagination of mans heart is evil from his Youth. *Now then, when we think thus of our selves, having sense thereof, then are our thoughts good ones, because according to the Word of God.* (146, marginal notations in brackets)

Correctly reading the Scripture, like "correctly" interpreting *The Pilgrim's Progress,* is useful only in a very limited, and paradoxical, way. The true mark of correct reading of the Scripture and the self is the conviction, the *"sense,"* of one's utter inability to read self or Scripture correctly. Reading, interpretation, and reflection should deposit one into a state of abjection, a "sensible" conviction of one's *"original . . . actual infirmities"* (147), the infirmity of an utterly corrupt imagination. Read correctly, the Scripture should convince us, with Calvin, that the human mind is nothing but "a perpetual forge of idols."

Ignorance confesses that he will "never believe that my heart is thus bad" (146), just as Christian and Hopeful could not bring themselves to admit that they had not really seen anything in the Perspective Glass. *"Therefore,"* says Christian, " . . . *when our thoughts of our HEARTS and WAYS agree with the Judgement which the Word giveth of both, then are both good, because agreeing thereto"* (146). The Word's judgment of human understanding is utter condemnation: "every imagination of the heart of man is only evil, and that continually" (146). To have "good thoughts" of one's self, then, is to think *"sensibly"* of one's self as *"crooked . . . not good, but perverse,"* in a word, as abjectly ignorant. Ignorance, as well he might, asks Christian to "Make out your meaning," but as Christian's response makes clear, meaning is hardly the issue. The issue, as always, is experience. Ignorance's problem, of course, is that he remains ignorant of the only thing anyone can be said to know—that one is utterly ignorant. *"Sensible"* conviction of one's abject state of ignorance is the prerequisite to "the Revelation of the Father."

> Why, the Word of God saith, That mans ways are crooked ways, not good, but perverse: It saith, they are naturally out of the good way, that *they have not known it*. Now when a man thus thinketh of his ways, I say when he doth sensibly, and with heart-humiliation thus think, then hath he good thoughts of his own ways, because his thoughts now agree with the judgment of the Word of God. (146, italics added).

If, as Bunyan seems to suggest, the reader's "way" is to interpret, then a correct interpretation of Scripture must yield the conviction that our "ways," all our efforts at interpretation, are "crooked ways," self-deceptive. As *"a Man cloathed with Raggs,"* Christian himself had made the early mistake of thinking that reading was a legitimate way. Indeed, the burden of "carnal imagination" that Christian so desperately seeks to shed first came to him "By reading this Book in my hand" (18). One of Bunyan's first marginal notations, "Hab. 2:2" (8), has often been mistaken by critics as indicating that Bunyan's Way is identified as an allegory of reading, that reading and "running" are somehow identified allegorically. Nothing could be further from Bunyan's point. At least initially, the "man cloathed with Raggs" is presented as *"standing in a certain place"* as he reads in "the Book." Reading initially makes him weep and tremble and "brake out with a lamentable cry," but it does not show him what to do (8). Reading makes him feel *"in myself undone,"* and drives him to distraction, but it neither constitutes nor indicates anything like the way. The man, we are told, reads as he walks "in the Fields," not in the way (9). Reading apparently makes him want to run, "yet he stood still, because, as I perceived, he could not tell which way to go" (9). The only perception yielded by reading and interpretation is, as he later tries to tell Ignorance, a sense of condemnation and judgment (9).

Even the "Parchment-Roll" that Evangelist gives the ragged man, which apparently represents reading of a somewhat different order, is capable only of aggravating his desire to *"Fly from the wrath to come,"* not of indicating which way to fly (10). This quotation from Matthew 3 registers quite nicely Bunyan's ambivalence about reading and interpretation. The words here are those John the Baptist addressed to the Pharisees: "But when he saw many of the Pharisees and Sadducees come to his baptism, he said unto them, O generation of vipers, who hath warned you to flee from the wrath to come?" One effect of the quotation is to locate the "Man cloathed with Raggs" in the position of a Pharisee—a zealous reader and interpreter of the law. Reading and interpretation apparently did nothing to save the poor Pharisees.

The issue here, as in Bunyan's debate with Edward Burrough, is not so much the content of the warning itself, the words, but the voice that speaks them—"*Who* hath warned you?" Until Christian can hear the words as voiced by Christ specifically to him, or more precisely, until the words are experienced as both spoken by and heard in the Spirit, they mean nothing. Reading is not only not the way, it cannot even point to the way. After reading the Parchment-Roll, Christian turns his attention to Evangelist, who tries to show him the way to the way:

> The Man therefore Read it, and looking upon *Evangelist* very carefully; said, Whither must I fly? Then said *Evangelist*, pointing with his finger over a very wide Field, Do you see yonder *Wicket-gate*? The Man said, No. Then said the other, Do you see yonder shining light? He said, I think I do. Then said *Evangelist*, Keep that light in your eye, and go up directly thereto, so shalt thou see the Gate; at which when thou knockest, it shall be told thee what thou shalt do. (10)[20]

The colloquy with Evangelist represents something other than reading and interpretation. It is Bunyan's similitude of the experience of the Word. The margin says simply, "Christ and the way to him cannot be found without the Word," but the similitude itself distinguishes clearly between the act of reading and the experience of the Word. Reading the Bible, as Worldly-Wiseman is made to remark with ironic accuracy, "unman[s] men" (18); re-making men is accomplished not through reading and interpretation, but by a work of grace. The Word is a shining light one cannot quite see, the very invisibility of which one must "Keep . . . in your eye." It is the invisible, unreadable "Gate" into the dazzling (un)certainty of "things not seen."

Even when Christian reads in his Book of the wonderful things promised to pilgrims (13), the most immediate result of such reading is that he falls into the "*Miry Slow*" of "*Dispond*" (14). Christian's eager reading to Pliable of the wonders promised in "his Book" is described by this episode as "being heedless" (14). The "burden" of reading and interpretation slows his flight and makes him sink in the mire, even as he reads of the "endless Kingdom to be Inhabited," and the "Crowns of Glory to be given" (13). Before Help pulls him out of the mire, he asks Christian, *"why did you not look for the steps?"* (15). Bunyan's margin glosses "the steps" as *"The Promises,"* prompting us to ask, what was Christian reading if not precisely "the promises" as recorded in his "Book"? The only answer, of course, is that reading is a profoundly different activity from looking and experiencing. Until Christian is freed from his dependence upon reading, interpretation, and all other worldly forms of understanding, he remains burdened.[21] Reading the promises, rather than simply standing on them, only plunges one deeper into "Dispond."

It is crucially significant that Bunyan's Interpreter confesses himself unable to relieve Christian of this burden: "He told him, As to the burden, be content to bear it, until thou comest to the place of Deliverance; for there it will fall from thy back it self" (28). Even the curriculum Christian experiences in Interpreter's House is one that simulates a movement beyond interpretation and toward experience. Christian begins his lessons by constantly asking "What means this?" (29, 30, 32), and is gradually led to experience the inadequacy of such a question and the answers it inevitably yields. As his lessons progress from emblems to emblematic dramas to three-dimensional drama puzzles, Christian discovers more and more the limitations of interpretation, and we gradually realize why the House of Interpreter is on the near side rather than the far side of new birth.[22] Christian's final lesson presents both a plethora of texts (see the margin on page 36) and, in a sense, no text at all, but a "Dream." What's more, it is not a dream to be interpreted, but to be experienced as one's own, yielding not a meaning, but the experience of being "put . . . in *hope* and *fear*" (37). Says Interpreter, "Keep all things so in thy mind, that they may be as a *Goad* in thy sides, to prick thee forward in the way thou must go" (37). Reading and interpreting things correctly is not the way; it is merely the *"Goad"* that pricks one on the way—that is, if one is truly "in the way" already.

According to Bunyan, interpretation, in itself, is always a dead end, and one must repeatedly experience it as a dead end, "sensibly, and with heart-humiliation." Experiencing this *mise-en-abyme* is precisely what reading and interpretation are for. When Bunyan warns his reader, "take heed / Of mis-interpreting: for that, instead / Of doing good, will but thy self abuse: / By mis-interpreting evil insues"

(164), he shows his reader the way to *"hope* and *fear."* All interpretation is misinterpretation; all readers are bound by their "original . . . actual infirmities" (147) to be misreaders. The only way to avoid misinterpretation is to experience a conviction of interpretation's inadequacy. The experience Bunyan hopes to offer his "Travailer" readers is frustration with travailing. The rest is "Revelation."

If no revelation is to be forthcoming, as Bunyan believes will be the case with most of his readers, and a reader finds herself interminably puzzled over how one correctly interprets a text that appears to announce one's utter inability to interpret anything correctly, then the text has succeeded in what is perhaps its primary goal:

> Would'st read thy self, and read thou know'st not what
> And yet know whether thou art blest or not,
> By reading the same lines?
>
> (7)

The "same lines," says Bunyan, offer images of "thy self" and "thou know'st not what." If one's experience of the self is just such abject conviction of self-ignorance and the self's ignorance, the utter loss of self (line 20), then presumably one may be "blest." Some, however, like Talkative and Ignorance, will discover nothing except *"the fruit of distracted braines"* (148), or mistakenly discover by reading that they are "blest" and so be finally cast into Hell, fully confident of their own salvation to the bitter end. Perhaps others may go to the pit having gathered from Bunyan's book just how unblessed they are. Whatever the case of any particular reader, Bunyan's narrative voice is content simply to look longingly after Christian and Hopeful, wishing himself "among them" (162), hoping that, like them, he has successfully pinned all his inward doubts and fears about his own way onto all the others, the vast majority of us false pilgrims who are shunned or even murdered by the likes of Mr. Great-heart, who litters the landscape of *The Second Part of The Pilgrim's Progress* with the dismembered carcasses of the faithless.

The metaphysics of insiders and outsiders constitutes the way as the self-abjection of insiders, an abjection achieved by exteriorizing all one's own inner vileness as the vileness of the outsider. Thus, the insider is "saved" from himself and is reborn as God, and the outsider becomes the old self one is saved from. "There but for the grace of

God, . . ." Without flesh-and-blood people to fill the damned roles of Christian's own exteriorized sin—Talkative, Ignorance, By-ends, Formalist, Giant Despair, (the list is endless)—there would be no way. Christian's abject conviction of ignorance is the way, both of his salvation and Ignorance's perdition. The one means nothing without the other.

"This Was the Story": The Threat of "Realism"

THE STORY OF LITTLE-FAITH and the three Sturdy Rogues, a story Christian tells to Hopeful in between their two encounters with Ignorance, has received almost no critical attention. When it is mentioned, it is usually cited as an example of the odd tendency of Bunyan's narrative to slip out of an allegorical mode and into narrative "realism."[23] Roger Sharrock calls the episode a "realistic scene of highway robbery."[24] Sharrock's point is not without merit, for, aside from the character and place names, there is nothing in the story "as it is" to suggest that Christian is speaking allegorically, or that allegoresis is called for in reading it. The story calls attention to no specific Scripture analogues, and Bunyan refrains from his usual practice of lining the margins with Scripture references. Christian's narrative style is exceedingly plain, its rhetorical figures limited to the homeliest sort of expressions: "white as a clout," "betook themselves to their heels," "shift for himself," and "scrabble upon his way." What's more, the story opens much as we might expect any bit of homely gossip or folktale to begin, with the simple statement: "The thing was this." And its coda is equally colloquial: "This was the story" (*PP*, 125–26).

Though Christian's anecdotal style invites his audience (Hopeful) and Bunyan's to expect a certain degree of homely realism, this is, of course, a rhetorical trap. For Christian and Hopeful, like all true pilgrims, are on a quest for reality, or more precisely, they are "travellers" on the road to becoming truly real. Since the truly real is everything on the other side of the "things of this world," what this world understands as realism is, strictly speaking, allegory. The more "realistic" the story sounds, the more thoroughly allegorical it is. When Christian begins with "The thing was this," we and Hopeful should be immediately aware of the potential equivocation in the word *thing*. Is it a thing as this world understands it, or truly a thing? If the former, it is, "strictly speaking," a sign of something else; if the latter, it is the reality of the next world. On this quest to be made truly real, the most persistent danger, as we have seen, is mistaking this world's things for true things. To paraphrase Faithful, there is, therefore, realism and realism.

The occasion for Christian's story is by now of a familiar sort. The pilgrims have just witnessed a man "bound with seven strong Cords" being carried by "seven Devils" "back *to the door* that they saw in the side of the Hill" (125), that is, he is being cast into Hell. Christian thinks he recognizes the poor fellow as "one *Turnaway* that dwelt in the *Town* of *Apostasy*," and, indeed, he carries a "Paper" on his back bearing the inscription, "*Wanton Professor, and damnable Apostate*." He hangs his head "like a Thief" (125). As is usual when they witness such scenes, "good *Christian* began to tremble, and so did *Hopeful* his Companion," for though they are fairly certain they are true pilgrims, this certainty rests, as we have seen, on still doubtful grounds. They only "thought they saw something like the Gate" of the Celestial City through the Shepherds' "Perspective Glass" (123), and as yet they know of no guarantee that they will not turn out to be apostates like Turnaway. Ignorance, after all, still dogs their heels, and their conversation with him, together with their false confidence about what they "thought" they saw in the "Perspective Glass," suggests that they are indeed quite liable to the sin of self-flattery. No doubt this is why the Shepherds specifically warn them to "*beware of the flatterer*" (123), a warning they promptly forget over the course of their interchanges with Ignorance and their argument between themselves over the meaning of the story of Little-faith (132–33). The pilgrims remain in hope and fear; they hope they are not apostates and hypocrites, and they fear that they might be.

Presumably it is such hope and fear that prompts Christian to recall the story of Little-faith being robbed by "three Sturdy Rogues," "*Faint-heart, Mistrust,* and *Guilt*" (125). In this story, these "three Sturdy Rogues" appear as highwaymen. The pilgrims' fear, then, is that they might be so racked with faint hearts, mistrust, and guilt that they turn out, like old Turnaway, to be thieves, robbing themselves and others (Bunyan's readers?) of whatever slight sense of assurance they possess. Their only hope, on the other hand, is that they are not thieves, but victims, and that Faint-heart, Mistrust, and Guilt are not them, or in them, but sufficiently exteriorized to be things of the world they are leaving behind. The measure of their progress toward becoming truly real will be the degree to which these "three Sturdy Rogues" are found to be external to them. Such threats are internal to the old man they are leaving behind because the old man, like the carnal-minded Jew, fails to recognize that he lives an allegorical existence, that his whole life in this world is an allegorical story of the true reality that only the newly born can experience. To the newly born, such thieves are simply no threat at all, just a story, not really things. As Bunyan's margin points out, the old man is both "Thief" and victim: "His own iniquities shall take the wicked himself, and he shall be holden with the cords of his sins" (Proverbs 5:22).

So Christian tells Hopeful this story because he finds it comforting. It reassures him that the "three Sturdy Rogues" are but a figment of a threat, that Faint-heart, Mistrust, and Guilt are, to the new man, mere phantoms of this world. To those who mistake this world for reality, however, they are all too real. Little-faith is a character who stands, as it were, with one foot in each world.

> The thing was this; at the entering in of this passage there comes down from *Broad-way-gate,* a Lane, called *Dead-mans lane;* so called, because of the Murders that are commonly done there. And this *Little-Faith* going on Pilgrimage, as we do now, chanced to sit down there and slept. Now there happened at that time, to come down that *Lane* from *Broad-way-gate,* three Sturdy Rogues; and their names were *Faint-heart, Mistrust,* and *Guilt,* (three Brothers) and they espying *Little-faith* where he was, came galloping up with speed: Now the good man was just awaked from his sleep, and was getting up to go on his Journey. So they came all up to him, and with threatening Language bid him *stand.* At this *Little faith* look'd as white as a clout, and he had neither power to *fight,* nor *flie.* Then said *Faint-heart,* Deliver thy Purse; but he making no haste to do it, (for he was loth to lose his Money) *Mistrust* ran up to him, and thrusting his hand into his Pocket, pull'd out thence a bag of Silver. Then he cried out, Thieves, thieves. With that, *Guilt* with a great Club that was in his hand, strook *Little-Faith* on the head, and with that blow fell'd him flat to the ground, where he lay bleeding as one that would bleed to death. All this while the Thieves stood by. But at last, they hearing that some were upon the Road, and fearing lest it should be one *Great-grace* that dwells in the City of *Good-confidence,* they be-

took themselves to their heels, and left this good man to shift for himself. Now after a while, *Little-faith* came to himself, and getting up, made shift to scrabble on his way. This was the story. (125–26)

This story epitomizes virtually every other episode of Christian's pilgrimage. Weary with traveling through this world, Little-faith allows his fears to get the best of him, and these worldly fears, mistaken for reality, literally beat him over the head and leave him for dead, having stolen his "Silver," his worldly possessions. Had he not been "loth to lose his Money," that is to say, were he unconcerned about the things of this world, the thieves would be no threat; they would not even exist.

Christian finds this story comforting, for Little-faith, however much he is prone to mistake the things of this world for reality, can never lose his "Jewels," the real things, the promises. Hopeful, on the other hand, finds the story very distressing: *"But did they take from him all that ever he had?"* asks Hopeful. "No," answers Christian, "the place where his Jewels were, they never ransackt, so those he kept still" (126). The thieves took most of his "spending Money," but left his "Jewels," apparently because they were not aware there were any Jewels to be had. These Jewels—also known as "his Certificate"—the thieves never saw, "though they mist it not through any good cunning of his, for he being dismayd with their coming upon him, had neither power nor skill to hide any thing; so 'twas more by good Providence then by his Indeavour, that they mist of *that good thing*" (126). The margin glosses *"that good thing"* by way of 2 Timothy 1:13–14 as "the form of sound words, which thou hast heard of me [Paul], in faith and love which is in Christ Jesus."[25] The "form of sound words," heard in faith, is "that good thing which was committed unto thee . . . by the Holy Ghost, who dwelleth in us." Little-faith's "Jewels," then, are what Luther calls the promises, spoken by the Holy Spirit and heard in faith. In other words, the Jewels, or Certificate, are things not of this world. The thieves miss them because they cannot see them. Indeed, Christian implies that most people cannot see them: "In all that Countrey where he was Robbed his Jewels were not accounted of" (127). Little-faith's "Money," as Sharrock glosses it, are his "assurances of faith," the ragged little bits of his own worldly evidences of salvation, his worldly tokens of salvation. These the worldly count as riches, especially

"Wanton" professors and apostates. These the world can see and steal from a pilgrim, but in "the world which is to come," they are worse than nothing. These are the temporal things that the Jews are alleged to have mistaken for the substance of God's promises, but which God's true Israelites know are nothing but drossy intimations of the real things promised. Little-faith—*"poor Man!"*—spends the rest of his journey grieving over the loss of such worldly things, quite forgetful that he had the real thing with him all along:

> It might have been a great comfort to him, had he used it as he should; but they that told me the story, said, That he made but little use of it all the rest of the way; and that because of the dismay that he had in their taking away his Money: indeed he forgot it a great part of the rest of the Journey; and besides, when at any time, it came into his mind, and he began to be comforted therewith, then would fresh thoughts of his loss come again upon him, and those thoughts would swallow up all. (127)

Little-faith, like the pilgrims who tell his story, is midway between the two worlds, between being an old man who grieves over the loss of those things that are really nothing—the mere temporal shadows of the truly real—and being a new man whose joy is in a reality that "in all that Countrey where he was Robbed" remains largely invisible. Christian understands the story as demonstrating that all the apparent obstacles in the way are, strictly speaking, nothings, but Hopeful doesn't quite get it.

Hopeful, after all, is a bit like Little-faith in that he, like "the Israelite of old," still tends to live by the hope instilled by the temporal signs of the promises, being all too prone to mistake the signs for the things signified, all too prone, that is, to slide from being an Israelite into being a Jew. And to be a Jew, Christian's story implies, is to be not one of little faith, but one of misplaced faith, to be an Esau, a false professor, an apostate, a hypocrite—in a word, to be hopelessly carnal. Like Paul, Bunyan emblematizes the Jew as the older, carnal-minded brother—Ishmael to the Christian Isaac, Esau to Jacob, even, perhaps, Cain to Abel.[26] For Bunyan, however, this designation includes all the many misbelievers of his age—established churchmen, Quakers, Catholics, Ranters, "Wanton Professors" of every stripe.

Hopeful's misstep is represented here as his failure to distinguish properly between the ontological status of Little-faith's Jewels and that of his Money. Hopeful, after all, grew up in the Town of Vanity, the site of the perpetual Vanity Fair. Vanity Fair is Bunyan's epitome of worldliness, wherein are sold *"all sorts of vanity,"* to wit: "Houses, Lands, Trades, Places, Honours, Preferments, Titles, Countreys, Kingdoms, Lusts, Pleasures, and Delights of all sorts, as Whores, Bauds, Wives, Husbands, Children, Masters, Servants, Lives, Blood, Bodies, Souls, Silver, Gold, Pearls, Precious Stones, and what not" (88). Coming from such a background, Hopeful is as likely as anyone to mistake the "things of this world" for things indeed, to mistake all this "what not" for what truly matters. In short, Hopeful is peculiarly liable to misunderstand what Christian means by Little-faith's Jewels. Truly real Jewels are none of these things. The language of Christian's story is, no doubt, equivocal, as language in this world unfortunately always is. Like the language employed by the thieving "three Sturdy Rogues," the language of this world is "threatening Language." It is also like the language Bunyan calls the "outside" of his dream, and the threat is that its potential for equivocation opens a way for precisely the sort of misinterpretation Hopeful falls into.

Hopeful remains anxiously fixated on Little-faith's "Jewels," and his fixation betrays, not Christian's confidence and comfort, but his own mistaking of the kind of thing *"that good thing"* really is. *"But 'tis a wonder,"* says Hopeful, *"that his necessities did not put him upon* selling, or pawning *some of his Jewels, that he might have wherewith to relieve himself in his Journey."* Christian's response to Hopeful's wonder is a sharp, almost damning, rebuke: "Thou talkest like one, upon whose head is the Shell to this very day: For what should he *pawn* them? or to whom should he sell them?" (127) The margin comments: "Christian *snibbeth his fellow for unadvised speaking."* Just what is "unadvised" about Hopeful's speaking is the burden of the rest of Christian's discourse on the episode.

Hopeful compounds his mistake by citing Scripture:

> *Hope. Why art thou so tart my Brother? Esau* sold his Birth-right, *and that for a mess of Pottage; and that Birth-right was his greatest Jewel: and if he, why might not* Little-Faith *do so too?* (128)

Because, Christian explains somewhat impatiently, Esau's "Birth-right" was not really a true thing at all. It belongs with that list of other "what not" that is the stuff of Vanity and its Fair:

> *Chr. Esau* did sell his Birth-right indeed, and so do many besides; and by so doing, exclude themselves from the chief blessing, as also that *Caytiff* did. But you must put a difference betwixt *Esau* and *Little-Faith,* and also betwixt their Estates. *Esau's* Birth-right was Typical, but *Little-Faith's* Jewels were not so. *Esau's* belly was his God, but *Little-Faith's* belly was not so. *Esau's* want lay in his fleshly appetite, *Little-Faith's* did not so. Besides, *Esau* could see no further then to the fulfilling of his lusts; *For I am at the point to dye,* said he, *and what good will this Birth-right do me?* But *Little-Faith,* though it was his lot to have but a *little faith,* was by his *little faith* kept from such extravagancies; and made to *see* and *prize* his Jewels more, then to sell them, as *Esau* did his Birth-right. You read not any where that *Esau* had *Faith,* no not so much as a *little:* Therefore no marvel, if where the flesh only bears sway (as it will in that man where *no* Faith is to resist) if he sells his *Birth-right,* and his Soul and all, and that to the Devil of Hell. (128)

I quote Christian's response at some length because it is a certain kind of raving, and raving must be allowed to go on a bit before it exposes itself as such. The paradoxical heart of Christian's (and Bunyan's) raving is his contention that Esau's "Birth-right" was merely "Typical," that is to say, not really a birth-right at all, at least not in the sense of reality ascribable to Little-faith's Jewels. Or, to put it another way, Esau's Birth-right is just that—a Birth-right, as opposed to a new-birth-right. Given this distinction, Esau's alleged line of reasoning makes perfect sense: *"I am at the point to dye,"* and, once dead, a Birth-right is truly a nothing. Only a new-birth-right is such a Jewel as the carnal-minded ones of this world can neither see nor prize, but which those newly born of faith rather than of flesh know as the real reality, the real inheritance or "family jewels" of which a carnal Birth-right is only a shadowy figure. What makes this explanation paradoxical is that precisely because Esau could and did sell his *Birth*-right, it is exposed as not a real Birth-right, "Inheritance," or "Jewels," but a mere type. And what qualifies Little-faith's Jewels or new-birth-right as really real is the quality of being unsellable, accounted as "nothing" by the carnal lights of this world. If Little-faith had, as Hopeful marveled he didn't, managed to sell his Jewels, they would have been exposed as never having been Jewels at all. Conversely, those like Esau, whose "minds are set upon their Lusts," and who will have their fleshly lusts "what ever they cost" (128), manage to sell something that is of infinite value "for a mess of pottage" or some other fleshly satisfaction. But, then, if they can sell it, it never really was anything to begin with.

Christian raves on:

> But *Little-faith* was of another temper, his mind was on things Divine; his livelyhood was upon things that were Spiritual, and from above; Therefore to what end should he that is of such a temper sell his Jewels, (had there been any that would have bought them) to fill his mind with empty things? . . . Though *faithless* ones can for carnal Lusts, pawn, or morgage, or sell what they have, and themselves out right to boot; yet they that have *faith, saving faith*, though but a *little* of it, cannot do so. Here therefore, my Brother, is thy mistake. (128–29)

Passing over, for the moment, Christian's contradictory characterization of Little-faith as first, one who "forgot" about his Jewels for "a great part of the rest of the Journey" due largely to his dismay over losing his Money (127), and then later as one whose "mind was on things Divine," Christian basically defines the things of this world, and those who credit them as real, as things for sale, indeed, things always already sold, things merely of use-value, not truly things, strictly speaking. This includes even the very selves who value such things; such people, asserts Christian, sell "themselves out right" without even knowing it. The once-born are doomed to the status of commodities—things of this world. Esau, then—and Hopeful as well if he does not recognize his mistake—turns out to be no better than any other nothing of this world, like all the other Hypocrites who must be stuffed into the "By-way to Hell" lest they be mistaken by true pilgrims for something real. Their unreality makes their damnation somewhat palatable, but they must also remain real enough for their damnation to count as real, else the pilgrims' salvation would lose its constitutive other.

Christian repeats his characterization of Hopeful as one "of the brisker sort, who will run to and fro in untrodden paths with the shell upon their heads" (129). Presumably, one with the "shell" on his or her head is one who remains in the allegory of this world's reality without knowing it, or put more simply, anyone who mistakes anything "this side the other world" (87) for something real. Richard Baxter, James Nayler reported, once leveled the same charge at Quakers, accusing them of "running away with the shell on [their] head."[27] It is much the same charge that Humphrey Ellis leveled against William Franklin and his "Allegorical Fancies." Nayler and Franklin both presumably mistook themselves for Christ and so cheated others into mistaking them for Christ. In doing so, they confused allegory with reality, mistaking what will come for what is. For Bunyan, such mistaking is the sign of a carnal mind, a mind like those belonging to the rulers of Vanity Fair—the Lord Old man, the Lord Carnal delight, and so on (94– 95). Such are Pharisees, Jews, Papists, and all the other "brisker sort" who cannot quite remember—or more likely, were never chosen to know—that this world is not really real.

Hopeful's mistake is, we are given to understand, largely the result of inexperience. He has not yet encountered the "three Sturdy Rogues" as Little-faith has, and, apparently, as Christian himself has (129–30). So, it seems, have David, Heman, Hezekiah, and Great-Grace himself, that is, Christ as he was tempted by Satan. So also have Paul[28] and Peter; indeed, anyone who has been reborn in/as Christ has undergone this text-experience in which their Jewels or new-birthright was proved real by virtue of its being "mist" by the thieving apostates of this world, not to mention the thieving apostasy of the carnal-minded old self (130–31). In fact, the story of Little-faith is the story of all the twice-born; for the once-born, the story is at once their reality and proof of their being less than really born as sons of God.

"No man," says Christian, "can tell what in that Combat attends us, but he that hath been in the Battle himself" (130). This is why Christian can only "tell" his experience as a story, rendered in a third-person mode that gradually reveals itself as an every-person mode, that is, for every person born of the Spirit and so worthy to be called a person at all. In other words, only Christ has really "been in the battle himself;" all others have been in it by imputation. So only Christ can "tell" the story (ventriloquized through Christian, Paul, and others) and only those newly born in Christ can hear the story as their own. To the rest, Bunyan's unblessed sort of reader, it remains incomprehensible, paradoxical, and self-contradictory. This we might call the damnation-effect of Bunyan's rhetoric.

Hopeful does not have to wait long for his experience. He and Christian no sooner finish their discourse about Little-faith than they also lose their way "at a place where they saw a *way* put it self into their *way*" (132), much as *"Dead-mans Lane"* put itself into Little-faith's way while he slept (125). And "the *Flatterer,*" "a man black of flesh, but covered with a very light Robe," comes down that other way and leads the pilgrims astray (133). Along comes "a shining One"—alias Great-Grace—and sets them on the "right way," but not before giving them a good whipping (134). Now Hopeful, who almost slipped away into being a carnal-minded Jew, proves instead to be, like Little-faith and Christian, an Israelite awaiting fulfillment of the promises, his Jewels, in the "world which is to come."

"Let nothing that is on this side the other world get within you," warns Bunyan's Evangelist; "and above all, look well to your own hearts, and to the lusts thereof; for they are deceitful above all things, and desperately wicked" (87). For Bunyan, the purity of Puritanism is the Calvinist theme of despising the world. The truly pious follow the sure way of "despising this present life and aspiring to celestial immortality" (*Institutes* 3.10.4). The millenarians, Fifth Monarchists, Quakers, and Ranters among whom Bunyan came of age during his army days drew from Protestantism's iconoclasm and the fierce literalism of its hermeneutics a faith in the imminent transformation of this world. Some, like William Franklin and Mary Gadbury, announced that their world, their language, their very flesh, had been transformed in the here and now, that the promise had been fulfilled and that their Jewels were now recognized for what they were. Such a transformation would have meant the end of religion, the end of politics, and the end of history so many believed the apocalypse promised.

Bunyan's "fall" into allegory has the effect of re-containing sectarian chiliasm, more firmly than ever before, in the binary frame of Christianity's two-world order. History, in this frame, does not end; it is emptied out, as if it never really was. It also re-installs difference and deferment with a vengeance. This world and the next, the City of Destruction and the Celestial City, are now figured as infinitely and interminably separate things, as different as unreality is from reality, non-being from being, idols from God. The world waits not so much for redemption, but for annihilation, an annihilation that somehow will prove that it never really existed to begin with. With reality projected so exclusively beyond the horizon of the present world, Bunyan's Christianity has little or no room for Jesus the man, the revolutionary, the merciful lover of humanity. It has become more a religion of brutality than of love, of metaphysics than of mercy. Even Bunyan's Mercie seems instinctively to know how to react to false professors who threaten the purity, the real reality, of true pilgrims:

> *Let them hang and their Names Rot, and their Crimes live forever against them; I think it a high favour that they were hanged afore we came hither, who knows else what they might a done to such poor Women as we are?* Then she turned it into a Song, saying,

> > *Now then, you three, hang there and be a Sign*
> > *To all that shall against the Truth combine:*
> > *And let him that comes after, fear this end,*
> > *If unto Pilgrims he is not a Friend.*
> >
> > (214)

Some are elected to be truly real, and the rest to hang as "a Sign" of the elect's reality. Though they are nothing more than shadowy types of true being to begin with, they do not simply evaporate as illusions, they must be brutally hanged, thrown into Hell. Paradoxically, they must pay a blood-price for never having truly existed. Allegorizing the world helps to make such brutality thinkable.

Christiana and Mercie

THOUGH FALSE PROFESSORS AND THE DECEITFUL HEARTS out of which they are generated make up Bunyan's largest class of threats to a true pilgrim's quest for reality, there is another class of "things this side the other world" that Bunyan's pilgrims must also fear. These are women. In the list of *"all sorts of Vanity"* to be found for sale at Vanity Fair, women are listed three times: "Whores, Bauds, Wives" (88). To be fair, the list also includes such "vanities" as "Husbands, Children, . . . Lives, Blood, Souls," but women are accorded special attention here by place and by number. To love such things is to love "what not." They threaten to perpetuate the pilgrim's attachment to this world of things that are really nothings. A pilgrim who properly loathes himself, his own life, blood, and soul, who has been newly born of the

Spirit and invested with Christ within and without, can hardly risk remaining attached to something as persistently this-worldly as a woman.[29] Be she whore, baud, or wife, the threat is really all the same.

When Christian comes to the cross, "three shining ones" strip away his "Raggs" and clothe him "with change of Raiment" (38). His burden gone, his sins forgiven, Christian is now cast in the role of Christ's bride, to be made one flesh with him. To be married to Christ requires that a man leave behind the shadowy image of true marriage that this world mistakes for the real thing. William Franklin, we recall from chapter 1, announced that when his flesh was "scrap't away" and replaced by the new flesh of Christ, he no longer had any fleshly connection to his wife and children. Divorce from the things of this world means divorce from wives, children, fathers, mothers, all fleshly ties, for only then can one be adopted as a son of God, and married to Christ. In *Grace Abounding*, Bunyan put it this way:

> by this Scripture [2 Corinthians 1:9] I was made to see, that if ever I would suffer rightly, I must first pass a sentence of death upon everything that can properly be called a thing of this life, even to reckon my Self, my Wife, my Children, my health, my enjoyments, and all, as dead to me, and my self as dead to them. *He that loveth father or mother, son or daughter, more than me, is not worthy of me*, Matt. 10:37. (par. 325)

To borrow Augustine's terminology, "everything that can properly be called a thing *in this life*" is precisely everything that is not, "strictly speaking," a thing at all. To achieve union with the only thing that qualifies as a thing, "strictly speaking," one must be divorced from all the things—that is, the nothings—of this life. The "Self," like a wife or child or parent, must come to be regarded as a nothing in preparation for its wedding to the only thing worthy of the designation.

Bunyan's Mr. Stand-fast speaks in the language of the beloved in the Song of Solomon as he readies himself to pass over the river to meet his true husband:

> I have formerly lived by Hear-say, and Faith, but now I go where I shall live by sight, and shall be with him, in whose Company I delight my self.
>
> I have loved to hear my Lord spoken of, and wherever I have seen the print of his Shooe in the Earth, there I have coveted to set my Foot too.

His name has been to me as a *Civit-Box,* yea sweeter then all Perfumes. His Voice to me has been most sweet, and his Countenance, I have more desired then they that have most desired the Light of the Sun. His Word I did use to gather for my Food, and for Antidotes against my Faintings. He has held me, and I have kept me from mine Iniquities. . . . *Take me, for I come unto thee.* (311)

Margaret Olofson Thickstun astutely reads Stand-fast's final speech as Bunyan's displacement of Christiana from the expected role of bride, and his substitution of a male as more appropriate to the role:

He appropriates for his hero Stand-fast's distinctly feminine language, language that in the logic of the allegory belongs in Christiana's mouth. Stand-fast, wearing Christiana's ring, rejoices in the person of the male Beloved, Christ, as he anticipates their union. . . . In this moment, Bunyan completes the displacement of the female implicit in the controlling metaphor of the second part. . . . Bunyan's transfer of the role of the Bride of Christ to Stand-fast excludes Christiana and all other women from that role.[30]

Bunyan's and Franklin's logics are much the same, except in the matter of timing. For Bunyan, full divorce from the flesh is only accomplished in death and full union with Christ in a world that is altogether other. The true pilgrim is, until death, in a constant state of betrothal, careful to keep his wedding garment free from any taint of this world. Nevertheless, the similarities of their logics leave women in much the same place of displacement, regardless of timing. Women are part of the fleshly world that must be left behind, except insofar as they are not really women at all.

Ironically, it is Mrs. Timorous who makes this point most clearly when she warns the newly "awakened" Christiana against going on pilgrimage: "pray for your poor Childrens sake, do not so unwomanly cast away your self" (181). It was, of course, precisely the "manly" thing to do when Christian "put his fingers in his Ears" in response to the cries of his wife and children to return (10). The margin there specifically invites us to compare Christian favorably with Lot's wife, who looked back on Sodom.[31] The margin also invites us to remember Jesus' warning in Luke 14:26: "If any man come to me, and hate not his father, and mother, and wife, and children, and brethren, and sisters, yea, and his own life also, he cannot be my disciple." In leaving his wife and children behind, Christian "plays the man" (240) and resolutely turns his back on the flesh. For Christiana to do likewise would indeed be "unwomanly." As Mrs. Timorous correctly points out, women may not "cast away" themselves as true pilgrimage requires without endangering "the Fruit of thy Body," the children (183).

Women are where the old man comes from. They are the literal tie that binds the old man to this world of destruction. They and the birth they effect are not really real. The shadowy type must pass away if one is truly to experience new birth. How then do women experience new birth? How do they go on true pilgrimage? The answer is that they don't; men must do it for them. Men are women's Christ-substitutes. They also stand in for women in the role of Christ's bride. Women are never truly elect; their salvation comes by way of following elected men in true submission and obedience.

Christiana and Mercie never experience a vision at the cross. Instead they listen silently to Great-heart explain the theology of imputed righteousness, taking Christian's experience as his text (209–12). The women are not relieved of their burden; we never hear that they carry any burden, for they *are* the burden; they are persistently flesh. They must remain so in order to marry (as Mercie is obliged to do), raise children, and attend to the poor, the sick, and the destitute of this world. This is their place:

> When Women keep their places, and Men manage their Worshipping God as they should, we shall have better days for the Church of God, in the World, *Jer.* 29:10, 11, 12, 13.[32]

Instead of being clothed with a new "raiment" in place of fleshly "Raggs," the women and children undergo the ritual cleansing of their bodies known in Jewish tradition as a mikvah, and they are clothed with nothing more mysteriously other-worldly than *"fine Linnen"* (207–8).[33] They are the Israelites who must remain in the flesh, submitting themselves to Jewish rituals that only dimly and imperfectly shadow the true transformations men experience.

At Interpreter's House, the women and children are exposed to lessons that are not only simpler and of a more domestic order than those Christian was exposed to (199–205, esp. 202), but which remain merely emblems for interpretation, unlike Christian's lessons, which progressed in complexity toward "actual" experiences beyond the reach of any interpretive method. Christian knew, as he tells Piety in the House Beautiful, that however much the things of Interpreter's House had ravished his heart, interpretation was not salvation: "I knew I had further to go" (48). For the women, as women, there really is no "further to go." The House Beautiful, and everything else they see on their way, remains emblematic, experience had second-hand, knowledge rather than experience, other men's experience. Even among the Shepherds, where Christian and Hopeful were invited to try their hands and eyes at the Perspective Glass, the women are offered nothing but more emblem lessons (285–86).

In place of the Perspective Glass, Mercie, "being a young, and breeding Woman," we are told, has a longing for the "Looking-glass" that hangs in the Shepherds' "Dining-room" (287). She is afraid that if she cannot have this glass, she may "Miscarry." The margin identifies the glass: *It was the Word of God.* Like the "Picture of a very grave Person" Christian saw at Interpreter's House, this "Glass was one of a thousand" (287, compare with 29). This is the closest Mercie, as a woman, can come to experiencing new birth in Christ. As she is about the womanly business of breeding in the flesh, she longs for a glass that will "present a man, one way, with his own Feature exactly, and turn it but an other way, and it would shew one the very Face and Similitude of the Prince of Pilgrims himself" (287). She is allowed to glimpse, in a gimmicky sort of mirror—her "experience" of the Word—herself as "a man," and as a man, therefore capable of being replaced by Christ, "the Prince of Pilgrims himself." But her desire for this "Glass," which is a far cry from the Perspective Glass offered to Christian or the experiences of "hope and fear" that move him beyond Interpreter's House, is figured here as the kind of quirky desire typical of pregnant women, as if they don't really know what they want, but only approximate truly godly desires in a persistently fleshly way. Mercie, so far as the narrative informs us, remains very much in this world, a "breeding woman."

If the story of Little-faith and his encounter with the "three Sturdy Rogues," Faint-heart, Mistrust, and Guilt, is the epitome of the story of the Prince of Pilgrims and all Pilgrims spiritually reborn as him, it is significant that Christiana and Mercie experience no such encounter. The task of keeping the things from "this side the other world" from getting "within" them is no task for a woman, for women quite simply are such things. Faithful is manly enough to resist the blandishments of Wanton, a version of Potiphar's wife (68), and Mr. Stand-fast manfully resists "the Mistriss of the World," Madam Bubble (300–301), but the women have a more impossible task—they must avoid being made "Women . . . for ever" (195). This is made painfully clear in *The Second Part*'s episode of attempted rape. Unlike Little-faith, who is robbed by personifications of his own worldly-mindedness but actually suffers no real loss, for his Jewels were of no account in this fleshly world, Christiana and Mercie find themselves threatened by "two very *ill-favoured ones* coming down a pace to meet them" (194). They assault the women sexually, "as if they would embrace them," and Christiana and Mercie kick them away, saying "we have no Money to loose being Pilgrims as ye see." The men reply that it is not money they seek, "but are come out to tell you, that if you will but grant one small request which we shall ask, we will make Women of you for ever." "We intend," they assure the women, "no hurt to your lives, 'tis another thing we would have" (194–95). Both the women then shriek "Murder, Murder," and the Reliever—their version of Great-grace—comes to their rescue.

Apparently the women have neither Jewels nor Money, neither the promises nor the assurances even Little-faith had. They certainly have no "parchment-roll" like Christian's. What they do have, what threatens to qualify them as "Women . . . for ever" is sexuality. Had these rapists succeeded as did Little-faith's thieves in getting what they came for, the women, we are assured, would have been eternally undone. The Reliever interprets the rapists' actions as attempts to "make my Lords People to Transgress" (195). Had they been raped, the transgression would have been Christiana's and Mercie's, because, says the Reliever, they are "but weak Women" and so they should have asked for "a Conductor" (196). Little-faith's Jewels cannot be stolen, for they are not things of this world. He can be robbed of his Money and no real harm is done him. The women, on the other hand, can be robbed of their salvation, precisely by what is effectively described as permitting themselves to be raped and so being made "Women" for ever, eternally disqualified from salvation as the "Bride of Christ." To be a forever a "Woman" is to be forever one of the things of this world, that is, a nothing.[34]

Christiana, of course, passes over into the next world, but not before she is effectively un-womaned. Unlike Christian, who set out for the Celestial City resolutely leaving all behind, Christiana must set all her worldly affairs in order. She is allowed ten days in which to consult with Mr. Great-heart, "her Guide," comfort herself that her children still bear the "Mark" of the elect, distribute her worldly goods among the poor, and surrender to Mr. Stand-fast "a Ring," presumably her wedding ring (305). Up to this point, she has pursued her pilgrimage as if it were a quest to be reunited with her dear husband, Christian. Indeed, the message that warns her to prepare for crossing over is addressed, not to Christiana the pilgrim, but to "one *Christiana,* the Wife of *Christian* the Pilgrim" (304). But union with Christ means becoming, not Christian's bride, but Christ's. In heaven, there will be no more marriage, only the true marriage of being made a member of Christ's body. Accordingly, Christiana gives her wedding band to Stand-fast, who speaks his own last words in the voice of the Shulamite wife, the true bride of Christ. No longer a wife, no longer a "young, and breeding woman," Christiana is un-womaned in preparation for her final journey. Only then can she fully receive the "Token" sent her by her true lover and husband, Christ. The "Token" is the closest Bunyan ever comes to a Petrarchan image: *"An Arrow with a Point sharpened with Love, let easily into her Heart, which by degrees wrought so effectually with her, that at the time appointed she must be gone"* (305). Christian waded into the depths of the River with one body and emerged transformed on the other side of death, but Christiana's body is even more "the body of this flesh" than Christian's. It must die twice: once as a woman, and then as an un-womaned being; only then is she fit to be truly a Bride of Christ: *"I come Lord, to be with thee and bless thee"* (306).

Christiana's crossing over is the closest Bunyan ever comes to representing the salvation of an old self—a body or a thing of this world. She is called into eternity, not as a pilgrim, but as "the Wife of *Christian* the Pilgrim," in apparent contradiction of the principle that wives, like all other things of this world, are really nothings and so can have no being in the next. By rights she ought to be the quintessential false professor, not just stubbornly attached to the things "on this side," but one of those things herself. Mercie, as long as she is a wife and a "breeding woman," is also one of those things, materially attached to the world of flesh and so disqualified from living "in Christ." Nevertheless, we are led to expect that she also will one day be "saved." In a sense, the word *saved* applies to Christiana and Mercie quite differently than it applies to Christian, Faithful, and Hopeful. These women, we are confident, will be saved from being "made women forever," but they are also—especially Mercie—saved for the peculiarly this-worldly labor of generating sons, the raw material for new birth (or not). However much Bunyan insists on an absolute distinction between this world and the next, a distinction under which all things "on this side" are nothings and all unseen things of the next are exclusively real, Mercie simply cannot be clearly assigned to one side or the other. For all her worldliness—she is a kind of good Samaritan, practicing what Evangelicals used disapprovingly to call a "social gospel," as opposed to a theological gospel—she cannot be absolutely lost, any more than Bunyan could afford the absolute loss of false professors, worldly wisemen, or Vanity Fair. Mothers, carnal mothers, are a kind of epitome of fleshliness, but they are also the "hard kernel" (to invoke Žižek once again) at the center of Bunyan's allegorical ideology that betrays the allegorical two-world ontology as impossible.

This hard kernel may be energetically denied, as Bunyan's treatment of Christiana's crossing tries to deny her womanhood, but it remains no less essential to the ideology even as it threatens to expose it as nonsense. Mercie, like Tamar, Ruth, Bathsheba, even the Virgin Mary, cannot be really newly born, but she cannot be destroyed either. If this is so, then the same needs to be said for all the other others constitutive of Christian's redeemed self, all the others upon which he pasted the exteriorized sinfulness of his old self, even the old self and the world that the gospel says "God so loved" (John 3:16). But Bunyan fails to acknowledge this; he fails, as orthodox Puritanism also failed, to acknowledge how much Christian needed an old self, a Jew-self, the false professor, and the misbeliever in order to know himself as really real. Puritanism can never purify itself of the shadowy types without purifying itself out of existence. Perhaps that is why it is relentlessly, sometimes hysterically, about the business of finding new others every day—"faggots," perverts, apostates, world-loving socialists, non-Christians and false Christians in endless variety. We would do better, I think, to teach ourselves to be content with being less than "really real" and so save everyone a lot of pain.

Notes

Chapter 1

1. Judith Butler, *Gender Trouble: Feminism and the Subversion of Identity* (New York: Routledge, 1990), 93.

2. Humphrey Ellis, *Pseudochristus,: Or, A True and Faithful Relation of the Grand Impostures, Abominable Practices, Horrid Blasphemies, Gross Deceits; Lately Spread Abroad and Acted . . . by William Franklin and Mary Gadbury, and Their Companions* (London, 1650), 11.

3. Sometime around 1647, Arise Evans, a Welsh minister, told the Deputy Recorder of London that he was the Lord his God. See Christopher Hill, *The World Turned Upside Down: Radical Ideas during the English Revolution* (New York: Viking, 1972), 200 (hereafter cited as *WTUD*); see also *A Catalogue of the Severall Sects and Opinions in England and other Nations* (London 1647), and Phyllis Mack, "Women Prophets during the English Civil War," *Feminist Studies* 8 (1982), 19–45.

4. Thomas Tany, *The Nations Right in* Magna Charta *Discussed with the Thing Called Parliament,* ed. Andrew Hopton (London: Aporia Press, 1988), 22.

5. On this particularly colorful figure, see Hill, *WTUD,* 181; David S. Katz, *Philo-Semitism and the Readmission of the Jews to England* (Oxford: Clarendon Press, 1982), 107–20; Richard L. Greaves and Robert Zaller, eds. *Biographical Dictionary of British Radicals in the Seventeenth Century,* 3 vols. (Brighton, Sussex: Harvester Press, 1983); Nigel Smith, *Perfection Proclaimed: Language and Literature in English Radical Religion, 1640–1660* (Oxford: Clarendon Press, 1989), 214–18, 229–307.

6. Robins, Tany, Muggleton, and Reeves were all fascinated with Jews and things Judaic. Tany, it is said, circumcised himself; Robins was reported to have "raised Cain, Judas, the prophet Jeremiah, and Benjamin the son of Jacob from the dead" (Katz, *Philo-Semitism*, 108). Tany and Robins appear along with assorted alleged Ranters in *A List of Some of the Grand Blasphemers and Blasphemies Which was given in to The Committee for Religion* (London, 1654), reprinted in Tany, *The Nations Right*, 33–34 (hereafter cited as *Grand Blasphemers*).

7. Lodowick Muggleton, *The Acts of the Witnesses of the Spirit* (London, 1699), 4, 21.

8. The language is Margaret Woodward's in Ellis, 39.

9. *The Cry of a Stone: or a Relation of Something Spoken in Whitehall by Anna Trapnel, being in the Visions of God* (London, 1654); and *Anna Trapnel's Report & Plea, or a Narrative of her Journey from London into Cornwal* (London, 1654).

10. On Nayler, see *A True Narrative of the Examination, Tryall, & Sufferings of James Nayler* (London, 1657) and Hill, *WTUD*, 186–207.

11. Some more instances from *Grand Blasphemers* are: "*Margaret Hollis*, singing antiquely, and in rude postures, said, *That that was Religion*. Committed to *New Prison*, 1651"; "*Mary Vanlop* said *She had served a false God, and had now found the true god to serve, who was a man whom she followed*. Committed to the *Gate-house*, 1651"; "*Mary Adams*, living about *Tillingham* in *Essex*, said about 1652. *That she was conceived with childe by the Holy Ghost, and that all the Gospel that had been taught heretofore, was false; and that which was within her, was the true Messias:* Was imprisoned and delivered (after sore travail, eight days together) of an ugly dead Monster, and her self after she had lain some time rotting and stinking, with filthy Botches and Boyls, took a Knife when she was alone, and ripped up her own Bowels, and so died, 1652"; "Mrs. *Gay* at *Knightsbridge* said, *That she could serve God as well in her bed, or at work in her Garden on the Lords dayes, as at any Ordinances at any meeting place*. About 1651 she was grievously afflicted without the use of her limbs, bed-ridden about a year, under a sad dispaire, and horrible torment of Devils, and so dyed."

12. John Bunyan, *Some Gospel Truths Opened*, in *The Miscellaneous Works of John Bunyan*, vol. 1, ed. T. L. Underwood and Roger Sharrock (Oxford: Clarendon Press, 1976), 15. John R. Knott Jr. notes that "the distinction between notional and experimental knowledge is a crucial one for Puritan thought" in *The Sword of the Spirit: Puritan Responses to the Bible* (Chicago: University of Chicago Press, 1980), 47. Knott repeats the point even more cogently in "'Thou must live upon my word': Bunyan and The Bible," in N. H. Keeble, ed., *John Bunyan: Conventicle and Parnassus: Tercentenary Essays* (Oxford: Clarendon Press, 1988), 156–57. See also Thomas Hyatt Luxon, "The

Pilgrim's Passive Progress: Luther and Bunyan on Talking and Doing, Word and Way," *ELH* 53 (1986): 73–98. In "Jordan" (II), George Herbert uses "notions" in much the same sense (*The Poems of George Herbert,* ed. F. E. Hutchinson [Oxford: Oxford University Press, 1961], 93, line 7). Bunyan, of course, records many instances of what are virtually physical experiences of the Word in his autobiography, *Grace Abounding to the Chief of Sinners,* edited by Roger Sharrock (Oxford: Oxford University Press, 1962), par. 204, 206 (hereafter cited as *GA*). See also Peter J. Carlton, "Bunyan: Language, Convention, Authority," *ELH* 51 (1984): 17.

13. John Calvin, *Institutes of the Christian Religion,* trans. Henry Beveridge, 2 vols. (Grand Rapids, Mich.: W. B. Eerdmans, 1983), 3.9.1–2 (hereafter cited as *Institutes*). Calvin emphasizes the ontological divide between this life and the next: "For there is no medium between the two things: the earth must either be worthless in our estimation, or keep us enslaved by an intemperate love of it."

14. In explicit opposition to the neoplatonism and monism of Catholic humanism, Calvin describes all of Creation, especially the human self, as constitutively not-God. What binds the knowledge of God and the knowledge of self so intimately together, says Calvin, is constitutive difference. "Man" comes to know himself truly by recognizing himself as radically not-God, and conversely he comes to recognize the true God as radically not-self (*Institutes,* 1.1.1–3). "Man" is not a synecdoche for God, a demigod, a fallen God, the divinity in the deepest recesses of his being eventually to be revealed. Rather, for Calvin, "Man" is quite strictly an image of God. Calvin's favorite metaphor for the traces by which God reveals himself in Creation is that of engravings, marks, traces as ontologically distinct from himself, as Saussure imagined writing was distinct from language. Expressions like "stamped," "inscribed" (1.3.1), "engraven" (1.3.3, 1.4.4, 1.5.1), "portrayed" (1.5.1), "images of the invisible world," "a language" (1.5.1), "structure," "proofs" (1.5.2), "a bright mirror," "a stamp" (1.5.5), "a picture" (1.5.10), a book (1.6.1), "this most glorious theatre" (1.6.2), "his image imprinted" (1.6.3) far outnumber expressions like "the divine presence within us" (1.5.6) and thus tend to register Calvin's sense of God's traces in the world as representational rather than immanent. Another frequent word, "manifestations," might equivocate between representation and immanence, but the weight of the expressions cited above tends to disallow a sense of immanence that comes too close to monism. God is not, for Calvin, consubstantial with his creation. Calvin's favorite trope both for Christ's humanity and human divinity is that of clothing. Man was originally "script of the divine attire" (1.1.1) and Jesus "hid under a humble clothing of flesh" (2.14.3). Each is an allegorical "veil" for the other. This world and those

in it at best represent God, and in representing God, remain ontologically other than God.

15. "When it is said that the Word was made flesh, we must not understand it as if he were either changed into flesh, or confusedly intermingled with flesh, but that he made choice of the Virgin's womb as a temple in which he might dwell. He who was the Son of God became the Son of man, *not by confusion of substance,* but by unity of person. For we maintain, that the divinity was so conjoined and united with the humanity, that the entire properties of each nature remain entire, and yet the two natures constitute only one Christ. If, in human affairs, anything analogous to this great mystery can be found, the most apposite similitude seems to be that of man, who obviously consists of two substances, neither of which, however, is so intermingled with the other as that both do not retain their own properties. For neither is soul body, nor is body soul" (*Institutes,* 2.14.1, italics added).

16. Lana Cable, "Milton's Iconoclastic Truth," in *Politics, Poetics, and Hermeneutics in Milton's Prose,* ed. David Loewenstein and James Grantham Turner (Cambridge: Cambridge University Press, 1990), 135.

17. Philip Knachel's Folger edition of *Eikon Basilike* (Ithaca, N.Y.: Cornell University Press, 1966) omits the frontispiece, but it can conveniently be found in Merritt Y. Hughes, ed., *John Milton: Complete Poems and Major Prose* (Indianapolis: The Odyssey Press, 1957), 816. *Eikon Basilike* was a stupendously successful best-seller, reaching 35 editions before the end of 1649 (Knachel, xiv).

18. Katz, *Philo-Semitism,* 121–22.

19. Muggleton, *The Acts of the Witnesses of the Spirit,* 61. Muggleton confessed that he passed several years outside of organized religion altogether. He simply could not bring himself to believe in the bodiless soul and the "God without a body" so prominent in Christian discourse (13–14, 59).

20. Quoted by Roland H. Bainton, "The Bible in the Reformation," in *The Cambridge History of the Bible,* ed. S. L. Greenslade (Cambridge: Cambridge University Press, 1963), 3:20.

21. See B. A. Gerrish, *The Old Protestantism and the New: Essays on the Reformation Heritage* (Chicago: University of Chicago Press, 1982), 116. Consistent with his doctrine that piety, or right belief and a proper attitude, is the prerequisite to knowing God and knowing self, Calvin insists that Christ is present in the physical elements of the Eucharist, and so in the person of the communicant, only if he or she has received the gift of correct belief. The fusing of sign (sacrament) and thing signified (the body and blood of Christ) is contingent upon piety and is inexplicable. Without piety, one receives only empty signs; with piety, the physical signs themselves are dispensable (Gerrish, 114). And

an important feature of piety, or correct belief, is zealously to maintain the distinction of Christ's "two natures" which are "united, but not confused" (*Institutes,* 2.14.4). The Johannine announcement, "The Word was made flesh," Calvin understands as one of those "modes of expression" improperly understood by shameful heretics and purveyors of "impious fiction" as confusing Christ's "two natures" (2.14.4–8). Christ's body was and is a "temple" for his divinity to dwell in, and as such the dwelling must be carefully distinguished from the dweller. What's more, the physical body of Christ, insists Calvin, has been and remains "in heaven" ever since the Ascension (*Institutes,* 4.17.26; see also Gerrish, 116). If Christ is present to and in Christians in this world, it is a Christ without a body. Whatever the subtleties, slippages, and contradictions of Calvin's and Luther's Christologies, popular Protestantism was clear on the absence of Christ's body from the world of lived experience: Franklin's judges told him "That he could not be the Christ, Christ being in heaven at the right hand of the Father, as the Scripture testifieth" (Ellis, 41).

22. Thomas Cranmer, *Book of Homilies* (London, 1647), B2.

23. René Descartes, *Discourse on Method and Selected Writings,* trans. John Veitch (New York: E. P. Dutton, 1951): "I observed that I could suppose that I had no body" (28). When Descartes considered theology as a possible course of study, he concluded that since the way to heaven "is not less open to the most ignorant than to the most learned, and that revealed truths which lead to heaven are above our comprehension . . . there was need of some special help from heaven and of being more than man" (6). Descartes makes explicit and then resists what people like Franklin and Nayler intuit and then act upon. See also Michel Foucault, *Madness and Civilization,* trans. Richard Howard (New York: Vintage, 1973) as well as Jacques Derrida, "Cogito and the History of Madness," in *Writing and Difference,* trans. Alan Bass (Chicago: University of Chicago Press, 1978), 31–63, and Felman, *Writing and Madness,* trans. Martha Noel Evans (Ithaca: Cornell University Press, 1985), 27.

24. Edmund Calamy, *The Monster of Sinful Self-Seeking, Anatomized* (London, 1655), 8.

25. "Were not the soul some kind of essence separated from the body, Scripture would not teach that we dwell in houses of clay, and at death remove from a tabernacle of flesh; that we put off that which is corruptible, in order that, at the last day, we may finally receive according to the deeds done in the body. These, and similar passages which everywhere occur, not only clearly distinguish the soul from the body, but by giving it the name of man, intimate that it is his principal part" (*Institutes,* 1.15.2).

26. "The bodies of men . . . in this life . . . they are vile bodies . . . bodies of vileness . . . the Greek . . . signifies *abjectum conditionem,* a vile and abject

condition." (Edmund Calamy, *The Doctrine of the Bodies Fragility* [London, 1655], 1). On the "abject" self in Christian thought, see Julia Kristeva, *The Powers of Horror: An Essay on Abjection,* trans. Leon S. Roudiez (New York: Columbia University Press, 1982), 1–6.

27. Hill, *WTUD,* 310–12; Cohn, *The Pursuit of the Millennium* (London: Secker and Warburg, 1957). Other recent studies of popular religion and culture in seventeenth-century England include Barry Reay, *The Quakers and the English Revolution* (New York: St. Martin's Press, 1985) and Barry Reay, ed., *Popular Culture in Seventeenth-Century England* (New York: St. Martin's Press, 1985); as well as Keeble, *John Bunyan,* and Smith, *Perfection Proclaimed,* cited above.

28. Hill, *A Tinker and a Poor Man: John Bunyan and His Church, 1628–1688* (New York: Alfred A. Knopf, 1989), 139.

29. Ellis, *Pseudochristus,* 56–62. Quakers, though not named specifically, seem also to figure in this allegedly anti-Christian group, as those who "set up a *teaching of the Spirit within themselves*" in contempt of Scripture (Ellis, 56).

30. I borrow these terms from Judith Butler's *Gender Trouble* as apt descriptions of the "subversive bodily acts" of radical antinomians like Franklin and Gadbury, but I also recognize that they do not apply here in quite the way Butler uses them. Ellis notwithstanding, it is hard to think that Franklin and Gadbury intended to parody (in the sense of make fun of) anything. Neither is their performance, strictly speaking, what Fredric Jameson calls pastiche ("Postmodernism and Consumer Society," in *The Anti-Aesthetic: Essays on Postmodern Culture,* ed. Hal Foster [Port Townsend, WA: Bay Press, 1983]). What's more, a serious pseudo-Christ—as I take Franklin to be—is not intentionally parodying "the very notion of an original" (Butler, 138), though I believe his claim to be the original ultimately has that effect.

31. Quoted from Luther's *Reply to Emser* by F. W. Loefscher in "Luther and the Problem of Authority in Religion," *Princeton Theological Review* 16 (1918): 529.

32. William Tyndale, *The Obedience of a Christian Man,* in *Doctrinal Treatises and Introductions to Different Portions of the Holy Scriptures,* ed. Henry Walter (Cambridge: Cambridge University Press, 1848; reprinted 1968), 304.

33. John Weemse, *Exercitations Divine, Containing Diverse Questions and Solutions for the Right Understanding of the Scriptures* (London, 1634).

34. John Calvin, *Commentaries on the Epistles of Paul to the Galatians and Ephesians,* trans. William Pringle (Edinburgh: The Calvin Translation Society, 1854), 135 (hereafter cited as *Commentaries on Galatians*).

35. See Hill, *WTUD,* chap. 11, and James I, *Basilikon Doron,* in *Images of English Puritanism: A Collection of Contemporary Sources 1589–1646,* ed. Law-

rence Sasek (Baton Rouge: Louisiana State University Press, 1989), 219; and John Taylor, *A Swarme of Sectaries,* in Sasek, 298. The term "lesbian rule" denotes "a mason's rule made of lead, which could be bent to fit the curves of a moulding" (*Oxford English Dictionary*). Aristotle uses the lesbian rule as an emblematic illustration of how a decree, if it is to be applied with equity to cases unanticipated by legislators, must be "adapted to the facts," just as a lesbian rule "adapts itself to the shape of a stone and is not rigid" (*The Nichomachean Ethics of Aristotle,* trans. David Ross [London: Oxford University Press, 1954], 5.10.7). In Reformation and Puritan literature, the term seems always to be used derisively, even though Protestant and Puritan hermeneutics and soteriology frequently encouraged the personal application of Scripture, read in the Spirit, to the individual Christian's experience. Perhaps there must always be something "lesbian" about personal, especially idiosyncratic, applications of Scripture, and it seems that having instituted and encouraged widespread personal Bible reading, Reformers soon came to fear many of its effects.

36. Samuel Parker, *A Discourse of Ecclesiasticall Polity* (London 1670), 75.

37. Margaret Woodward's "literal" understanding of Franklin's accession to a glorified body is careful to preserve his original (carnal?) hair, following Jesus' promise to his disciples in the apocalyptic section of Luke 21:8–28, specifically verse 18. Such hyperliteralism was not uncommon among sectarians, and, I will argue, proceeds according to a very perceptible (if perverse) logic from even mainstream Puritan teaching and preaching. Ellis himself readily interpreted the whole Franklin-Gadbury affair as a literal fulfillment of Luke 21:8: "for many shall come in my name, saying, I am Christ; and the time draweth near."

38. I refer to Louis Althusser's list of "Ideological State Apparatuses" in his essay "Ideology and Ideological State Apparatuses (Notes toward an Investigation)," in *Lenin and Philosophy and Other Essays,* trans. Ben Brewster (New York: Monthly Review Press, 1971), 143. Of course, Althusser's distinction between public and private institutions (144) does not map very well onto seventeenth-century England, where the church, and even the family, are not private or nonpublic in the way we have come to recognize—or misrecognize—them. William Dell's *Right Reformation: or The Reformation of the Church of the New Testament, Represented in Gospel-Light* (London, 1646) is a fascinating example of an early attempt to redefine ecclesiastical powers as entirely ideological rather than repressive and to exclude the state from power over the properly reformed Christian. But even Dell assigns the magistrate absolute repressive power over "those that are *outwardly wicked,*" the state "having power over their *persons, estates,* and *lives,*" as opposed to their souls (*Right Reformation,* 125). In Franklin's case, the ideology of inwardness has

failed to keep him and his followers in order because they have interpreted it outwardly; therefore the repressive arm of the state exercises its full force. Dell was a popular preacher in the Army and in London; he invited Bunyan to preach to his London congregation in 1659, and he published with Giles Calvert, a printer often distrained and prosecuted for printing Quaker pamphlets. See also Greaves and Zaller, *Biographical Dictionary of British Radicals*.

39. For a very clear (if partisan) summary of Christian hermeneutics, see A. J. Maas, "Exegesis (Biblical)," in *The Catholic Encyclopedia* (New York: The Encyclopedia Press, 1913), especially 5:693–94.

40. For a very useful discussion of Paul's concepts of the body and the flesh, see John A. T. Robinson, *The Body: A Study in Pauline Theology*, Studies in Biblical Theology (Chicago: Henry Regnery Company, 1952), especially 31–32.

41. The quotation is from the title of A. T. Lincoln's study of Pauline eschatology, *Paradise Now and Not Yet: Studies in the Role of the Heavenly Dimension in Paul's Thought with Special Reference to His Eschatology* (Cambridge: Cambridge University Press, 1981).

42. See Hill, *WTUD*, 77–78.

43. John Calvin, *Commentaries on the Epistle of Paul the Apostle to the Romans*, trans. John Owen (Edinburgh: The Calvin Translation Society, 1849), 221.

44. Robinson, *The Body*, 79–80. See similar language in Victor Furnish's commentary on 2 Corinthians in *II Corinthians: The Anchor Bible*, vol. 32, trans. Victor Paul Furnish (Garden City, N.Y.: Doubleday, 1984), 332–33.

45. "My little children," Paul addresses the Galatian converts, "of whom I travail in birth again until Christ be formed in you . . ."

46. Barbara Lewalski, *Protestant Poetics and the Seventeenth-Century Religious Lyric* (Princeton: Princeton University Press, 1979), 132–39. Lewalski cites examples from Calvin, Luther, Perkins, Donne, and others of the way a Protestant of the seventeenth century was "likely to view himself as a correlative type with the Old Testament Israelites, located on the same spiritual [that is, ontological] plane and waiting like them for the fulfillment of all the signs in Christ at the end of time" (132). Though Lewalski pursues this to quite different conclusions, I take this to amount to a virtual allegorization of the Puritan self and its worldly experience, much as medieval Christian exegesis had allegorized the ancient Israelites, their history, and their worship.

47. John Calvin, *The Psalmes of David and others*, [trans. Arthur Golding] (London, 1571), pt. I, folio 164· as quoted in Lewalski, *Protestant Poetics*, 133.

48. Ellis writes that Gadbury, unlike Franklin, signed her recantation and confession "by making her mark, she not having skill to write her name" (Ellis, 45). Her inability to write does not necessarily imply an inability to read, but there is no indication in Ellis's account that she could or did read.

49. Ellis, 8; for Sedgwick, see Greaves and Zaller, *Biographical Dictionary of British Radicals*. Gadbury is also said to have frequented the sermons of Henry Jessey and John Goodwin. Jessey was both a Baptist and a Fifth Monarchist, and was involved in a project to secure the return of the Jews to England. According to Richard Greaves ("Conscience, Liberty, and the Spirit: Bunyan and Nonconformity," in Keeble, *John Bunyan*, 35), Jessey was among those London preachers recommended by Bunyan and the Bedford congregation to anyone sojourning in London. Jessey contributed a statement of support to Bunyan's *Differences in Judgement about Water Baptism No Bar to Communion* (1673). Sedgwick was a Bedfordshire native, army chaplain, and millenarian, fascinated with the likes of Lodowick Muggleton and James Nayler. See John Reeve, *Sacred Remains: or, A Divine Appendix; Being A Collection of Several Treatises, Epistolary and Publick* ([London] 1657), 1–4.

50. William Sedgwick, *The Spiritual Madman, or A Prophesie Concerning, The King, the Parliament, London, the Army; of the admirable fulnesse, and compleatnesse, of the restauration, and satisfaction of all Interests* ([London], 1648), 6, 4–5.

51. William Sedgwick, *Zions Deliverance and her Friends Duty: or The Grounds of Expecting, and Means of Procuring Jerusalems Restauration. In a Sermon Preached at a Publicke Fast, Before the Honourable House of Commons* (London, 1643), 11.

52. See Ivy Schweitzer's illuminating discussion of this figure in New England Puritan poetry and sermons in *The Work of Self-Representation: Lyric Poetry in Colonial New England* (Chapel Hill: University of North Carolina Press, 1991), 22–35.

53. Richard Sibbes, *The Complete Works*, ed. Alexander Balloch Grosart (Edinburgh: James Nichol, 1862–1963), 4:265

54. See the chapter on Sibbes in Knott, *The Sword of the Spirit*.

55. William Blake offers a graphic version of such equivocation in his illustrations of Bunyan's Christian and his "burden" in *The Pilgrim's Progress* (illustrated with 29 watercolor paintings by William Blake, edited by G. B. Harrison [New York: Limited Editions Press, 1941]). In plate 2, the burden appears as a physical deformity on Christian's back, complete with vascular and muscular connections. At the Slough of Despond (plate 5) it looks like a separate human (dead?) body. As Christian listens to Worldly-Wiseman and reads in his "Book," it appears as a deforming hump (plate 7). Finally, at the

Wicket Gate (plate 10) and at the Cross (plate 14), it looks like a detachable rucksack. A more accessible selection of Blake's watercolors (including those cited here) is collected in *The Pilgrim's Progress from This World to That Which is to Come,* illustrated with watercolors by William Blake (New York: The Heritage Press, 1942). Blake illustrates Bunyan's burden as registering in its various shapes and forms the back and forth process of Christian's othering from himself and his flesh. As pictures, the illustrations also register the imprecision of the categories of literal and figurative.

56. J. S. Preus, *From Shadow to Promise: Old Testament Interpretation from Augustine to the Young Luther* (Cambridge, Mass.: Harvard University Press, 1969), 33.

57. Bernhard Blumenkranz, "Augustin et les juifs," *Recherches Augustiniennes* 1 (1958), as quoted in Jill Robbins, *Prodigal Son/Elder Brother: Interpretation and Alterity in Augustine, Petrarch, Kafka, Levinas* (Chicago: University of Chicago Press, 1991), 114. Robbins's book opens with a brilliant analysis of Augustinian hermeneutics and its sense of "the Judaic," though she nowhere considers that Protestant hermeneutics and its sense of "the Judaic" might be different. J. S. Preus's overview of medieval hermeneutics details how Augustine's categories shape medieval hermeneutics largely until Luther's scholia on the Psalms. See also Harold Bloom, "'Before Moses Was, I Am': The Original and the Belated Testaments," in *Notebooks in Cultural Analysis,* vol. 1, ed. Norman F. Cantor and Nathalia King (Durham, N.C.: Duke University Press, 1984), 3; Mark Taylor, *Erring: A Postmodern A/theology* (Chicago: University of Chicago Press, 1984), 55–56. None of these scholars takes special note of Reformation Christianity, which, I will argue, is significantly different.

58. Preus, 16–20. Augustine continues: "The promises there announced . . . are earthly and temporal, good things of this corruptible flesh, even though they may be figures (*figurentur*) of the eternal and heavenly goods belonging to the New Covenant. Whereas now there is promised a good of the heart itself, a good of the mind, a spiritual good which is an intelligible good" (quoted in Preus, 18).

59. "Out of the theological and historical limbo of 'umbra' to which the people of Israel had been consigned in most medieval exegesis, a 'remnant' emerged, which Luther called the 'faithful synagogue,' and which became the concrete example to which even the Christian church itself should conform. The word of promise, and faith as *expectatio,* gradually undercut tropology as the 'sensus ultimatus" of Luther's exegesis, allowing the letter—the clear and naked words of the text—to take on a theological significance not accorded them before, and requiring not grace as *intellectus* and *caritas,* but faith. It was

the word of promise, not *conformitas christi* via tropological signification, that led Luther away from medieval theology to the exclusive '*sola* fide' and '*solo* verbo' of Reformation theology." (Preus, 268)

60. *The Soul's Conflict,* in Sibbes, *The Complete Works,* 1:277.

61. Thus Calvin dwells at length on the human inability to "read" God's allegory in Creation, even in himself, without the aid of the Spirit's revelation in Scripture (*Institutes,* 1.5.11).

62. *Exposition on the Psalms* LVI.9. Translated by Robbins in *Prodigal Son,* 6.

63. It is tempting in the light of arguments I will pursue in chapter 3 to see in Sibbes's use of the word *carry* an example of Pauline and Puritan redefinitions of birthing and motherhood as "carnal" allegories of true birth and true spiritual motherhood, which are insistently masculine experiences, but the *Oxford English Dictionary* offers no contemporary examples of this sense of the word *carry.*

64. "The Author's Apology for His Book," in *The Pilgrim's Progress from this World to That which is to Come,* ed. James Blanton Wharey, 2d ed. by Roger Sharrock (Oxford: The Clarendon Press, 1967), 1 (hereafter cited as *PP*).

65. This is a stronger version of Hill's observation that "just as Oliver Cromwell aimed to bring about the kingdom of God on earth and founded the British Empire, so Bunyan wanted the millennium and got the novel" (*A Tinker and a Poor Man,* 368). That is, Bunyan reinstalled the allegory that registers this world as fiction.

66. Holding all these contradictions both apart and together is allegory, what Paul de Man called the "rhetoric of temporality," which installs and maintains deferral and so difference. Using de Man's terms, we could say that Reformation thought, especially in its Puritan versions, pushes asymptotically closer to symbolism and a cult of the transcendental moment outside of time, but insofar as it remains orthodox, it always retreats from the threshold of such transgression even as it locates its hope and the object of its faith on the other side of an allegorical ontological divide.

> In the world of the symbol it would be possible for the image to coincide with the substance, since the substance and its representation do not differ in their being but only in their extension: they are part and whole of the same set of categories. Their relationship is one of simultaneity, which, in truth, is spatial in kind, and in which the intervention of time is merely a matter of contingency, whereas in the world of allegory, time is the originary constitutive category. . . . Whereas the symbol postulates the possibility of an identity or identification, allegory designates primarily a distance in relation to its own origin, and, re-

nouncing the nostalgia and the desire to coincide, it establishes its language in the void of this temporal difference. In so doing, it prevents the self from an illusory identification with the non-self, which is now fully, though painfully, recognized as a non-self. ("The Rhetoric of Temporality," in *Blindness and Insight: Essays in the Rhetoric of Contemporary Criticism*, 2d ed., rev. [Minneapolis: University of Minnesota Press, 1983], 206–7)

Christianity, however, never, even in its most reformed mode, renounces nostalgia and desire. Even as reformers preach an experimental understanding of the Word, their own orthodoxy insists that the Word is never fully and immediately experienced in what we familiarly call the here and now. They preserve allegorical ontology even as they rail against allegorical exegesis and a faith based on tropes. If the Word is always literal, then experience itself is but an allegorical shadow of the life to come.

67. Stanley Fish, *Self-Consuming Artifacts: The Experience of Seventeenth-Century Literature* (Berkeley: University of California Press, 1972), 264

68. I refer to the theory Fish elaborates in his "Appendix" to *Self-Consuming Artifacts*, "Literature in the Reader: Affective Stylistics," 383–427. Fish calls his method of reading and interpretation "not a method at all" (425), which, I will argue, is precisely what Bunyan tries to recommend—a method of reading that denies it is a method.

Chapter 2

1. Augustine, *On Christian Doctrine*, trans. D. W. Robertson Jr. (Indianapolis: Bobbs-Merrill, 1958), 2.13.20, 47. (Hereafter cited as *CD*).

2. Christopher Kendrick, "Milton and Sexuality: A Symptomatic Reading of *Comus*," in *Re-membering Milton: Essays on the Texts and Traditions*, ed. Mary Nyquist and Margaret W. Ferguson (New York: Methuen, 1987), 44.

3. For a very intelligent account of the metaphysics that underwrites Milton's attacks on the Bishops as "more fleshly," see Stephen M. Fallon, *Milton Among the Philosophers: Poetry and Materialism in Seventeenth-Century England* (Ithaca: Cornell University Press, 1991), 83–89.

4. *CD*, 1.1.3; in Robertson's translation, p. 9. Subsequent references to this text will be noted parenthetically by book, chapter and paragraph, as well as by Robertson's page number.

5. Similar expressions are found in 2:17–18, 4:14–15, 8:17, 12:17, 21:4, 26:54, and 27:9, not to mention those in the other gospel accounts.

6. As I rewrote this chapter, David Koresh, who called himself Christ, was still holed up in his Mount Carmel compound near Waco, Texas, waiting for God to announce "the fullness of time" and the "end of history."

7. In *Tetrachordon*, Milton tells us that it "is generally beleev'd" that "even in the jolliest expressions" the Song of Songs is meant "to figure the spousals of the Church with Christ" and "sings a thousand raptures between those two lovely ones far on the hither side of carnall enjoyment" (Don M. Wolfe, gen. ed., *Complete Prose Works of John Milton* [New Haven: Yale University Press, 1953–1982], 2:597).

8. Lewalski (*Protestant Poetics*, 117) advances this possibility but then dismisses it by saying, "From a literary point of view, at least, it is not." Neither reformers nor sectarian preachers like Bunyan were much in the habit of choosing a "literary" over a "Godly" or "Gospel" perspective in such matters, and this is perhaps why Bunyan uses the terms "typology" and "allegory" quite interchangeably, and why, rather than simply dubbing *The Pilgrim's Progress* a typology, he instead feels obliged to construct for it an elaborate defense of allegory and allegoresis in his "Author's Apology." The authors Lewalski treats are clearly much more literary-minded than Bunyan.

9. Erich Auerbach, "Figura," in *Scenes from the Drama of European Literature*, reprinted in *Theory and History of Literature*, vol. 9 (Minneapolis: University of Minnesota Press, 1984), 11–76.

10. Richard Sibbes, a popular but thoroughly orthodox Puritan, put it this way: "Who keeps Christ alive in this world, but a company of Christians that carry his resemblance? . . . He lives in them, and Christ is alive no otherwise in the world then in the hearts of gracious Christians, that carry the picture and resemblance of Christ in them" (*The Complete Works*, 4:264).

11. Calvin's title for Book 1, chapter 5 of the *Institutes* is "The knowledge of God conspicuous in the creation and continual government of the world." "Creation" and "continual government" or the march of providential destiny are treated here as virtually equivalent kinds of evidence, equally "conspicuous" to any qualified observer. A qualified observer regards both synchronically, as if from a position outside of both.

12. Sir Philip Sidney, *Apologie for Poetrie*, in *English Literary Criticism: The Renaissance*, ed. O. B. Hardison, Jr. (New York: Appleton-Century-Crofts, 1963). Sidney supposes that it is not "too sawcie a comparison to ballance the highest point of mans wit with the efficacie of Nature," as long as we "giue right honor to the heauenly Maker of that maker [the poet], who hauing made man in his owne likenes, set him beyond and ouer all the workes of that second nature, which in nothing hee sheweth so much as in Poetrie, when with the force of a diuine breath he bringeth things forth far surpassing her dooings, with no small argument to the incredulous of that first accursed fall of *Adam:* sith our erected wit maketh vs to know what perfection is, and yet our infected will keepeth vs from reaching vnto it" (105). Calvin is far less sanguine than

Sidney about the erectedness of human wit ("a perpetual forge of idols") and would have taken Sidney's comparison as not only "too sawcie," but impious.

13. The pamphlet literature of the civil war and interregnum years is full of accusations and counter-accusations of atheism; see Hill, *WTUD*. See also *Religions Lotterie, or the Churches Amazement* (London, 1642) in Sasek, *Images of English Puritanism,* 330–34. Bunyan admits in his "Conclusion" to *Grace Abounding* that he was continually tempted throughout his life to "question the being of God" (102).

14. See Auerbach, 54 and 58, for examples.

15. Also note the "more real" and the "true reality" in Auerbach, 71.

16. Auerbach, 52. See also Robbins, *Prodigal Son,* chap. 1, and Preus, *From Shadow to Promise,* 10, 33.

17. I use the word *enjoy* here in Augustine's sense as that activity proper to things that do not also represent other things, which is as much as to say things that are not words or signs.

18. Lewalski, 132.

19. Another even more crucial constitutive other (using Slavoj Žižek's term, we might call it "the big Other") is, of course, God. We will consider below Calvin's epistemological version of the constitutive self/God binary. See Žižek's brief analysis of the difference between Jewish and Christian responses to God in *The Sublime Object of Ideology* (London: Verso, 1989), 114–116.

20. See Preus, 198–99 and 268–69.

21. Augustine put it this way: "The Jew carries a book, from which a Christian may believe. Our librarians is what they have become, just as it is customary for servants to carry books behind their masters, so that those who carry faint and those who read profit. . . . The appearance of the Jews in the holy scripture which they carry is just like the face of a blind man in a mirror; he is seen by other, by himself not seen." (*Exposition on the Psalms* LVI.9, translated by Jill Robbins in *Prodigal Son,* 6). Thus "the Jew's" reading of Scripture is tantamount to non-reading—carrying, or blindness—compared with the Christian's reading of the Scriptures. "The Jew" cannot see himself in Scripture, because the self that is there is the Christian, or Christ. Augustine does not even allow "the Jew" misreading, only non-reading or blindness.

22. *D. Martin Luthers Werke: Kritische Gesamtausgabe* (Weimar: H. Bohlau, 1883 ff.), 4.400.1–5 (hereafter cited as *WA* by volume, page, and line), as translated by Preus, 221.

23. Calvin asserts the essential identity of old and new covenants: "The covenant made with all the fathers is so far from differing from ours in reality

substance, that it is altogether one and the same: still the administration differs" (*Institutes,* 2.10.2). He also rejects the "senseless and pernicious notion, that the Lord proposed nothing to the Jews, or that they sought nothing but full supplies of food, carnal delights, abundance of wealth, external influence, a numerous offspring, and all those things which our animal nature deems valuable" (2.10.23). But in the next chapter, he invokes Paul's "allegory of the two sons of Abraham," to prove that the "Old Testament . . . begets fear" and "bondage," while the "New" is "productive of confidence and security," and thus, "freedom" (2.11.9).

24. *Institutes* 2.11.4–5. Pointing to Christ "with the finger," as Calvin puts it, marks a kind of asymptotic limit to the antirepresentational or antimediational project of mainstream Protestantism. On the one hand, it carries the rhetorical sense of absolutely direct ostention, something like Dr. Johnson kicking the stone. On the other hand, ostention itself, the *pointing* of the finger, is still a mediating act, the witnessing (albeit minimalist) of one person's knowledge or sight to another. Also, Calvin acknowledges quite frequently that the risen Christ is very literally and insistently absent from this world, and thus particularly resistant to acts of ostention.

25. Following Paul's explanation in Galatians 4:1, Calvin likens "the Jews to children, and Christians to grown men. . . . What irregularity is there in the Divine arrangement, which confined them to the rudiments which were suitable to their age, and trains us by a firmer and more manly discipline? The constancy of God is conspicuous in this, that he delivered the same doctrine to all ages . . . His changing the external form and manner does not show that he is liable to change. In so far he has only accommodated himself to the mutable and diversified capacities of man" (*Institutes* 2.11.13). This passage registers the ambivalence attendant upon the Protestant rehabilitation of "the Jew." Insofar as "the Jew" is eventually to become a Christian, he is less "manly," less "firm," and less mature. And those Jews who refuse to "grow up" or become "more manly," who "remain contented with existing shadows" and do "not carry their thoughts to Christ, the Apostle charges them with blindness and malediction" (1.11.10). That is, they are damned to eternal childishness, unmanliness, and destruction. This is what it means when "The Apostle makes the Israelites our equals" (1.10.5)?

26. This is the persistent theme of Edmund Calamy's *The Monster of Sinful Self-Seeking, Anatomized:* "He that beates downe his Body, and brings it into subjection . . . that weares and fires out his body in a service of God . . . this is the true . . . and blessed selfe-seeker" (8–9). "Therefore he that seeks to get his Soule *beautified* with *grace,* to be made Christ's picture, and a real member of his body, this Man, and this Man onely, seeks himselfe" (8). True self-seeking, then, is self-abjection in the service of being "reborn" as Christ.

27. The phrase is from Thucydides, *History of the Peloponnesian War,* translated by C. F. Smith (Cambridge, Mass.: Harvard University Press, 1962), 1.22.4. It is quoted by Joel Fineman in "The History of the Anecdote: Fiction and Fiction," in *The New Historicism,* edited by H. Aram Veeser (New York: Routledge, 1989), 52, as "not only exemplary of, but also constitutive of, in an historically significant way, Western historiographic consciousness."

28. Auerbach even compares this view of Israelite (non)history to "the procession of prophets in the medieval theater and in the cyclic representations of medieval sculpture" (52).

29. See note 1 to chapter 6, below.

30. Such terms appear throughout Preus. The "full literal" sense proposed by English Reformers like Whitaker and Weemse is discussed in detail in chapter 3, below.

31. Martin Luther, as quoted in Lewalski, 117.

32. Maas, "Exegesis," *The Catholic Encyclopedia,* 5:693. Maas's outline of scholastic hermeneutics follows Thomistic and Augustinian categories quite faithfully, and so is a useful "trot" for my purposes.

33. Dante, *The Letter to Can Grande,* in *Literary Criticism of Dante Alighieri,* trans. and ed. Robert S. Haller (Lincoln: University of Nebraska Press, 1973), 112.

34. Thomas Aquinas, as quoted in Lewalski, 115.

35. For Barthes on myth as "a type of speech" or metalanguage, see "Myth Today" in *Mythologies,* selected and translated by Annette Lavers (New York: Hill and Wang, 1972), 109–159, especially 111–117.

36. See chapter 1, above.

37. Quoted from Luther's *Reply to Emser* by F. W. Loefscher in "Luther and the Problem of Authority in Religion," *Princeton Theological Review* 16 (1918): 529.

38. *WA* 4.272.16–24, as quoted in Preus, 247.

39. Preus quotes from *WA* 3.368.22–24: "Christus est finis omnium et centrum, in quem omnia respiciunt et monstrant, ac si dicerent: Ecce iste est, qui est, nos autem non sumus, sed significamus tantum." He also quotes *WA* 4.248.39–41: "Et hec est ratio, quare ps. 18 et 118 verba Dei dicuntur 'iudicia' et 'iudicia iustificationis,' quia iudicant et iustificant diversos. Et hoc totum, quia Christum predicant, qui est iudicium et iustitia."

40. The theme song of *Paris is Burning,* which repeats and celebrates the injunction "To Be Real," strikes me as a latter-day—and politically differently situated—version of this radical sectarian anxiety. In a very general sense, this is the anxiety of groups whom the dominant culture persistently defines as and

treats as "unreal." The drag queen who competes at balls by dressing and walking exactly like a Marine drill sergeant is both acting out and parodying this desire to "be real" in the dominant culture's terms. So also, perhaps, the mechanic preacher or rope-maker who performs, like Nayler, a kind of Christ-drag.

41. See Katz, *Philo-Semitism,* 43–88.

42. Maas identifies the most frequently disputed passages: Psalm 2:7; Isaiah 53:4,8; Daniel 9:27; John 11:51 and 2:19 (*Catholic Encyclopedia* 5:693).

43. *Metaphysics,* as quoted in Derrida, "White Mythology," in *Margins of Philosophy,* trans. Alan Bass (Chicago: University of Chicago Press, 1982), 248.

44. Bunyan, *PP,* 1.

45. Mitchell Dahood, S.J., trans. and ed., *Psalms I: The Anchor Bible,* vol. 16 (Garden City, N.J.: Doubleday, 1965), 7.

46. See Dahood, 11–12, and his reference to Gerald Cooke.

47. Perhaps the most popular and authoritative reference Bible among Christian evangelicals and fundamentalists of the twentieth century has been the New Scofield Reference Bible (ed. C. I. Scofield [New York: Oxford University Press, 1969]). Of the "Messianic" Psalms, the Scofield editors write, "These Psalms, either in whole or in part, speak of the Messiah. . . . The inspired interpretation of this [verses 2–7] is in Acts 4:25–28, which asserts its fulfillment in the crucifixion of Christ" (607).

48. *Luther's Works,* vol. 12, ed. Jaroslav Pelikan (St. Louis: Concordia, 1955), 51–52.

49. Contra Erasmus, Luther argued energetically for the overwhelming clarity and plainness of Scripture: "But that in Scripture there are some things abstruse, and everything is not plain—this is an idea put about by the ungodly Sophists, with whose lips you also speak here, Erasmus; but they have never produced, nor can they produce, a single article to prove this mad notion of theirs. Yet with such a phantasmagoria Satan has frightened men away from reading the Sacred Writ, and has made Holy Scripture contemptible, in order to enable the plagues he has bred from philosophy to prevail in the Church." Luther admits, however, that some places are obscure due to a general ignorance of "vocabulary and grammar," but aside from that, "The subject matter of the Scriptures . . . is all quite accessible. . . . If the words are obscure in one place, yet they are plain in another" ("On the Bondage of the Will," in *Luther and Erasmus: Free Will and Salvation,* ed. E. Gordon Rupp and Philip S. Watson [Philadelphia: Westminster Press, 1969], 110–111).

50. Henry George Liddell and Robert Scott, *Greek-English Lexicon,* revised and augmented by Sir Henry Stuart Jones and Roderick McKenzie (Oxford:

Clarendon Press, 1968). My thanks to Peter Bien for helping me make out the many senses of the word.

51. On Yahwism's constitutive anti-monism, see Michael Fishbane, "Israel and the 'Mothers,'" in *Garments of Torah: Essays in Biblical Hermeneutics* (Bloomington: Indiana University Press, 1989), 49–63.

52. Muggleton, *The Acts of the Witnesses of the Spirit*, 61.

53. Perhaps this is why Milton represents Adam as describing Eve's birth in terms strongly suggestive of an erotic "conversation" between himself and God (*Paradise Lost* 8:450–72) (hereafter cited as *PL*). Adam speaks quite literally when he addresses Eve as "Daughter of God and Man" (*PL* 9:291).

54. See Derrida, "White Mythology," 235–37.

55. Daniel Boyarin ("'This We Know to Be the Carnal Israel': Circumcision and the Erotic Life of God and Israel," *Critical Inquiry* 18 [1992]: 474–83) (hereafter cited as "Circumcision") distinguishes between the ontology of middle- and neo-platonism associated with Philo and the Christian Fathers and that of the Rabbis and their midrashim. Each ontology gives rise to and requires its own hermeneutic and produces its own anthropology. The former's hermeneutic is allegorical—the Platonic metaphysics of signification; the latter's resists this Platonic metaphysics and so "escapes the logic of the supplement," that is, the treatment of materiality, language, the body, and woman as supplementary to the intelligible, which alone is really real. Midrashic hermeneutics, says Boyarin, "sees the Bible as a self-glossing work and hermeneutics as a process of connecting concrete signifiers—not as a process of replacing concrete signifiers with their spiritual meanings" (480). Luther, it might be said, is attracted to a midrashic hermeneutic, one that does not displace "historical specificity" with an "unchanging ontology," one in which the material words of promise, as orally spoken, are really the promise rather than merely signs of the promise; but Luther cannot abandon the two-world ontology of Pauline Christianity that privileges the signified over the signifier. However much, then, he might be attracted to a signifier-based hermeneutic (like midrash), what Luther produces is simply a more thoroughly equivocal hermeneutic, riddled with ever more evident contradictions and aporias. These contradictions and aporias play themselves out in sectarian Protestantism as the self-consumption, or deconstruction, of Christianity in the West.

Chapter 3

1. That Paul's exegesis is very much in the tradition of midrashic interpretation but departs from it in important ways has long been recognized. See Dan Cohn-Sherbok, "Paul and Rabbinic Exegesis," *Scottish Journal of Theology* 35 (1982): 117–19 for a brief review of relevant literature. See also Hans Dieter

Betz, *Galatians: A Commentary on Paul's Letter to the Churches in Galatia* (Philadelphia: Fortress Press, 1979), 238–52.

2. See John L. McKenzie, S.J., trans. and ed., *Second Isaiah: The Anchor Bible,* vol. 20 (Garden City, N.Y.: Doubleday, 1968), 113.

3. Roger Sharrock, in his commentary on *PP,* suggests that "some features of the latitudinarian attitude of Edward Fowler (*Design of Christianity,* 1671) which Bunyan wrote against in *A Defence of the Doctrine of Justification by Faith* have been incorporated in this portrait" of Worldly-Wiseman (314).

4. William Tyndale, *The Obedience of a Christian Man* (Antwerp, 1528), folio 132ᵛ.

5. As quoted in Lewalski, *Protestant Poetics,* 122.

6. Janel M. Mueller, in her introduction to *Donne's Prebend Sermons* (Cambridge, Mass.: Harvard University Press, 1971), notes that though this careful distinction between the "sense" and the "use" of Scripture meanings came to be typical in "the preaching manuals of Donne's day," Donne himself apparently avoided maintaining such an absolute distinction and "often announced his intention of making 'the right use of the right sense' of his text." "It is rarely possible," Mueller claims, "to find a dividing line between amplification and application in his preaching" (42). Donne appears more aware than most of his contemporaries of the impossibility of maintaining what Tyndale wants to see as a crucial, and absolute, distinction. "That the one [application or use?] should subsume the other [amplification or sense?] is, of course," continues Mueller, "a further consequence of his Anglican view that there is a continuum and not a hierarchy of meaning in Scripture" (42). It is hard to see how subsumption can take place in the absence of any hierarchy. If "continuall application" was "the central function of the Church's ministry and the sole objective of the Christian life" (43), then application or use must "subsume" amplification or sense in such a manner as to render any sense incommensurate with Christian use non-sense.

7. Martin Luther, *Commentary on Galatians* [1535], in *Luther's Works,* vol. 27, 430.

8. *Luther's Works,* 27:425–26. In his 1519 edition of the *Commentary,* Luther is even more explicit in denying that Paul's practice here offers any precedent for the scholastic method of fourfold exegesis, which he refers to as a "game," generally permissible, but fraught with dangers when pursued rashly or taken to be foundational in matters of doctrine: "these interpretations should not be brought forward with a view to establishing a doctrine of faith. For that four-horse team (even though I do not disapprove of it) is not sufficiently supported by the authority of Scripture, by the custom of the fathers, or by grammatical principles." (*Luther's Works* 27:311). Calvin also advances the

ornament/argument distinction in *Commentaries on Galatians,* 134. See also William Perkins's warning that allegories "are to be used sparingly and soberly; let them not be far-fetched, but fitting to the matter in hand; they must be quickly dispatched; they are to be used for the instruction of the life and not to prove any point of faith" (*The Arte of Prophesying,* in *The Works of William Perkins,* ed. Ian Breward [Appleford, Abingdon, Berkshire: Sutton Courtenay Press, 1970], 340–41).

9. For examples, see Ernest De Witt Burton, *A Critical and Exegetical Commentary on the Epistle to the Galatians* (Edinburgh: T. & T. Clark, 1921), 251; and James D. G. Dunn, *The Theology of Paul's Letter to the Galatians* (Cambridge: Cambridge University Press, 1993), 124.

10. These include G. Walter Hansen, "Abraham in Galatians: Epistolary and Rhetorical Contexts," *Journal for the Study of the New Testament,* Supplement Series 29 (Sheffield: Sheffield Academic Press, 1989), 154–63, 210; Leonhard Goppelt, *Typos: The Typological Interpretation of the Old Testament in the New,* trans. Donald H. Madvig (Grand Rapids, Mich.: W. B. Eerdmans, 1982), 139–40; J. Bligh, *Galatians: A Discussion of St. Paul's Epistle* (London: St. Paul, 1969), 395; A. T. Hanson, *Studies in Paul's Technique and Theology* (Grand Rapids, Mich.: W. B. Eerdmans, 1974), 101; F. F. Bruce, *The Epistle of Paul to the Galatians: A Commentary on the Greek Text* (Exeter: Paternoster Press, 1982), 217; and Ronald Y. K. Fung, *The Epistle to the Galatians* (Grand Rapids, Mich.: W. B. Eerdmans, 1988), 217–20. These all follow the allegory/typology distinction articulated in R. P. C. Hanson, *Allegory and Event: A Study of the Sources and Significance of Origen's Interpretation of Scripture* (London: SCM Press, 1959), 7, which is essentially the same as Whitaker's, Auerbach's and Lewalski's versions.

11. Hanson, for example. Andrew T. Lincoln, in *Paradise Now and Not Yet,* while explicitly following Hanson's distinction, advances the more ingenious Lutheran notion that Paul's exegesis is basically a typological "cake" with "some allegorical icing" (14). But this "allegorical icing," he admits, is precisely the "real tension [contradiction] between type and antitype in his midrash" (13).

12. Like Fung (219) and against H. J. Schoeps (*Paul: The Theology of the Apostle in the Light of Jewish Religious History,* trans. Harold Knight [Philadelphia: Westminster Press, 1961], 234–35, 238–39), Lincoln insists that it is his "deep concern" with salvation-history, or as Fung puts it, "faith in Christ" (219), that keeps Paul's allegory from being "capricious" or "fanciful" (Lincoln, 14; Fung, 219) like Philo's or those of the Alexandrine school.

13. See Gerald L. Bruns, "Midrash and Allegory: The Beginnings of Scriptural Interpretation," *The Literary Guide to the Bible,* ed. Robert Alter and

Frank Kermode (London: Fontana Press, 1989), 637–41. See also Boyarin, "Circumcision," 477–500.

14. C. K. Barrett, *Freedom and Obligation: A Study of the Epistle to the Galatians* (London: SPCK, 1985), 22–27.

15. Bruns, 191. See also *Midrash Rabbah: Genesis,* trans. Rabbi Dr. H. Freedman (London: Soncino Press, 1939), 1:xiii.

16. This is the *New English Bible* translation quoted by Hans Dieter Betz in his *Commentary,* 270. Betz also notes that while traditional translations often "tend to avoid" Paul's obviously violent obscenity here, Luther's translation of 1519 did not: "Tell those who are disturbing you I would like to see the knife slip."

17. We should recall here that Calvin followed Paul's suggestion when asserting that God's two covenants, old and new, are essentially identical, but that Christianity is still "a firmer and more manly discipline" or version (see above, chap. 2).

18. *Midrash Rabbah: Genesis,* 53:11 in Freedman translation, 1:470.

19. *Midrash Rabbah: Genesis,* 53:13, in Freedman translation, 1:471.

20. *Midrash Rabbah: Genesis,* 53:12, in Freedman translation, 1:471. See also Jacob Neusner, *Genesis Rabbah: The Judaic Commentary to the Book of Genesis: A New American Translation* (Atlanta: Scholars Press, 1985), 2:254. Esau, of course, was held to be another such example of a "son of Abraham" who was cut off for this worldly-mindedness.

21. Daniel Boyarin, in his recently published *Carnal Israel* (Berkeley: University of California Press, 1993), carefully traces out the many ways rabbinic traditions distinguished between flesh and spirit short of forging the absolute bipolarity that invites allegory.

22. Bruns, "Midrash and Allegory," 194–95, and Boyarin, "Circumcision," 479–80.

23. *Midrash Rabbah: Genesis,* 47:3, in Freedman translation, 1:400.

24. Beverly R. Gaventa, "The Maternity of Paul: An Exegetical Study of Galatians 4:19," in *The Conversation Continues: Studies in Paul and John in Honor of J. Louis Martyn,* ed. Robert T. Fortna and Beverly R. Gaventa (Nashville: Abingdon Press, 1990), 196.

25. William Whitaker, *A Disputation on Holy Scripture Against the Papists,* trans. William Fitzgerald for the Parker Society (Cambridge: Cambridge University Press, 1849), 405–8.

26. Quoted in Lewalski, 121.

27. The quoted phrases are from Lewalski, 117: "The new Protestant emphasis is clear: it makes for a different sense of the Bible as a unified poetic text,

and for a much closer fusion of sign and thing signified, type and antitype. The characteristic Protestant approach takes the Bible not as a multi-level allegory, but as a complex literary work whose full literal meaning is revealed only by careful attention to its poetic texture and to its pervasive symbolic mode—typology."

28. Lewalski, 138. The Donne quotation is from *Sermons,* ed. G. F. Potter and Evelyn Simpson, (Berkeley: University of California Press, 1953–1962), 7:356.

29. Quoted in Lewalski, 140.

30. Perhaps, as Joel Fineman has suggested in "The History of the Anecdote," it is precisely in the Renaissance and Reformation that we should look for the beginnings of "New" Historicism, that modern interpretive practice most invested in blurring, if not eliding, the difference between "historical" events and literary representations as signifiers of cultural "reality."

Chapter 4

1. John Donne, *Devotions upon Emergent Occasions,* 9. Expostulation (Ann Arbor: University of Michigan Press, 1959), 60–61.

2. George Herbert, "The Holy Scriptures," in Hutchinson, *The Poems of George Herbert,* 50.

3. Daniel Boyarin and Jonathan Boyarin, "Diaspora: Generation and the Ground of Jewish Identity," *Critical Inquiry* 19 (1993): 695. The following quotation is also from this page.

4. Boyarin and Boyarin, 696.

5. Boyarin and Boyarin, 697.

6. Boyarin and Boyarin, 696, note 8.

7. Žižek, *The Sublime Object of Ideology,* 126. See also Paul's version of the Church as Christ's body in 1 Corinthians 12:12–31 and Romans 12:4–5.

8. Boyarin and Boyarin, 694; see also Galatians 3:26–29.

9. See above, chapter 3, n. 16.

10. In *Areopagitica,* Milton advances an image of the body of Truth as a body that can tolerate only "neighboring differences, or rather indifferences"; real difference "should be extirpate" (Stephen Orgel and Jonathan Goldberg, eds., *The Oxford Authors John Milton* [New York: Oxford University Press, 1991], 270. See also Stanley Fish's reading of *Areopagitica* in "Driving from the Letter: Truth and Indeterminacy in Milton's *Areopagitica,*" in *Re-membering Milton,* ed. Nyquist and Ferguson, 246–47.

11. The phrase is part of the full title of Bunyan's famous allegory of "the

Way / and Race of Saints," *The Pilgrim's Progress from This World to That which is to Come: Delivered under the Similitude of a Dream,* 10th ed., 1685.

12. I borrow the phrase from the title of A. T. Lincoln's study of Pauline eschatology, *Paradise Now and Not Yet,* and his description of the deferred status of the "saint," 194.

13. Thomas Tany, *TheaurauJohn His Aurora in Trandagorum in Salem Gloria, Or the discussive of the Law & the Gospell betwixt the Jew and the Gentile in Salem Resurrectionem* (London, 1655) 55.

14. Katz gives a useful and brief summary of the careers of Tany and Robins in *Philo-Semitism,* 107–20.

15. For the best account to date of the seventeenth-century English search for a universal language and Hebrew studies, see Katz, *Philo-Semitism,* 43–88. Thomas (ThoreauJohn) Tany believed that he had miraculously learned original "pure language" or "*Radaxes*" and "simblims" (*TheaurauJohn His Aurora,* 2, 6, 54–55). He claimed that he was himself "the Lords gimell," or key (19). He also thought English was particularly well suited to rendering Hebrew (A2). I include a small sample of "the pure language": "obedient alma honasa hul; generati alvah ableuvisse insi locat amorvissem humanet rokoas salah axoret eltah alvah hon ono olephad in se mori melet eri neri meleare; okoriko olo ophaus narratus asa sadoas loboim olet amni Phikepeaa ebellrer elma bosai in re meal olike'(54–55).

16. Boyarin and Boyarin put it this way: "Once Paul succeeded, 'real Jews' ended up being only a trope. They have remained such for European discourse down to the present and even in the writings of leftists whose work is *explicitly* opposed to anti-Semitism—and even the writings of Jews" (697). Ivy Schweitzer argues that the widespread Puritan practice of imagining the self's relation to God under the figure of the bride of Christ had much the same effect of de-realizing real brides and real women. See *The Work of Self-Representation,* 22–35.

17. *Institutes,* 1.1.1. This is not to suggest, contra Dowey and Gerrish, that Calvin entertains any notion that God can be properly known without, or before, revelation, but that he tries to imagine what knowledge of God must have been like for those to whom God revealed himself before the particular forms of revelation known as the Law and the Gospel. Calvin is convinced that knowledge of God and knowledge of self is hopelessly flawed without benefit of revelation. See Edward A. Dowey Jr., *The Knowledge of God in Calvin's Theology* (New York: Columbia University Press, 1952) and Gerrish, "Theology Within the Limits of Piety Alone," in *The Old Protestantism and the New,* 196–207.

18. Calvin's Latin here is: "*Caeterum quum multis inter se vinculis connexae*

sint, utra tamen alteram praecedat, et ex se pariat, non facile est discernere," from Ioannis Calvini, *Opera Quae Supersunt Omnia,* vol. 2, ed. William Baum, Edward Cunitz, and Edward Reuss, in the series *Corpus Reformatorum,* vol. 30 (Brunsvigae: C. A. Schwetschke and Son, 1864).

19. On this, see Fishbane, "Israel and the 'Mothers,'" cited above. Milton's monism is much more redolent of Puritan radicals than of Protestant orthodoxy.

20. *Midrash Rabbah: Genesis* distinguishes between Isaac's blessing—the promise of fathering "twelve tribes"—and Ishmael's blessing—the promise of fathering "twelve princes"—by saying, "In truth those [Ishmael's] were *nesi'im* (princes) in the same sense as you read, *As* nesi'im [E. V. *'vapours'*] *and wind,* etc. (Prov. xxv, 14). But these [Issac's] were *matoth* (tribes) as you read, *Sworn are the* matoth [E. V. *'rods'*] *of the word. Selah* (Hab. iii, 9)." Rabbi Freedman further glosses *nesi'im* as meaning Ishmael's princes' "glory would be transient, and they would soon pass away," but Isaac's "tribes would endure like rods that are planted" (*Midrash Rabbah: Genesis,* 47:5). Presumably, God will "heed" (17:20) Abraham's pleading for Ishmael (20:18) in a manner similar to the way he heeded Abram's pleading for Sodom in chapters 18–19. In any case, Ishmael's blessing is said to be a vaporish simulacrum of Isaac's blessing; this is very reminiscent of medieval Catholic interpretations of the "Old" and "New" covenants. See Robbins, *Prodigal Son,* 1–20.

21. E. A. Speiser, trans., *Genesis: The Anchor Bible,* vol. 1 (Garden City, N.Y.: Doubleday, 1964), 124.

22. Derrida, "Violence and Metaphysics: An Essay on the Thought of Emmanuel Levinas," in *Writing and Difference,* 80.

23. Boyarin and Boyarin, 721.

24. Paul's remainder "me" reminds one a bit of the Lacanian pre-subjective or proto-subjective *moi,* the bodily imago that will be displaced into the unconscious with the advent of the subject formed by the symbolic order and upon its lack ("The Mirror Stage as Formative of the Function of the I as Revealed in Psychoanalytic Experience," in *Écrits: A Selection,* trans. Alan Sheridan [New York: Norton, 1977], 2: "This jubilant assumption of his specular image by the child at the *infans* stage, . . . would seem to exhibit in an exemplary situation the symbolic matrix in which the *I* is precipitated in a primordial form.")

25. Susan Handelman, "Jacques Derrida and the Heretic Hermeneutic," in *Displacement: Derrida and After,* ed. Mark Krupnik (Bloomington: Indiana University Press, 1983), 108.

26. "Fear not, Abram, I am your shield" (Genesis 15:1); "Fear not, for God

has heard the voice of the lad" [to Hagar concerning Ishmael] (21:17); "Fear not, for I am with you and will bless you and multiply your descendants" [to Isaac] (26:24); "Fear not, for now you will have another son" [to Rachel concerning Benjamin, at whose birth she died] (35:17); "I am God, the god of your father; fear not to go down into Egypt" [to Jacob] (KJV 46:3).

27. See Paul Ricoeur, *Essays on Biblical Interpretation,* ed. Lewis S. Mudge (Philadelphia: Fortress Press, 1980), 78–79, and "Fatherhood: From Phantasm to Symbol," in *The Conflict of Interpretations: Essays in Hermeneutics* (Evanston: Northwestern University Press, 1974), 484.

28. Boyarin and Boyarin, 715.

29. John 3:1–10, 7:50, and 19:39 present Nicodemus as a figure of radical ambivalence, unable to think the absolute distinction of flesh (*sarkos*) and spirit (*pneumatos*) (3:6), asking "How can this be?" (3:9). In 7:50, Nicodemus is identified as "one of them," presumably of the crowd following Jesus, but he is also a Pharisee and tries to cite "the Law" (51) in Jesus' defense. In 19:39, he is among those who attend to Jesus' crucified body. John Bunyan calls him "a night professor" in *The Jerusalem Sinner Saved* (in *The Works of John Bunyan,* ed. George Offor [Glasgow: Blackie and Son, 1860], 1:74.)

30. My reading of Tamar's story owes a great deal to Bal's brilliant reading in *Lethal Love: Feminist Literary Readings of Biblical Love Stories* (Bloomington: Indiana University Press, 1987), 89–103). She also conceives of the Joseph story, and particularly the "metaleptic" chapter 38, as an emblematic problematization of the "question of the subject" (98). Bal reads Tamar as "the woman . . . used for her indispensable share in the course of history, as the sidestep that restores broken chronology" (102), but the chronology has to do with the formation of the patriarchal subjectivity, not her own.

31. For this latter observation, I am indebted to my colleague James Heffernan.

32. The *Midrash Rabbah: Genesis* (85:4) suggests that Er was wicked "because he plowed on roofs," which Freedman glosses as "a delicate expression for unnatural intercourse, so that his wife should not conceive."

33. "Thy signet," says *Midrash Rabbah: Genesis,* "alludes to royalty, . . . Thy Cord alludes to the Sanhedrin, . . . And Thy Staff alludes to the royal Messiah" (85:9).

34. Hitherto in Genesis the word "righteous" [*tsedaqah*] has been applied to Noah (7:1), to the hypothetical remnant of Sodom for whose sake Yahweh would have spared a city renowned for sexual perversion (18:23–32), and to Abimelech, who narrowly escaped adultery with the wife of Abraham (20:4). Given this record of the word's connotations of sexual purity, Judah's applica-

tion of it to a woman who literally "played the harlot" (*zanah*, 38:24) and was pregnant by her father-in-law signals the depth of his reinterpretive recognition of himself and his kin.

35. See *Midrash Rabbah: Genesis*, 85:13.

36. E. A. Speiser's comment that chapter 38 "is a completely independent unit" having "no connection with the drama of Joseph" (Speiser, 299) reflects source criticism's sense of biblical narrators as "custodians of diverse traditions," though occasionally capable of "keen literary sensitivity" in the placement of what are essentially "preserved" materials. Robert Alter, in *The Art of Biblical Narrative* (New York: Basic Books, 1981), 3–13, uses this apparently "interpolated story" to demonstrate his sense of a biblical narrator's conscious artistry. Mieke Bal, in *Lethal Love*, 96, somewhat enigmatically suggests that chapter 38's (dis)placement is both a "significant" editorial and/or compositional "act, motivated and related to the endorsement of paralepsis as sign" and that it represents "a case of lapsus, a slip, of the intervention of the unconscious, which, far from eliminating the episode for the sake of clarity, has dictated its position at this place" for very specific reasons.

37. The expected sequence of the story is interrupted, "disarranged," says *Midrash Rabbah: Genesis* (85:2), "so that it might not be said that the narrative is mere fiction, and that all might know that it was composed under divine inspiration." Since Tamar's story is the most dramatic of the narrative's interruptions, it is precisely in the event of this story's displacement that "divine inspiration" is most clearly signaled.

Chapter 5

1. Gabriel Vahanian, "God and the Utopianism of Language," in *Lacan and Theological Discourse*, ed. Edith Wyschogrod et al. (Albany: State University of New York Press, 1989), 120.

2. Fish, *Self-Consuming Artifacts*, 264.

3. For an articulation of such accusations and fears, see N. H. Keeble, "'Of him thousands daily sing and talk': Bunyan and His Reputation," in Keeble, *John Bunyan*, where Keeble scoffs at (and fears) the idea that "Bunyan the literary gamester is about to succeed Bunyan 'the greatest imaginative writer of [*his*] age'" (263, bracket and contents are Keeble's). The first response to Fish's claims, John R. Knott Jr.'s "Bunyan's Gospel Day: A Reading of *The Pilgrim's Progress*" (in *English Literary Renaissance* 3 [1973]:443–61), set the tone for much of the Bunyan industry's response to Fish by accepting without question Bunyan's own allegory-driven equivocation on the word *real*. On the one hand, Knott wants to argue that Bunyan really does present an image of pro-

gress in *The Pilgrim's Progress,* a progress "all the way from the 'carnal' world in which the narrative began up to the contemplation of a transcendant [*sic*] world whose reality is validated by the Word" (461), but he acknowledges, on the other hand, that for Bunyan, "the visible world of ordinary experience" is "an alien, and ultimately insubstantial country through which God's people must journey" to real reality (461). If the faithful journey through an "insubstantial country," how substantial is their journey? At many points in his argument, Knott implies that the very substantiality of Bunyan's landscape in *The Pilgrim's Progress* depends directly upon a reader's own belief "in the fundamental truth of Scripture" (454). But of course Scripture (according to Bunyan) is bent on teaching the ultimate insubstantiality of "this World." This tendency to define the "right reader" of Bunyan as one who shares his faith and avoids questioning his allegorical metaphysics continues to be a feature in much Bunyan scholarship. Recent examples are James F. Forrest, "Allegory as Sacred Sport," and Barbara A. Johnson, "Falling Into Allegory: The 'Apology' to *The Pilgrim's Progress* and Bunyan's Scriptural Methodology," both in *Bunyan in Our Time,* ed. Robert G. Collmer (Kent, Ohio: Kent State University Press, 1989), 112, 124. For important exceptions to this tendency, see Vincent Newey, "'With the eyes of my understanding': Bunyan, Experience, and Acts of Interpretation," and Valentine Cunningham, "Glossing and Glozing: Bunyan and Allegory," both in Keeble, *John Bunyan,* 189–240.

4. I allude here to Slavoj Žižek's Lacanian definition of the Real as "that which resists symbolization: the traumatic point which is always missed [in dreams as in ideologies] but none the less always returns, although we try— through a set of different strategies—to neutralize it, to integrate it into the symbolic order. In the perspective of the last stage of Lacanian teaching, it [the Real] is precisely the symptom which is conceived as such a kernel of enjoyment, which persists as a surplus and returns through all attempts to domesticate it, to gentrify it, . . . to dissolve it by means of explication, of putting-into words its meaning." (*The Sublime Object,* 69). The Real is what is impossible to say and, at the same time, the absolute ground of all saying.

For useful historical treatments of the debate about "the verbal condition of man" among seventeenth-century religious radicals, see Katz, *Philo-Semitism,* chapter 2, and Smith, *Perfection Proclaimed.* For Tany, see *Theaurau-john Tani His Second Part of His Theous-Ori Apokalipika: Or God's Light declared in Mysteries . . . Wrote by me Magi Tani Est* (London, 1653).

5. By calling his autobiography a "Relation," Bunyan invites readers to fit it into a once highly popular genre—that of the "True Relation" or "Strange News." For scores of examples, see Donald Goddard Wing, comp., *Short-Title Catalogue . . . 1641–1700,* 2d ed. (New York: Index Committee of the Modern

Language Association of America, 1972–1988). Bunyan's full title is: *Grace Abounding to the Chief of Sinners: or, A Brief and Faithful Relation of the Exceeding Mercy of God in Christ to his Poor Servant John Bunyan.*

6. In "The Author's *Apology* For His Book," which prefaces *The Pilgrim's Progress,* Bunyan writes: "I writing of the Way / And Race of Saints in this our Gospel-Day / Fell suddenly into an Allegory" (1).

7. Bunyan, *Some Gospel Truths Opened* and *A Vindication of Some Gospel Truths Opened,* in *The Miscellaneous Works of John Bunyan;* Edward Burrough, *Truth Defended* (London, 1656); *Stablishing Against Quaking* (London, 1656); and *The Memorable Works of a Son of Thunder and Consolation* (London, 1672), a posthumous collection. John Knott Jr. outlines quite cogently Bunyan's doctrinal differences with the Quakers in "'Thou must live upon my word': Bunyan and the Bible," in Keeble, *John Bunyan,* 154–55. Though I agree with his outline, I am arguing that for Bunyan, and for Puritans more generally, distinguishing between the "literal" life of the historical Christ and the equally literal life of the "Christ within" was never as easy as Knott makes it appear here. Knott notes that "Bunyan's great accomplishment . . . was to give substance to this unseen world [the Kingdom described in Scripture] and to make it seem . . . *more real* than the Bedfordshire setting from which Christian and those he encounters emerge" (165, italics added), and that this "great accomplishment" is effected by way of allegory, but he shrinks from concluding that only allegory can offer Bunyan a "solution" to the difference between the Quaker's "Christ within" and the "historical" or scriptural Christ. And this "solution," by rendering the word *real* equivocal, tends to privilege the reality of the "Christ within" even as it avoids denying the reality of the "Christ without."

8. This is much the same as Richard Bauman's observation in *Let Your Words Be Few: Symbolism of Speaking and Silence among Seventeenth-Century Quakers* (Cambridge: Cambridge University Press, 1983): "Quakerism may be seen as the carrying of the Protestant tendency [to reject all mediating institutions] to its logical extreme" (29). A desire, running counter to this generally Protestant tendency, to preserve some sense of the "outwardness" of both the Scriptures and Christ—what Bunyan calls "the Christ without"—underlies Bunyan's controversy with the Quakers. This desire, both in Bunyan and in other Puritan writers, seems to me to have been largely frustrated, and this frustration may account for the shrillness of Bunyan's attack on Burrough and Quakerism (see Bauman, 25).

9. George Puttenham, *The Art of English Poesie* (1589), in Hardison, *English Literary Criticism,* 178.

10. "Epistle to the Reader," originally prefaced to George Foxe's *The Great*

Mystery of the Great Whore (1659), and reprinted in *Memorable Works;* italics added.

11. *A Vindication Of Some Gospel Truths Opened,* in Offor, *The Works of John Bunyan,* 2:183.

12. Perhaps this is why so much of his writing dwells in such excruciating detail upon the torments of a "lost soul" and upon hell.

13. Bunyan also describes his temptation to "blaspheme the Ordinance, and to wish some deadly thing to those that then did eat thereof" (par. 253).

14. Ranters, with whom Bunyan had some familiarity both in books and in person (*GA,* par. 44–45), were especially fond of cursing and blaspheming, often claiming that such behavior constituted a more sincere form of worship than any religious observance they had ever seen in church or at conventicles. See Christopher Hill, *WTUD,* esp. chaps. 9 and 10; A. L. Morton, *The World of the Ranters: Religious Radicalism in the English Revolution* (London: Lawrence & Wishart, 1970); Jerome Friedman, *Blasphemy, Immorality, and Anarchy: The Ranters and the English Revolution* (Athens: Ohio University Press, 1987); and *Grand Blasphemers,* 33–34.

15. I am indebted to my colleague Peter Saccio for this last suggestion.

16. Atheism seemed a very logical position to Bunyan precisely because he had thought at such length and depth about the problem of intentionality: "Though we made so great a matter of *Paul,* and of his words, yet how could I tell but that in very deed, he, being a subtle and cunning man, might give himself up to deceive with strong delusions, and also take both that pains and travel to undo and destroy his fellows?" (*GA,* par. 98). It is impossible not to hear in this passage a "mechanick preacher's" version of Descartes' "Divine deceiver." Bunyan's use of dream-vision allegory is also reminiscent of Descartes' worry about how we know when we're waking or sleeping, what is allegory and what is "reality." Descartes, like Bunyan, was desperate for certainty and assurance. See René Descartes, *Meditations on First Philosophy,* 2d ed., trans. Ronald Rubin (Claremont, Calif.: Arete Press, 1986), especially the First and Second Meditations.

17. *A Relation of the Imprisonment of Mr. John Bunyan,* in *GA,* 113.

18. *Institutes,* 1.1.1 (the second sentence); and Galatians 4:19–31. See also chapter 4 above.

19. Another Justice indulges here in a little irrelevant teasing, asking Bunyan, "How should we know, that you do not write out your prayers first, and then read them afterwards to the people?" (114).

20. Sharrock notes that Kelynge, a staunch Royalist, spent much of the interregnum in prison, and became in 1660 a notoriously vigorous prosecutor of

"Fifth Monarchy men and regicides, showing himself harsh and insulting to Sir Henry Vane and others" (*GA,* 159–60). He was a member for Bedford in Charles II's first parliament. Vane, writes Barry Reay, "was said to favour Quakers; one it was even rumoured, had anointed him king." Vane is on record as a supporter, along with Baptist Henry Denne, Henry Stubbe, and Fifth Monarchist Morgan Llwyd, of tolerance for Quakers (*The Quakers and the English Revolution,* 84, 87). Vane was thought to be, like virtually all Quakers, "an implacable enemy of the ministry." After serving years in prison with Quakers and having been released at least partly due to organized Quaker efforts, Bunyan quietly dropped his polemic against them. See Hill, *A Tinker and a Poor Man.*

21. Bunyan's mention of "babbling" here echoes the Geneva Bible's (1602) gloss on Matthew 11:5, where "two foule faults in prayer" are identified as "ambition, and vaine babling."

22. Bunyan glosses "God useth means" in a footnote: "If any say now that God useth means; I answer, but not the Common Prayer-book, or that is none of his institution, 'tis the spirit in the word that is Gods ordinance" (115).

23. In *I Will Pray with the Spirit,* in *Miscellaneous Works,* vol. 2, ed. Richard L. Greaves (Oxford: Clarendon Press, 1976), Bunyan meditates upon the *"sensible feeling"* that is the mark of sincere prayer: "a sence of the want of mercy, by reason of the danger of sin. The soul, I say, feels, and from feeling, sighs, groans, and breaks at the heart" (237). As in Donne's "Batter my heart three-person'd God," sincere prayer requires absolute abjection, if not annihilation, of the self ("Holy Sonnet 14," in *John Donne: The Complete English Poems,* ed. A. J. Smith [New York: Penguin Books, 1986], 314).

24. Bunyan says of his *Pilgrim's Progress,* "This Book it chaulketh out before thine eyes, / The man that seeks the everlasting Prize" (6). The "Prize," of course, is the replacement of the self by Christ in "New-birth."

25. Felicity Nussbaum, in "'By These Words I was Sustained': Bunyan's *Grace Abounding* (*ELH* 49 [1982]: 18–34) and Peter J. Carlton, in "Bunyan: Language, Convention, Authority" (*ELH* 51 [1984]: 17–21), offer largely complementary analyses of Bunyan's habit in *GA* of figuring Scripture experience as violent assaults upon his person. Carlton calls them "disclaiming locutions" designed to help Bunyan deny the subjectivity of his "spiritual" experience and so render it objectively authoritative. Nussbaum argues that Bunyan elevates the authority of ecstatic experience above the authority of Scripture. The first makes the problematic assumption that "subjective" experience would carry, for Bunyan, less authority than "objective" experience; the second renders a Bunyan unconsciously in agreement with Quakers over the status of Scripture authority. See also my essay, "The Pilgrim's Passive Progress."

26. Perhaps Bunyan wants to experience what Derrida calls the "impossibility" of "an echo that would somehow precede the origin it seems to answer—the 'real,' the 'originary,' the 'true,' the 'present,' being constituted only on the rebound from the duplication in which alone they can arise. . . . The 'effect' becomes the cause" (*Dissemination*, translated by Barbara Johnson [Chicago: University of Chicago Press, 1981], 323). Bunyan experiences the "originary" (though he calls it "original") Word of God in what Derrida might call the "plupresent," an impossible tense in which the infinitely past is imagined as now and the infinitely absent as present. This is Bunyan's version of the impossible "Real" of Christian metaphysics. This analysis of the echo figure in Bunyan is deeply indebted to the far more elaborate analyses Jonathan Goldberg presents of other seventeenth-century texts in *Voice, Terminal, Echo: Postmodernism and English Renaissance Texts* (New York: Methuen, 1986), especially 12–13. Goldberg, in turn, is indebted to John Hollander's *The Figure of Echo: A Mode of Allusion in Milton and After* (Berkeley: University of California Press, 1981). Goldberg's chapter on Herbert (chap. 5) has been especially useful for suggesting new ways to read Bunyan.

27. Derrida, *Dissemination,* 323

28. Paragraphs 50, 52, 56, 59, and 61 contain different versions of this outcry. In paragraph 56, it is "I knew not where I was." Bunyan's *A Map Shewing the Order and Causes of Salvation and Damnation* (Offor, *Works,* vol. 3, insert at page 374) labels a particular soteriological stage "where at the soul is cast down . . . which occasioneth satan to tempt to despair . . . which driveth the soul to the promise" with the framed tag, "what shall i do to be saved." It is also during this period that Bunyan dallies with Ranterism (par. 44–45), a temptation he confesses was peculiarly "suitable to my flesh." Bunyan begins here to work through his particular brand of antinomianism.

29. N. H. Keeble very nicely describes both the "by-the-by, incidental" tone of Bunyan's narrative here and the "revolutionary" significance Bunyan gradually assigns to this "casual" incident in "'Here is her Glory, even to be under Him': The Feminine in the Thought and Work of John Bunyan," in *John Bunyan and His England, 1628–88,* ed. Anne Laurence, W. R. Owens, and Stuart Sim (London: The Hambledon Press, 1990), 131–33. In the same volume (125–30), Elspeth Graham's "Authority, Resistance, and Loss: Gendered Difference in the Writings of John Bunyan and Hannah Allen" recognizes this episode as a crucial stage in Bunyan's conversion, emphasizing the significance "that it is a group of women who stimulate Bunyan into a new phase of understanding." Graham also calls attention to Bunyan's anxiety over language in interesting ways. Neither Keeble nor Graham subject the episode and Bunyan's allegorical permutations upon it to detailed analysis. When Graham notes that Bunyan's "encounter with the poor women of Bedford made a

'feminised' spirituality possible" (129), she seems to ignore the fact that the Protestant discourse of conversion has *always* portrayed the self-abjecting stage of conversion as a feminizing experience, and that when "their discourse is finally assimilated into his own fatherly one" (129), Bunyan is not retreating from a protofeminist position, but is following the familiar pattern by which self-abjection and humiliation is figured as a woman's experience and being made "one with Christ" a man's experience. Women's experience, then, serves as a figure for the as yet not fully regenerated state of being in the world. Men's experience of authority, fulfillment, and domination is a figure for being in the next world.

30. I am borrowing Joel Fineman's senses of the words *whole* and *hole* as they appear in his groundbreaking essay, "The History of the Anecdote," 61.

31. I use *happening* and *event* as terms to offer a provisional distinction between things finally indistinguishable, since, as Fineman demonstrates from Thucydides's history, any absolutely contingent happening is instantly transformed into an event belonging to a "genericizing narrative context" upon its recognition as significant, even before, as in Bunyan's case, that significance is articulable (Fineman, 52–53).

32. See also how this pun on *calling* lies at the center of Bunyan's dispute with Justice Kelynge (*Imprisonment*, in *GA*, 117–18).

33. I refer, of course to Stanley Fish's landmark reading of *The Pilgrim's Progress* in *Self-Consuming Artifacts*, chapter 4.

34. This offers another explanation for Joan Webber's conviction that in *GA* Bunyan "makes allegory and realism touch briefly, before rejecting the former method for the present." Webber suggests that Bunyan's persona, his *I*, "functions as a representative human being in an allegorical situation" (*The Eloquent "I": Style and Self in Seventeenth-Century Prose* [Madison: University of Wisconsin Press, 1968], 22, 44). I'm suggesting that Bunyan imagines an exchange of respective epistemological status between allegory and raw experience that requires the self to be reborn out of this world and into allegory.

Chapter 6

1. So Coleridge accounted for the apparent unevenness of Bunyan's allegory (*Miscellaneous Criticism*, ed. T. M. Raysor [London: Constable & Co., 1936], 31).

C. S. Lewis complained that Bunyan's characters occasionally "step out of the allegorical story altogether" and "talk literally and directly about the spiritual life" they are supposed to represent ("The Vision of John Bunyan," *The Listener* 68 [1962]: 1006–7). Wolfgang Iser says that Bunyan's characters "fall out of their allegorical character" in order to lend realism to the narrative (*The*

Implied Reader: Patterns of Communication in Prose Fiction from Bunyan to Beckett [Baltimore: Johns Hopkins University Press, 1974], 13). Sir Charles Firth similarly praised such "lapses" from strict allegory as an "improving tendency" (*Essays Historical and Literary* [Oxford: Clarendon Press, 1938], 171–72). J. G. Patrick sees "no symbolic conflict" in Christian's battle with Apollyon ("The Realism of *The Pilgrim's Progress*," *Baptist Quarterly* 13 [1949–50]: 19). Daniel Gibson Jr. notes "the streamy nature of association" in Bunyan's allegory that knits together "paradoxical elements" ("On the Genesis of *The Pilgrim's Progress*," *Modern Philology* 30 [1935]: 382). David Mills echoes Stanley Fish's analysis when he says that "Bunyan used allegory . . . to produce its own demise," arguing that much of the narrative is "not allegorical but ironic" ("The Dreams of Bunyan and Langland," in *The Pilgrim's Progress: Critical and Historical Views,* ed. Vincent Newey [Totowa, N.J.: Barnes and Noble, 1980], 150, 180). Richard Dutton claims the narrative is uneven, "ranging from graphic vividness to desperate obscurity, from a simplistic handbook on Christian behavior to intense Calvinist dogma, from sheer clumsiness to dexterous paradox" ("'Interesting but tough': Reading *The Pilgrim's Progress*," *Studies in English Literature* 18 [1978]: 445). Brian Nellist patronizes the mechanic preacher by allowing that his allegory should not be held to the standards of "traditional allegory" ("*The Pilgrim's Progress* and Allegory," in Newey, 132–53). Thomas E. Maresca simply denies that *PP* is an allegory at all ("Saying and Meaning: Allegory and the Indefinable," *Bulletin of Research in the Humanities* 83 [1980]: 257). Christine Sizemore argues that Bunyan's allegorical style was still developing as he wrote *PP* and that *Holy War* demonstrates a more fully mature and consistent approach to allegorical expression ("Puritan Allegory and the Four Levels of Bunyan's *Holy War*," *Christianity and Literature* 24 [1973]: 20–35). In what is still one of the best books on Bunyan, U. Milo Kaufmann concludes that *PP* is not consistently allegorical, nor was it meant to be, but contains "three diverse modes of narration . . . the mythic, the allegorical, and the literal-didactic" (*The Pilgrim's Progress and Traditions in Puritan Meditation* [New Haven: Yale University Press, 1966], 5).

2. Bunyan takes an epigraph from Proverbs 29: "Where there is no vision the people perish."

3. See *The Doctrine of Law and Grace Unfolded,* in *Miscellaneous Works,* 2:23: "Now there are but two Covenants; therefore it must needs be, that they that are under the Curse, are under the Law; seeing those that are under the other Covenant, are not under the Curse, but under the Blessing. *So then, they which be of faith, are blessed with faithful Abraham,* but the rest are under the law, *Gal.* 3:9." Bunyan applies Paul's logic in such a way as to reclassify all misbelievers as "under the Law," that is, as "Jews." Richard Coppin made precisely the same point in his argument at Rochester Cathedral in 1655. Accused by estab-

lished churchmen of turning the Scriptures "into an Allegory" by claiming to be literally part of the risen body of Christ, Coppin immediately cites Galatians and the "two Covenants" in his defense (*Truth's Triumph* [London, 1656], 39). His opponents are left speechless, because once this world's "reality" has been allegorized—"The Disciples had but a carnal [allegorical] knowledge of Christ" (41)—there is little more they can say.

4. Knott, *The Sword of the Spirit*, 153. Barbara A. Johnson recently quoted this from Knott's book in support of her contention that "Bunyan captures what the real world is like to someone whose perception of it is altered by grace" ("Falling into Allegory," in Collmer, *Bunyan in Our Time*, 124). The alteration grace presumably brings to one's perception of the real world is precisely the conviction that it is not real, so that Bunyan, according to Johnson, "can speak both figuratively and accurately about a Christian's experience in this world" because the only way to speak accurately about life in this world is to speak of it as figures. This is Christianity's "figural view of reality," as Auerbach put it. Bunyan's allegory, Johnson insists, "is not really feigning at all," but "offers the most direct mimesis possible of the way a Christian, as opposed to a non-Christian, experiences his life" (125, 129). And direct mimesis of an allegory must always look like an allegory. Johnson has quite uncritically accepted the Protestant (now evangelical fundamentalist) "figural view of reality," as have many Bunyanists. Johnson, like many Bunyanists, shares Bunyan's conviction that everything this side of the "world which is to come" is allegorical, so to speak literally about it is to transmit the allegory. These critics also tend to flatten out Bunyan's own sense of anxiety and desperation concerning the allegorical status of this life, for Bunyan, unlike most of them, realized how threatening this conviction is to any theory of revelation.

5. Fish, *Self-Consuming Artifacts*, 233, 264.

6. See Luxon, "The Pilgrim's Passive Progress."

7. Once we realize this, it is hard not to wonder why so many Bunyanists labor so hard to find themselves at odds with Fish's reading of *The Pilgrim's Progress*, since Fish is even more evangelistic than most of them. See Forrest's and Johnson's essays in Collmer, *Bunyan in Our Time*.

8. The sentence that follows this has always intrigued me; it sounds almost mystical: "The many levels on which this basic experience occurs would be the substance of a full reading of *The Pilgrim's Progress*, something the world will soon have whether it wants it or not." This is a truly weird sentence. At first I thought that Fish was promising—somewhat less than modestly—a forthcoming volume on Bunyan. Since that has never appeared, I then fantasized that it was a prophecy of my own work. This was, of course, an egocentric fantasy I have since been cured of. I now believe that Fish had in mind here an

apocalyptic threat. He uses the word *substance* here much as seventeenth-century sectarians used it to indicate spiritual experience. Accordingly, the only way "the world" would ever be treated to "the substance of a full reading of *The Pilgrim's Progress*" would be for it to undergo apocalyptic rapture, the rending of all seven veils. This, at any rate, is my current experience of Fish's sentence, and it accounts quite fully for the uncanny feeling the sentence generates even on a first reading.

9. Sidney is more explicit about this familiar dodge when he defends poets against the charge of being "the principall lyars" by answering (with some apparent anxiety): "paradoxically, but, truely, I thinke truely, that of all Writers vnder the sunne the Poet is the least lier, and, though he would, as a Poet can scarcely be a lyer. . . . for the Poet, he nothing affirmes, and therefore neuer lyeth" (*Apologie*, in Hardison, *English Literary Criticism*, 127–28).

10. "The Authors Way of Sending Forth His Second Part of the Pilgrim," 167; see also 169.

11. See *A Vindication* and *Some Gospel Truths Opened*.

12. Warren A. Quanbeck, "Luther's Early Exegesis," in *Luther Today: Martin Luther Lectures* (Decorah, Iowa: Luther College Press, 1957), 1:52–53. I am indebted to Richard Strier for directing me to Quanbeck's piece.

13. *Luther's Works*, 11. 433. For the Lutheran character of much of Bunyan's theology, and especially his theories of Scripture understanding, see Richard L. Greaves, *John Bunyan: Courtenay Studies in Reformation Theology* 2 (Grand Rapids, Mich.: W. B. Eerdmans, 1969), though Greaves is careful to note that "no single theological label without careful qualifications will fit Bunyan" (150). Some recent criticism, especially of *Grace Abounding*, has remarked on Bunyan's Lutheran attitudes toward Scripture reading: Dayton Haskin, "Bunyan, Luther, and the Struggle with Belatedness in *Grace Abounding*," *University of Toronto Quarterly* 50 (1981): 304; Rebecca S. Beal, *"Grace Abounding to the Chief of Sinners*: John Bunyan's Pauline Epistle," *Studies in English Literature* 21 (1981): 147–60; and Knott, *The Sword of the Spirit*, 132–35.

14. Richard Baxter, *Practical Works*, ed. G. R. Henderson (London: Henry G. Bohn, 1854), 1:41.

15. So Bunyan describes his allegory in his prefatory "Apology": "This Book, it chaulketh out before thine eyes, / The man that seeks the everlasting Prize" (*PP*, 6). As such, Bunyan's allegory should be taken to have much the same status as the "Old Testament" covenant, which—according to Calvin—was a kind of "rough draught" of the Christian's nearly finished portrait (*A Commentarie on the Whole Epistle to the Hebrewes*, trans. C. Cotton [London, 1605], 201). See also Lewalski's discussion of this figure (*Protestant Poetics*, 127).

16. Keeble writes that "Nonconformity's commitment to God and to man

resulted in that literary equipoise exemplified in different ways in the 'realistic allegory' of Bunyan" (*The Literary Culture of Nonconformity in Later Seventeenth-Century England* (Athens: University of Georgia Press, 1987), 284.

17. See *PP*, 143, and *GA,* par. 204–8.

18. Sharrock, *PP*, 337; Hill, *A Tinker and a Poor Man*, 130–35 and 223–35. See also Richard F. Hardin, "Bunyan, Mr Ignorance, and the Quakers," *Studies in Philology* 69 (1972): 496–508.

19. Although I have called this effect the "inner latitudinarian," Bunyan was just as apt to see this as an effect of Quaker trust in the "Christ within." See *Some Gospel Truths*.

20. Evangelist's gesture with his finger invites comparison with Calvin's assurance that "where Christ can be pointed to with the finger, there the kingdom of God is manifested" (*Institutes,* 2.11.5). Calvin is trying to distinguish here between the shadowy revelations of "the Law and the Prophets" and those enjoyed by Christians, but Bunyan's Evangelist manages to point to something "the Man clothed with Raggs" cannot see.

21. This puts me slightly at odds with Dayton Haskin's sense of Christian's burden in "The Burden of Interpretation in *The Pilgrim's Progress*" (*Studies in Philology* 79 [1982]: 256–78).

22. For a rather fuller reading of Christian's episode in Interpreter's House, see my "Calvin and Bunyan on Word and Image: Is There a Text in Interpreter's House?" *English Literary Renaissance* 18 (1988): 438–59.

23. See note 1 above.

24. Sharrock, *John Bunyan* (London: Edward Arnold, 1966), 58.

25. Though Paul was probably not the author of the Pastoral Epistles, Bunyan almost certainly read them as his.

26. See Robbins, *Prodigal Son*.

27. *An Answer to a Book called the Quaker's Catechism put out by Richard Baxter* (London, 1656), 10–11.

28. Christian reports that he once heard Great-Grace "say, (and that when he was in the Combat) *We despaired even of life,*" which is a quotation from 2 Corinthians 1:8, thus identifying Great-Grace, Paul, and Christ in one allusive stroke (130).

29. Here it is useful to recall that in the first part, Charity cleared Christian of all responsibility for the apparent damnation of his wife and children with much the same formula by which Christian cleared himself of any responsibility for the "blood" of Talkative: "If thy Wife and Children have been offended with thee for this, they thereby shew themselves to be implacable to good; and thou hast delivered thy soul from their blood" (*PP*, 52); see also *PP*,

85 and above, 249–50. This interchange with Charity was added in the second edition of *The Pilgrim's Progress.*

30. Margaret Olofson Thickstun, *Fictions of the Feminine: Puritan Doctrine and the Representation of Women* (Ithaca: Cornell University Press, 1988), 104.

31. The image of Lot's wife as the epitome of all those who look back toward Vanity Fair, the City of Destruction, or "the things of this world" returns again as "a *Woman* transformed into the shape of a Pillar" on page 108. Lot's wife marks the place where Christian and Hopeful encountered false pilgrims like Mr. Save-all, Mr. Mony-love, Hold-the-World, and By-ends. All these, in other words, are unmanly, that is, "effeminately" attached to this world.

32. Bunyan's *A Case of Conscience Resolved,* in *Miscellaneous Works,* vol. 4, ed. T. L. Underwood (Oxford: Clarendon Press, 1989), 329.

33. On the significance of the mikvah here, see Thickstun, 98.

34. Kathleen M. Swaim, in *Pilgrim's Progress, Puritan Progress: Discourses and Contexts* (Urbana: University of Illinois Press, 1993), works very hard at avoiding this conclusion. She argues that Mercie, not Christiana, focuses the theological and soteriological issues of *The Second Part,* a narrative that she admits is more domestic, "muted and humdrum" (187), less theological and "transcendental" than the first part. Mercie, as Swaim would have it, represents "Bunyan's version of the female heroic" (191), and as such, figures a kind of female Christ: "Mercy's characteristic activity of clothing the naked, . . . becomes enfolded into service to Christ (Matthew 25:36, 38) and ultimately into the savioral role itself" (196). I have been arguing that Bunyan's soteriology will not admit "sympathetic ministering to the basic human needs of others" (196) as having any soteriological value, nor is such activity seen as peculiarly Christlike, certainly not "savioral." Becoming a "Mother in *Israel*" (*PP,* 219), as both Mercie and Christiana do, is not quite the same as being reborn in or as Christ. It is close, however, to figuring the status of being married to Christ; as Bunyan put it, "that I was flesh of his flesh, and bone of his bone" (*GA,* par. 233), borrowing Adam's description of Eve in Genesis. Perhaps this is why, even in Swaim's account, Mercie is incapable of representing "the individual believer," and must remain content with figuring the as yet unraptured "church or conventicle as a whole" (193).

Index

Abraham, 111–13, 115–17, 119, 121; Paul's allegory of (*see* Paul: and allegory of Abraham)

agency, 163–64

allegory: and Christianity in general, 26, 34, 167, 220n. 66; and de Man, 219–20n. 66; and history, 62, 85, 95–96; 'living allegories,' 16, 21; medieval, 25, 63–65; radical Puritan rejection of, 8–22, 108; and Puttenham, 132–33; and realism, 190–99, 240–41nn. 34, 1; and Reformers, ix–x, 8, 40–43; of the self, 29–30, 105–9, 110–11; and typology, 34–83, 97–101; 221n. 8, 228nn. 10, 11. *See also* Bunyan: and allegory; hermeneutics; Paul: and allegory of Abraham

Alter, Robert, 234n. 36

Althusser, Louis, 215n. 38

anecdote, 150–53. *See also* Fineman

antinomianism, 86–87, 181, 214n. 30, 239n. 28

apocalypse, 14

Aquinas, Thomas, 64, 73, 98

Aristotle, 67, 68, 215n. 35

atheism, 50, 153, 222n. 13, 237n. 16

Auerbach, Eric, 43–44, 47, 50, 51–62, 222nn. 14, 15, 242n. 4

Augustine, 25, 26, 34, 218nn. 57, 58; and Jews, 222n. 21; and semiotics, 35–37, 64–65, 201

autobiography. *See* Bunyan: Works: *Grace Abounding*

Bal, Mieke, 125, 233n. 30, 234n. 36

baptism, 14. *See also* mikvah

Barker, Francis, 6

Barrett, C. K., 85

Barthes, Roland, 64–65

Bauman, Richard, 236n. 8

Baxter, Richard, 175, 198

Beal, Rebecca S., 243n. 13

Bedford congregation, 143, 152–53, 157, 239–40n. 29

Betz, Hans Deiter, 226–27n. 1, 229n. 16

Bible: quotations from: Acts, 69, 163; Colossians, 13, 14, 58; 1 Corinthians, 13, 14, 58, 59; 2 Corinthians, 12–13, 58, 180, 201;